Refining the Common Good

How has Islam as a set of beliefs and practices shaped the allocation of oil revenues in Arab Gulf monarchies? In turn, how has oil wealth impacted the role of Islamic doctrine in politics? *Refining the Common Good* explores the relationship between Islamic norms and the circulation of oil wealth in Gulf monarchies. The study demonstrates how both oil (revenues) and Islam (as doctrine) are manipulated as tools of state power and how religious norms are refined for the sake of achieving narrow secular interests. Miriam R. Lowi examines different institutionalized practices financed by hydrocarbon revenues and sanctioned, either implicitly or explicitly, by Islam, and provides evidence from Kuwait, Qatar, Oman and Saudi Arabia to show how these practices are infused with political purpose. The dynamic relationship between oil wealth and Islamic doctrine contributes to the management and control of society, and the consolidation of dynastic autocracy.

Miriam R. Lowi is Professor of Comparative and Middle East Politics at The College of New Jersey. She is the author of *Oil Wealth and the Poverty of Politics: Algeria Compared* (Cambridge University Press, 2009) and *Water and Power: The Politics of a Scarce Resource in the Jordan River Basin* (Cambridge University Press, 1993).

Cambridge Middle East Studies

Editorial Board

Charles Tripp (general editor)
Julia Clancy-Smith
F. Gregory Gause
Yezid Sayigh
Avi Shlaim
Judith E. Tucker

Cambridge Middle East Studies has been established to publish books on the nineteenth- to twenty-first-century Middle East and North Africa. The series offers new and original interpretations of aspects of Middle Eastern societies and their histories. To achieve disciplinary diversity, books are solicited from authors writing in a wide range of fields including history, sociology, anthropology, political science, and political economy. The emphasis is on producing books affording an original approach along theoretical and empirical lines. The series is intended for students and academics, but the more accessible and wide-ranging studies will also appeal to the interested general reader.

A list of books in the series can be found after the index.

Refining the Common Good
Oil, Islam and Politics in Gulf Monarchies

Miriam R. Lowi
The College of New Jersey

Shaftesbury Road, Cambridge CB2 8EA, United Kingdom

One Liberty Plaza, 20th Floor, New York, NY 10006, USA

477 Williamstown Road, Port Melbourne, VIC 3207, Australia

314–321, 3rd Floor, Plot 3, Splendor Forum, Jasola District Centre,
New Delhi – 110025, India

103 Penang Road, #05–06/07, Visioncrest Commercial, Singapore 238467

Cambridge University Press is part of Cambridge University Press & Assessment,
a department of the University of Cambridge.

We share the University's mission to contribute to society through the pursuit of
education, learning and research at the highest international levels of excellence.

www.cambridge.org
Information on this title: www.cambridge.org/9781009463317
DOI: 10.1017/9781009463324

© Miriam R. Lowi 2024

This publication is in copyright. Subject to statutory exception and to the provisions
of relevant collective licensing agreements, no reproduction of any part may take
place without the written permission of Cambridge University Press & Assessment.

When citing this work, please include a reference to the
DOI 10.1017/9781009463324

First published 2024

A catalogue record for this publication is available from the British Library.

Library of Congress Cataloging-in-Publication Data

Names: Lowi, Miriam R., author.
Title: Refining the common good : oil, Islam and politics in Gulf monarchies /
  Miriam R. Lowi.
Description: Cambridge ; New York : Cambridge University Press, 2024. |
  Includes bibliographical references and index.
Identifiers: LCCN 2024012528 (print) | LCCN 2024012529 (ebook) | ISBN
  9781009463317 (hardback) | ISBN 9781009463287 (paperback) | ISBN
  9781009463324 (ebook)
Subjects: LCSH: Islam and politics–Arab countries. | Islam and state–Arab
  countries. | Gulf Cooperation Council. | Arab countries–Politics and
  government.
Classification: LCC BP173.7 .L686 2024 (print) | LCC BP173.7 (ebook) |
  DDC 322/.109536–dc23/eng/20240516
LC record available at https://lccn.loc.gov/2024012528
LC ebook record available at https://lccn.loc.gov/2024012529

ISBN 978-1-009-46331-7 Hardback
ISBN 978-1-009-46328-7 Paperback

Cambridge University Press & Assessment has no responsibility for the persistence
or accuracy of URLs for external or third-party internet websites referred to in this
publication and does not guarantee that any content on such websites is, or will
remain, accurate or appropriate.

For my mother, Naomi Paltiel Lowi (1926–2020),
in loving memory

Contents

List of Tables		*page* viii
Acknowledgments		ix
Note on Transliteration		xiv
Map of Gulf Monarchies and Neighboring States		xv
1	Oil and Islam in the Gulf	1
2	Islamic Norms, Interpretations, Applications	30
3	The State and the Political Economy of Distribution	47
4	Society Responds	74
5	Imported Labor: Building/Appeasing the Nation	88
6	Charity as Politics "Writ Small"	112
7	Islamic Banking and Finance: A Political Economy of Accumulation	140
8	Reflections on Islam and Politics in the Oil Era	167
	Appendix	175
	Bibliography	177
	Index	204

Tables

1.1	Rent abundance in 4 GCC states, select years	page 6
1.2	Population and per capita income, 2017	7
1.3	Oil and LNG rents per capita, GCC states and select others, select years	8
1.4	Foreign nationals in Gulf monarchies, 2020	26
3.1	Price of gasoline (/gal.), select countries, select years	50
3.2	Nationals as proportion of public sector, select GCC states, select years	53
5.1	Foreigners as percentage of labor force, select years	91
5.2	Foreigners as percentage of total population, select years	92
5.3	Non-GCC Arabs as proportion of foreign population, select GCC states, select years	96
5.4	Labor force by nationality and employment sector, select GCC states, 2022	97
7.1	Islamic bank assets as percentage of domestic market, select GCC states, select years	155

Acknowledgments

In spring 2008, I visited the Gulf for the very first time. I went there to conduct research for a book I had been asked to write on oil and its various effects on the politics, economy, society and international relations of Middle Eastern and North African states. For some years I had been studying the political economy of oil-exporting states, with a focus on Algeria, and the relationship between oil and political instability. In the book I wrote on that topic, Saudi Arabia was one of the comparators. However, I could not possibly write a broad, textbook-like study of the sort I had agreed to without some fieldwork in the Gulf monarchies, home to roughly 40 percent of the world's oil and natural gas reserves.

Arriving first in Saudi Arabia and then in Kuwait, I was immediately struck by the hyperbolic visual landscape and the "debauchery of merchandise." I was also struck by the heavy presence of Islam. In this environment, so different from what I experience elsewhere in the Middle East and North Africa, I could not help but wonder how oil-driven abundance impacted the way Gulf Arabs lived and Gulf rulers governed as Muslims. Beyond that, I was curious about whether Islamic norms and the circulation of oil wealth had any effect on each other. In other words, how, if at all, did the teachings of Islam impact government policies related to the spending of oil revenues, and how, if at all, did the latter impact the former? Was there a connection between ideology (belief) and political economy? And if there was, what might that reveal about politics in the Gulf monarchies? With a generous external grant and leaves from my home institution, I returned to the Gulf multiple times from 2012 – for stays ranging from three weeks to five months in Kuwait, Qatar, Oman, Saudi Arabia and the UAE – to conduct the research for this new project. While I began by asking how oil revenues were distributed and Islamic norms deployed by ruling elites, the research agenda evolved considerably over time and in unexpected ways.

In the years it took to research and write this book, I have incurred innumerable debts. It gives me great pleasure to finally have the opportunity to record my gratitude to the many individuals and institutions that helped me along the way. However, as indebted as I am to others for their many contributions to my work, I alone am responsible for the printed product, including any errors or omissions herein.

Before traveling to the region, several colleagues, most of whom are Gulf scholars, shared advice and experiences, and recommended people to meet and institutions to visit. Several of the connections I made this way turned out to be key interlocutors and, in some cases, have become good friends. For their generosity in introducing me to their contacts and providing all sorts of helpful advice about conducting research in the Gulf, I acknowledge (the late) Chris Boucek and (the late) Mary Ann Tetreault, and thank Greg Gause, Steffen Hertog, Amaney Jamal, Toby Jones, Amélie LeRenard, Pascal Menoret, Gwenn Okruhlik and J. E. Peterson.

In the early stages of the research, as I immersed myself in the study of Islamic thought on the one hand and the place of Islam in the historical development of the Gulf monarchies on the other, I benefited from helpful discussions with Thomas Hegghammer and Qasim Zaman, both of whom directed me to important sources, as well. I had productive conversations with ulama at Al Azhar University in Cairo, and especially with the late Dr. Mohamed Kamal Imam, who was particularly helpful with elucidating dimensions of the normative tradition relative to natural resources. In the Gulf, I continued to meet with prominent religious scholars with whom I clarified my understanding of variations in interpretations and applications of norms. I am grateful to them for their guidance and their patience.

Also in the early stages, a key dimension of what would become my central argument took shape through conversations with Neve Gordon. At one point, in response to my meanderings, Neve said something like the following: "Oh, so what you're arguing is essentially this: ..." I listened carefully and then said, "Hmmm ... yes, that's it; you're right." Sincere thanks to Neve for helping me clarify my thoughts and put them into words.

The field research in the Gulf was both productive and illuminating, though challenging at times. In each country, I met with and interviewed an array of people: members of government (ministers, technocrats and other experts) – past and current – members of royal families, oil industry technocrats, Islamic scholars – both official (that is, of the regime) and independent – social critics and activists, university professors and other scholars, journalists, industrialists, bankers, representatives or key members of foundations, associations and international organizations and members (past or then current) of religious movements. I visited government offices, charitable foundations and welfare associations, and international governmental and non-governmental organizations. My greatest debt is to the many people who met with me – often several times – and shared their knowledge and insights, and answered my many questions. Not only that, but so many of them connected me with others whom they thought would be important interlocutors. While I do not name them so as to protect their identities, I am deeply grateful to them, and I hope that if they have the occasion to read this book, at least parts of the analysis will ring true to them. Furthermore, a few of those whom I initially met for my work have become dear friends, most notably Hatoon Al-Fassi and Mu'taz Al-Khatib.

My home institution, The College of New Jersey (TCNJ), supported this research through yearly course reductions and two year-long leaves. On the basis of a proposal on the earliest iteration of this research, the Carnegie Corporation of New York named me "Carnegie Scholar" and awarded me a generous grant through its Carnegie Scholars program on the Muslim World (grant no. D-08084). The Corporation's support, as well as its flexibility as the project evolved, allowed me to both extend one of my leaves from my home institution by a full semester and spend a total of eleven months in the Gulf over four years and four separate trips. Furthermore, my work in the Gulf was facilitated by two important invitations. In spring 2012, I was a visiting research fellow at the King Feisal Center for Research and Islamic Studies in Riyadh. The director at that time, Dr. Yahya Ibn Junaid, most graciously opened doors for me and set up meetings with individuals and institutions I could not have arranged on my own. And in spring 2015, I was a visiting research scholar at the Arab Center for Research and Policy Studies in Doha. I benefited from the many resources of the Center and had fruitful discussions with its director, Dr. Azmi Bishara, and with several of the resident scholars. My office mate Murad Diani deserves special mention. In addition to graciously providing assistance and hospitality, he greeted me in our office each morning to the uplifting music of Sheikh Imam. I am most grateful to these individuals and institutions.

Different parts of the research for this book were presented at annual meetings of the Middle East Studies Association (2015, 2017 and 2019), as well as at other scholarly venues. I wish to acknowledge the following for inviting me and showing interest in my work: the Lilly Family School of Philanthropy, Indiana University-Purdue University (October 2018); Beth Baron and the Middle East and Middle East American Center (MEMEAC) at the Graduate Center of City University of New York (March 2018); Amaney Jamal and the Workshop on Arab Political

Development, Mamdouh Bobst Center, Princeton University (October 2015); Azmi Bishara and the Arab Center for Research and Policy Studies, Doha (April 2015); the Center for International and Regional Studies, Georgetown University – Doha campus (April 2015); the Faculty Senate Colloquium for Research and Creative Activity at The College of New Jersey (March 2013). I am especially grateful to the following scholars for insightful comments on my research that suggested new dimensions and encouraged me to rethink, revise and elaborate: Fulya Aypadin vom Hau, Azmi Bishara, Sarah Chartock, Hatoon al-Fassi, Amaney Jamal, Mu'taz al-Khatib, Leena Rethel, Kevin Mazur, Jillian Schwedler and (the late) Amira Sonbol.

Early versions of Chapters 5 and 6 of this book were published as journal articles in 2017 and 2018. I wish to thank the *Journal of Muslim Philanthropy and Civil Society*, as well as Brill Publishing House and the journal *Sociology of Islam* for allowing me to include parts of those articles in the book.

I have been lucky to have had some wonderful students over the years. While working on this book project, I was able, on two separate occasions, to engage the best of them in my scholarship. I conducted two semester-long research seminars on my book manuscript at different stages of its completion. In spring 2019, with four of the eight chapters written, six hand-picked students contributed to my work by commenting on draft chapters and updating information, collecting data for the remaining chapters and organizing and analyzing interview materials. In spring 2023, with a first draft of the entire manuscript and a book contract in hand, another group of seven exceptional students helped me improve the manuscript. They created most of the tables, read and analyzed relevant newly published scholarship, and suggested where the text would benefit from further elaboration. With heartfelt thanks, I acknowledge Jenna Aziz, Emma Becker, Nancy Bowne, Ryan Brubaker, Steven Cummins, Matt Duca, Eric Gibney, James Mcelroy, Brooke Schwartzman, Olivia Snow, Courtney Strauch, Anjali Thakker and Eric Yavorsky. Four individuals deserve special mention: Eric Gibney proposed the new title of the book; Matt did yeoman's work on statistical tables in the months after graduating; Ryan worked as my research assistant during the summer of 2019; and Courtney expertly constructed the index in the last months before the manuscript was sent to production. I am grateful to all thirteen students for their many contributions to this volume, and for the pleasure it was to work with them and learn from them.

Also at TCNJ, Susan Scibilia, the Political Science department's program assistant, has been a great help to me. She has routinely assisted with all sorts of tasks, especially those that require more sophisticated computer literacy than what I possess, and has tolerated both my limitations and my distractedness with patience and a smile. As for my department colleagues, they have always been collegial and supportive. At Cambridge University Press, I thank my editors, Maria Marsh and Natasha Burton, for their professionalism and care in shepherding the manuscript through the production process from the outset.

Several friends and colleagues read drafts of chapters at various stages or drafts of articles based on this research and offered helpful feedback. I wish to acknowledge Zahra Baber, (the late) Michael Bonner, Nathan Brown, Sarah Chartock, Kristin Smith Diwan, Greg Gause, Clement Henry, Timur Kuran, Pete Moore, Gwenn Okruhlik, Amy Singer, Rafieh al-Talaei, Charles Tripp, Kristian Ulrichsen, John Waterbury, Isabelle Werenfels, Qasim Zaman. Laurie Brand and Arang Keshavarzian, as well as two anonymous reviewers read the penultimate draft of this book and made suggestions that allowed me to improve the manuscript significantly. I am most grateful to them. The publication of this book owes much to the timely interventions of Beth Baron and Homa Hoodfar. They did not allow me to abandon the manuscript when I was inclined to do so, when all that remained to write were the introduction and conclusion. I thank them for their wise counsel and gentle insistence.

As this may well be my last book, I mention here my dearest friends: Laurie Brand – devoted listener, reader and collaborator; Isabelle Werenfels, with whom I share North Africa, scholarly engagement and a special closeness despite the ocean between us; Fairlie Gibson, who has been there ever since our Cairo days; Suzanne Flom and Margie Mendell, who have been (like) the very best of family for the longest time. I thank all of them for enriching my life with their friendship.

Finally, and most importantly ... Abdellah Hammoudi discussed at length with me the conceptualization of this project in its earliest stages and has been a wonderful interlocutor and companion throughout. With all my heart, I thank him and our beloved Jazia and Ismael for the joys of life *en famille*.

Note on Transliteration

This book follows the transliteration system of the *International Journal of Middle East Studies*, with some modifications. I do not use diacritics, but in most cases I use long vowel markers, the glottal stop hamza (') and the pharyngeal fricative ayn ('). However, in an effort to simplify, I minimize these where possible and especially in personal names, names of institutions and organizations. I tend to spell the names of institutions and organizations as they appear on their business cards or the documents they produce in the English language. For common Arabic words that have entered the English lexicon, I tend to use the conventional English spelling (waqf but *awqāf*, zakat but *ṣadaqa* and hajj). Common place names like Doha, Dhofar and Jeddah are not transliterated. Finally, I use "Al" to refer to "House of" as in Al Sa'ud (House of Sa'ud) and Al Sa'id or Al BuSa'id (House of Sa'id or BuSa'id).

Map of Gulf Monarchies and Neighboring States

* also known as Persian Gulf
Source: Original map in German: Furfur translation to English: Ham105, CC BY-SA 4.0, via Wikimedia Commons with modifications

1 Oil and Islam in the Gulf

Introduction

For centuries, Islam as religion, normative system and foundation of social and political practice prevailed in a more or less vast territory that extended and contracted, stretching from the frontiers of China to North Africa and from Southern Europe to sub-Saharan Africa. The last of the Muslim caliphates, the Ottoman Empire oversaw a territory that, on the eve of World War I and its demise, encompassed much of what is now commonly referred to as the Middle East. While the Empire's politics is said to have been based upon "a mixture of religion and dynastic loyalty" (Ochsenwald 1984, 3), in the predominantly Arabic-speaking lands that it ruled from the sixteenth century, authority was largely decentralized such that there was considerable local autonomy over both politics and the "domain of Islam" (Lapidus 1996, 12). Although little is known about the lives of villagers and nomadic groups in Ottoman lands, it is fair to say that for town dwellers and political elites, Islam tended to play a substantial role in daily life. And in the Arabian Peninsula, where it had emerged in the Hijaz in the west, in Mecca and Medina in the seventh century, Islam enjoyed pride of place. Indeed, according to an eminent scholar of nineteenth-century Arabia, religion was surely a "chief motivating force" in that region's social history (Ochsenwald 1984, ix).

The discovery of oil in the Gulf region, beginning in Persia (under the Qajar dynasty) in 1908, Iraq (a British-mandated territory) in 1923, followed by Bahrain (a British protectorate) in 1932, and Kuwait (a British protectorate) and Saudi Arabia in 1938, represented a dramatic development. Within a few decades, the availability of a seemingly unlimited (and increasingly highly valued) source of energy and of capital provoked the persistent encroachment of foreign powers coveting that resource; and their exploitation of oil engendered novel settlement patterns and urbanization, novel employment structures and practices. The new reality profoundly restructured societies shaped by Islam, among other forces, and already affected in different measures by contact with the west, colonial domination and the insinuation of particularist identities. The exploitation of oil by imperial powers impacted not only local economies and social relations but also the organization of governance within emergent or newly created states and their interactions with the outside world. For some analysts – most notable among them Daniel Yergin (1991) and Leonardo Maugeri (2006) – oil came to define an era.

Much has been written about oil and its effects on politics, society and the economy; much has been written about Islam, Islam and politics, and Islam in the Middle East and North Africa (MENA). Virtually nothing has been written about connections between oil and Islam apart from Saudi Arabia's "recycling of petrodollars" to export its ruling politico-religious ideology and spread Saudi influence, Gulf states' spending oil revenues to encourage radical "Islamist" movements, and more recently, Saudi Arabia's and the United Arab Emirates' use of oil revenues to suppress the Muslim Brotherhood.[1] The research on which this book is based grew out of my earlier critical engagement with the rentier state framework and related "resource curse" literature that address the challenges faced by states and societies where government revenues and national welfare are dependent upon the export of a single high-valued natural resource (Lowi 2009).[2] It was inspired by my puzzling over possible impacts "oil" and "Islam" have had on each other in states where they co-occur and are prominent. In considering the Gulf monarchies, I began by asking myself how, if at all, has Islam, as a normative system, code of conduct and set of practices, shaped the allocation of oil revenues, and how, if at all, has oil, or rather the allocation of revenues from the sale of oil, impacted Islamic doctrine – the set of beliefs, its juridical interpretations or practices. Additionally, I wondered how the spectacular wealth derived from oil and natural gas, from both their export and the investment of (surplus) rents, has affected the way Gulf rulers govern and Gulf Arabs live as Muslims today.

In posing these questions, I focus on Islam as a tool of governance and statecraft, hence on ruling elites. I study the "petro-monarchies" of the Arabian Peninsula, member states since 1981 of the Cooperation Council for the Arab States of the Gulf, colloquially known as the Gulf Cooperation Council (GCC). Although several Muslim-majority

---

[1] See, for example, Noreng (1997); Rashid (2010); Al-Rasheed (2002). For an eclectic discussion, see Haykel (2015,125–47). For a multilayered study of one of Saudi Arabia's "missionary project(s)," see Farquhar (2017). Note that Foley (2010) mentions both Islam and oil in the title of his book but says little about a relationship between them.

[2] The "classics" of the rentier state framework include, *inter alia*, Mahdavy (1970), Beblawi et al. (1987). For a review of the "resource curse" literature in its early stage, see Ross (1999).

Introduction 3

countries of North and sub-Saharan Africa, Central and Southeast Asia have also experienced important effects attendant to the exploitation of oil reserves, it is arguably in the Arabian Peninsula, the cradle of Islam, where Islam and oil, both independently and together, have contributed to the structuring of politics and social life more deeply and broadly, and over a longer period of time than elsewhere.[3] Consider the following: In 2018, the six Gulf monarchies, with a combined population of 27 million citizens (and 29 million expatriates), accounted for roughly 30 percent of the world's proven oil reserves and 21 percent of its natural gas, down from 40 percent and 25 percent, respectively, eight years before. Their hydrocarbon sectors accounted for, on average, about 73 percent of combined total exports (ranging from a low of 50 percent in Bahrain and the United Arab Emirates [UAE] to a high of more than 90 percent in Kuwait and Qatar), at least 70 percent of total government revenues in all but one country (UAE), and more than 40 percent of GDP in all but two (Bahrain and UAE) (Ollero et al. 2019, 54–9).

No doubt, the relative abundance of oil and natural gas, designated as "common property resources," in and along the shores of the Arabian Peninsula has contributed enormously over the past fifty years to the power of the centralizing state and its international visibility. Moreover, ruling elites of these hydrocarbon-rich states insist, to varying degrees and in multiple ways, upon their commitment to the faith and, in some cases, assert that their own legitimacy derives from Islamic codes. For example, in their constitutions, the governments of Kuwait and Qatar cite the *Shari'a* as a main source of legislation, as does the government of Oman in its Basic Law. Saudi Arabia goes even further, stipulating in its Basic Law that its constitution is the *Qur'an* and the *Sunnah* (practices of the Prophet Mohamed).[4] As the dominant, indeed the sole recognized religion intrinsic to state-building, Islam in Gulf monarchies has not only been a source of legitimation for rulers but more so than elsewhere in the MENA region, except perhaps Iran since 1979, it has been absorbed within state institutions and intertwined with national identity and public norms.[5]

Although Gulf rulers broadcast their adherence to the religious tradition, some of their practices, as will be evident in the chapters that follow, do not appear to align with its principles. This, however, is

---

[3] For oil's role in modernization and development in the broader Middle East, see, for example, Cammett et al. (2015); Henry et al. (2001).
[4] Césari (2014) points out that most MENA states include Islam in their constitutions. She suggests that doing so is a means to both legitimize their power, since the state thereby assumes the role of guardian of the faith, and deny religious diversity (31–2).
[5] I borrow this latter insight from Césari (2014, xv) and apply it here to the Gulf monarchies.

neither surprising nor unusual, nor unique to Islam. As with other religions as well as secular moralities, Islam has guiding principles relative to, for example, redistributing wealth and protecting the most vulnerable members of society, and these principles have been interpreted and institutionalized in many different ways. Moreover, the behaviors of a community tend to be more closely connected to economic and social structures in place than they are to religious doctrine, even though, at its inception, doctrine was largely a response to those structures (Rodinson 1978, 164). As for rulers, interests related to their office, as in retaining political power and access to resources, outweigh religious principles in guiding their behavior, although religion (and religious discourse) may provide a cover for secular interests (Gill and Keshavarzian 1999).[6]

In this book, I, like other scholars (for example, Tabaar 2018; Platteau 2017; Zeghal 2012; Mandaville and Hamid 2018), am less concerned with "Islamic intentionality and sincerity" than with the ways in which religion, not unlike oil revenues, is used by ruling elites as a tool to advance particular interests.[7] As with any ideology or type of group affiliation/identification, religion – its doctrine, symbols, norms of behavior or practices – can be mobilized by well-placed individuals to pursue their goals and advance their priorities. Hence, I ask the following: Given that wealth circulation practices of Gulf monarchies, avowedly Muslim states, do not typically adhere to principles of the faith, how, then, are oil revenues allocated and religious norms manipulated, and for what purposes? To explore this central question, I examine four government-sponsored institutionalized practices associated with welfare and/or development, financed by oil and gas revenues and sanctioned, either implicitly or explicitly, by Islam – government subsidies and transfers, the employment of foreign labor, charitable giving, Islamic banking and finance – in Kuwait, Qatar, Oman and Saudi Arabia, four of the six GCC states. I have chosen to focus on these four because they offer interesting variation. As for Bahrain and the UAE, while I refer to them at times and especially in the examination of Islamic finance, I omit them from much of the evidentiary portion of this study because of particular confounding features that could bias outcomes. Unlike the other Gulf monarchies, Bahrain has a Shi'a majority population but a Sunni political elite and

---

[6] As an example, Madawi al-Rasheed (2012, 204–6) describes a "theology of obedience" whereby official religious discourse in Saudi Arabia has served to depoliticize society.

[7] While my attention in this study is on ruling elites and not religiously inflected (dissident) movements in the Gulf, it is worth noting that the literature on the latter and the strategies they employ to achieve their goals is vast. See, *inter alia*, Hegghammer (2010); Freer (2018); Al-Rasheed (2007).

sectarianism in governance; hence, state narratives and distributive practices are informed, in large measure, by sectarian considerations.[8] The UAE is a federation of seven states with six ruling families, each with autonomy over local resources, revenue streams and fiscal policy. The seven emirates manifest considerable heterogeneity in terms of income, level of development and natural resource endowment. While one emirate (Abu Dhabi) has most of the petroleum reserves (95 percent), the others have very little, if any at all. Oil-poor Dubai has the highest level of development in the federation, whereas a few of the northern emirates depend on subsidies and grants from the federal government. No doubt, each of the Gulf monarchies has unique features. I suggest, however, that apart from Bahrain and the UAE, none – not even Kuwait with its functioning parliament for much of its post-independence history, nor Oman with its Ibaḍi[9] religious establishment – has features that skew outcomes of the practices I am investigating.

I argue that in the four states, not only hydrocarbon rents but also religious (discourse and) doctrine and the related notion of community (*umma*) are instrumentalized for the sake of achieving political goals. They are manipulated by ruling elites in ways that allow for privileging themselves and their ambitions while managing, dominating and controlling society. Family, associates and loyalists are favored; real or potential adversaries are appeased; and those who are considered to be different, distant or disassociated are snubbed (if not punished). In exploring connections between oil revenues[10] and Islamic norms through an examination of four government-sponsored, institutionalized practices, I show that in the contemporary period, regime behavior is not merely detached from religious principles, but more significantly, norms are either reconfigured or their interpretation revised for the sake of narrow (political) interests. Maintaining dynastic states is the priority; oil and Islam are its principal tools.

---

[8] While sectarianism is institutionalized in Saudi Arabia, as well, insofar as discriminatory policies and practices prevail toward its Shi'a minority communities (representing 10–15 percent of the total population), Bahrain's situation is quite unique given the political-demographic imbalance and the regime's perceived (structural) vulnerability. In Oman, sectarianism has been deterred by the very deliberate promotion by the former sultan of a universal or, in Amal Sachedina's (2021, 11) terminology, "desectarian" Islam in which the basic principles of the faith are emphasized. On sectarianism in the Gulf, see Potter (2014). For a rich treatment of sectarianism in Bahrain and Britain's central role in its institutionalization, see Alshehabi (2019).

[9] Ibaḍi (al-Ibāḍīya) are a sect in Islam, distinct from Sunni and Shi'a. For a rich treatment see Hoffman (2012).

[10] In this book, I use "oil" as a shorthand for crude oil and liquid natural gas.

Table 1.1 *Rent abundance in 4 GCC states, select years*

	Oil/Gas as % Exports		Oil/Gas as %Gov.Revenue		Oil/Gas as %GDP	
	2012	2018	2012	2018	2012	2018
Kuwait	95.5%	93.8%	93.6%	89.6%	64.5%	54.1%
Oman	83.6	74.4	84.7	78.2	44.9	40.8
Qatar	92.5	88.2	77.1	83.3	58.1	47.4
KSA	87.4	80.2	91.8	67.5	45.2	43.2

Source: Ollero et al. (World Bank Group), Gulf Economic Monitor, Dec. 2019

Oil and Islam as Tools of State Power

The four Gulf states treated in this study – Kuwait, Qatar, Oman and Saudi Arabia – are oil- and gas-exporting, dynastic autocracies and (in the latter two cases, absolutist) monarchies, dependent on foreign powers for protection but also as buyers of their hydrocarbon resources (oil and natural gas) and suppliers of their manifold imports that include projects, expertise, labor, consumption goods, weapons, etc. Classic rentier states,[11] they were, until recently, absolutely dependent on their narrow resource base and the external environment: Their petroleum sectors account for the majority of exports and, in most cases, government revenues, as well (Table 1.1).[12] And since rent accrues directly to the state and rent-derived income predominates in government finances, engaging in distribution, as in the extension of goods, services and financial facilities, has remained a primary task of national governments and an important source of their legitimacy.

Especially since the new millennium, however, burgeoning income from rising oil and gas prices, from 2000–08 and 2009–14, has facilitated lucrative international investments and the expansion of important savings/wealth funds (nourished by surplus rents and returns on investments), thereby diversifying government revenue sources somewhat (Bazoobandi 2012; Seznec et al. 2019).[13] Adam Hanieh (2018, 31) reports that while precise data is lacking, "(A) conservative estimate puts

---

[11] Rentierism refers to the predominance of rent-derived income in government finances, combined with the tendency for distribution to take precedence over production as the principal task of the state.
[12] However, by the early 1980s, Kuwait was already earning more from its foreign investments than from its oil exports (Bazoobandi 2011, 66).
[13] Official figures of their sovereign wealth funds are not published. Note, as well, that some portion of the international investments is the work of private Gulf capitalists and not the national governments.

Table 1.2 *Population and per capita income, 2017*

	Total Pop.	GNI p.c. (PPP*)
Bahrain	1.5 mill.	$46,190
Kuwait	4.2	66,102
Oman	4.6	41,230
Qatar	2.7	127,602
Saudi Arabia	33.0	55,650
UAE	9.5	71,690

* expressed as purchasing power parity, US$
Source: IMF: World Economic Outlook database; World Bank Indicators database

the collective value of disposable wealth and foreign assets of GCC governments, sovereign wealth funds, private Gulf firms and individuals at well over US$6 trillion by 2016." With their spectacular wealth and bold ventures across the globe, these "petro-monarchies" have become increasingly integrated as prominent players in global capitalism; however, Bahrain and Oman are not in quite the same league as the other four. Furthermore, while their oil and gas reserves are among the largest in the world, their populations are relatively small. Apart from Saudi Arabia, which had a population of 33 million in 2017 (of which 20 million, or 60 percent, were citizens), Oman had 4.6 million (of which 55 percent citizens); Kuwait had 4.2 million (31 percent citizens); and Qatar had 2.7 million (11.5 percent citizens).[14] The combination of small size with vast hydrocarbon endowments and other important sources of national income accounts for high per capita income. In 2017, in fact, three of the six Gulf monarchies ranked among the top ten countries in the world in terms of per capita income. Qatar, with a citizen population of just over 300,000, held first place (Tables 1.2 and 1.3).[15]

While there was no modern state to speak of in the Arabian Peninsula prior to imperialist powers' discovery of oil beginning in the 1930s, revenues from the sale of oil became critical for the tasks of

---

[14] At that time, 11.5 percent of the total population of the UAE and 47 percent of the total in Bahrain were citizens.

[15] Michael Herb (2014, 10–15) contends that the proper measure for rentierism is per capita rent income. He points out that on the basis of this measure *per citizen*, Kuwait, Qatar and the UAE are the world's richest rentier states, while Oman and Saudi Arabia follow close behind. (He refers to the former as belonging to the category of "extreme" rentier states and the latter as "middling.") Thus, Qatar's per capita income of $127,000 in 2017 would have been significantly higher if only its citizen population were considered.

Table 1.3 Oil and LNG rents per capita (in 2022 USD),* GCC states and select others,** select years

Year	Saudi Arabia	Qatar	Kuwait	Oman	UAE	Bahrain	Eq. Guinea	Brunei	Norway	Trinidad-Tob.
1980	$38,802	***	$37,447	$10,009	$56,721	$18,727	$0	$28,707	$7,703	$9,633
1990	$12,111	***	$13,840	$10,870	$28,055	$8,793	$0	$13,167	$7,932	$2,471
2000	$10,489	$33,531	$26,205	$12,310	$15,683	$6,069	$3,437	$12,177	$12,093	$1,891
2010	$9,742	$30,555	$27,424	$10,175	$9,404	$5,425	$6,492	$11,345	$11,630	$3,022
2020	$4,701	$16,327	$11,310	$4,432	$8,775	$2,987	$1,135	$5,339	$4,241	$1,053

* Data manually adjusted for regional inflation; "rents" defined as revenues minus costs as stated in World Bank (2021)."
** Sample of oil-/gas-rich, low-population states in different world regions
*** World Bank inflation measures for Qatar in 1980 and 1990 not available

Sources: derived from World Bank Indicators for: oil rents (% of GDP), natural gas rents (% of GDP), GDP deflator (base year varies by country), GDP (current US$), population, total

state-building. They initially supplemented and eventually superseded royalties from the British Crown, as well as revenues from the hajj in the case of Saudi Arabia, from pearling in Kuwait, Qatar and Oman, and from both long-distance/maritime and internal trade in all four. In each country, the state is coterminous with a single family – the al-Saʿud (Saudi Arabia), al-Sabaḥ (Kuwait), al-Thani (Qatar), al-BuSaʿid (Oman)[16] – that had enjoyed some prominence pre-oil and eventually came to dominate politically, at least in part with the intervention and certainly the backing of first Britain, and later, the United States (Sluglett 2002, 150). Until today, the latter, with the United States in the lead since the 1980s, have provided military protection, as well. Thus, ruling families have enjoyed powerful foreign patrons and access to vast sums from external sources.

The rentier state/resource curse literature has offered several insights about the supposed peculiarities of these states and the ways in which dependence upon oil extraction and export has impacted the economy, as well as politics and society.[17] Hossein Mahdavy (1970), in his seminal article, points out that in most environments, the government, as overseer of the public good, "owns" subsoil minerals. Hence, rents from the sale of oil and natural gas quite naturally accrue to the government. Furthermore, as rents increase, the public sector grows in size and importance, and the government's power and authority grow and become increasingly centralized. It is worth noting, however, that in the Arabian Peninsula, the foreign companies that explored for oil singled out a prominent family in each locale and deliberated with them alone. Backed by their home governments, they eventually offered the family a share of the oil sales in exchange for a concession: the exclusive right to continue exploiting the resource in that territory (Crystal 1990; Vitalis 2007). Thus, imperial powers reinforced the stature and prerogatives of a single family, and the preferred member within it, thereby paving the way for the latter's assumption of autocratic control over what would eventually become an independent state.[18]

---

[16] In Oman, however, as will become evident, the late sultan Qābūs bin Saʿīd (1970–2020) ruled without sharing power with family members, although relatives figured among his important allies (Valeri 2009, 94–5).

[17] See, *inter alia*, Ross (2012); Sachs et al. (1995).

[18] As Tim Mitchell (2009, 2011) has proposed, in response to a claim of the resource curse literature that oil wealth fosters authoritarian governance (Ross 2001), the latter may be symptomatic of behaviors and relationships that occurred or were initiated from outside the oil-producing state. He argues that "production arrangements" imposed by the European and American oil companies on host governments were crafted for their own benefit and that of their governments. And several of these arrangements, as noted, favored autocratic rule.

Classic rentier states, Gulf monarchies are said to enjoy "revenue autonomy" since the bulk of their revenues comes from rents that accrue directly to them from external sources (and eventually, from returns on their foreign investments made possible with surplus rents). Hence, they perceive no need to extract from their populations to carry out the tasks of governance.[19] And typically, they fail to disclose to the public the actual size of the rents they receive. It is generally assumed that only a portion of the real oil and gas revenues appears in the national accounts and government budget (Alshehabi 2017). However, this "secrecy" is not a "quality" of oil revenues, as Ross (2012, 59–62) claims; it is more closely associated with the behavior of autocrats.

Gulf monarchies also enjoy, in Terry Karl's (2007) words, "discretionary power over spending" in that the government, headed by a single family, decides how to allocate the revenues. In Kuwait, however, its fully elected National Assembly, unique among the Gulf monarchies, enjoys some influence over policy-making. Thus, the government determines who gets what and who is excluded. Insofar as these states' social spending is concerned, it includes the generalized distribution of free or subsidized goods and services to the citizen population, as well as allowances to members of key social groups. By spreading wealth in this manner, it has been argued, rentier states buy broad-based, public support – in other words, the legitimation of their rule. Hence, oil rents can be considered as a tool that is used for political purposes. Furthermore, as rents are indeed instrumentalized by autocratic rulers to achieve their goals, this sort of distribution is coercive in function and objective. Rather than reflective of a "social contract" (Crystal 1990) or "ruling bargain" (Kamrava 2014) in which citizens agree to forego political participation in exchange for material benefits (including low taxation), it is meant, as Albertus et al. (2018) argue, to render citizens/subjects dependent on their rulers for their survival. Thus, distribution enforces submission, while neutralizing (potentially) rival elites. As such, "coercive distribution" is an effective "strategy for authoritarian consolidation" (17).[20] In short, oil revenues are utilized by ruling elites to enhance their monopoly of power.

Not unlike oil revenues, any ideology, whether nationalist, religious or universalist-humanist, can be exploited by privileged persons – what

---

[19] See Chaudhry (1997, 143–44) on the end of tax collection in Saudi Arabia in the mid-1970s. However, see Hertog (2010, 77) for a critique of Chaudhry's claims.

[20] No doubt, some portion of rents can be allocated for the creation of and support for productive enterprises, as Hertog (2010) argues in his discussion of the few "islands of efficiency" in Saudi Arabia. While this phenomenon may be rare, it demonstrates the importance of choice, even among oil-exporting states, rather than the commodity determinism that has infused some of the rentier state/resource curse literature. See, Lowi (2009, 37–40).

Maxime Rodinson (1978, 222–23) refers to as "profiteers of the ideology" and Charles Tilly (2003, 30) refers to as "political entrepreneurs" – for the pursuit of their own self-interested goals. Thus, the sacred can be invoked and instrumentalized for secular political ends. The politicization of religious traditions, including via the mobilization of religious communities, has been the subject of much research and debate (for example, Gill 2001; Grzymala-Busse 2012; Wald et al. 2004; Mandaville 2001; Rouhana et al. 2021). Within this body of literature, the instrumentalist approach proceeds from the observation that new forms of governance and major changes in policy behavior tend to be accompanied by "supporting patterns of ideological, religious, or moral justification" (Hasenclever and Rittberger 2000, 660).

As a normative framework, Islam presents a set of beliefs with which the *umma* (the community of believers) closely identifies and which is meant to govern their behaviors. And since the inception of Islam in the seventh century, adherents have mobilized to spread, if not impose, its teachings. While grassroots mobilization in the name of the faith has dominated the social-scientific study of Islam and politics in recent decades, my focus in this book is on Islam as statecraft, Islam in governance.

Given the significance of Islam in the MENA as a source of identification and a resource for mobilization, authoritarian states, no matter their political tendency, need to engage directly or indirectly with Islam. As Nathan Brown (2015, 42–4) points out, not only is religion "a public matter and therefore woven into the structure of the modern state" but also, in the MENA region, it often provides "an important anchor" for discussions about "justice, morality, political and social behavior." Furthermore, being authoritarian, most states of the region "tend to see regime survival as inextricably linked to religious legitimacy" conferred via descent from the prophet as in the case of Morocco; a historic alliance with a religious movement as in Saudi Arabia; the seizure of power by religious forces as in Iran since 1979; or the expression of allegiance (*bayʿa*) of the ʿ*ulama* (religious scholars or chief religious authorities) as in most other states. Furthermore, it is typical, in both secular and "religious" states in the Muslim world, for governments to "coopt religion – and religious leaders – as part of national development agendas or to protect the state against interpretations of religion that may undermine their authority" (Mandaville and Hamid 2018, 5). Thus, the state's regulation of religion has much to do with the ruler's priority to hold onto power.[21]

---

[21] Nada Moumtaz (2021, 225) underscores that beyond the Muslim world, secular states routinely engage in regulating religion and she cites, as an example, the extension of tax

In the modern state, instrumentalists argue, the use of religious rhetoric, including the fanning of religious symbols or practices, tends to be a cover for parochial (and often, institutional) interests related to such things as access to political power and resources. Whether we consider conflicts between the state and religious forces (Gill and Keshavarzian 1999; Platteau 2011), struggles among competing political factions (Tabaar 2018), reform agendas of authoritarian rulers (Zeghal 2012) or the foreign policy behavior of rival states (Mandaville and Keshavarzian 2018), religion can be exploited and manipulated – indeed, repurposed – for the sake of secular political ends.

Across the Middle East and North Africa, in fact, the modern state, in order to consolidate and expand its rule early on in the state-building process, expropriated Islamic institutions, such as the *awqāf/ḥabūs* (religious endowments or charitable trusts) and *madrasa/madāris* (traditional schools for higher education), that had been the exclusive domain of the religious clergy. In so doing, it undercut the authority of the *'ulama*, transforming them into civil servants. At the same time, it began providing public services – social welfare, education and justice – that were equivalent to services formerly provided by religious institutions (Césari 2014, 49–51). Furthermore, in all matters related to the rulers' agenda, the *'ulama* were either enticed to cooperate, or at least acquiesce, via the distribution of material benefits, or they were coerced to do so to avoid facing harsh consequences.

Thus, as Jocelyne Césari (2014) elucidates, Islam was nationalized: Religious institutions and the services they had provided were appropriated by the state and incorporated into (the system of) governance, while rulers arrogated to themselves the religious legitimacy traditionally enjoyed by the *'ulama*. And the compliant *'ulama*, "servants of the state," endorsed the ruler's policies and practices and the particular understanding of Islam that he was promoting. In these ways, Islam not only became "a tool for the elaboration of the nation-state" (30), but the religious tradition was made to cohere with state interests and programs and not the other way around (83–4). That is to say, states promote a particular understanding of Islam that suits their interests; this is true whether we consider Bourguiba's Tunisia, Qaddafi's Libya, Qaboos Al Saʿīd's Oman or Al Saʿūd's Saudi Arabia.

In her discussion of reform relative to the "woman question" in Tunisia (from the 1920s until 1987) and particularly, the wearing of

---

exemptions to religious organizations in France and the United States. Regulation of this sort is, no doubt, a response to the relative bargaining power of religious and political actors (Gill 2001, 132).

the *hijab*, Malika Zeghal (2012) shows how political elites, whether secularists like Habib Bourguiba or Islamists like Rached Al-Ghannouchi, appropriated Islamic narratives and instrumentalized the religious tradition for their own political purposes. During the confrontation with the French colonial power, Bourguiba, the nationalist leader, encouraged the wearing of the *hijab* as symbolic of the "nation under occupation" (3). In that context, the practice reflected Tunisians' distinctive identity and their resistance to French influence. However, with independence, this same political leader – now head of state – imposed a host of reforms of Islamic institutions. Among them, he insisted upon the removal of the *hijab*, symbolic of the new status of the Tunisian woman with rights and access to the public sphere. For Bourguiba, enforced unveiling also reflected the people's submission to the strong nation-state and its modernist agenda. Thus, Islam was institutionalized as a political resource, and a religious symbol (*hijab*) – interpreted one way and then, another – was deployed as a political instrument to achieve a particular goal in one context and later, a new goal in a very different context. While this served the secular nationalist-reformist agenda of the post-colonial authoritarian state, Zeghal goes on to show that it also paved the way for the Islamist opposition, with their own conceptions of the tradition, to do likewise – in their advocacy for wearing the hijab, for example – for their own political purposes (21). Indeed, the religious tradition can be appropriated and instrumentalized in various (and contrasting) ways, and at times, with unanticipated outcomes.[22]

In his rich study of factional politics in the Islamic Republic of Iran, Mohammad Ayatollahi Tabaar (2018) demonstrates that the instrumentalization of Islam is a strategy, derivative of strategic thinking for the sake of pursuing interests and achieving goals. He explains regime behavior through an examination of how elites transform, manipulate and make use of "religious narratives" in their efforts to meet the challenges of elite competition and achieve political ends. In his analysis, religious ideology is not only instrumentalized, but it is also "constructed"; it is crafted and molded by elites in response to changing opportunities and perceptions of threat, and for the purpose of attaining their political objectives. And new behaviors to advance elites' interests follow from the newly crafted religious narrative (2–20). He clarifies, further, that religion is instrumentalized not necessarily for the sake of creating a just, morally grounded society as per the teachings of Islam but rather for secular

---

[22] For example, see Sells (2021, 297) for a discussion of Wahhabi doctrine, disseminated widely by the Saudi monarchy, as inspiration for Al-Qaeda and the Islamic State, among other dissident "Islamist" movements.

pursuits: in the case of factional politics in Iran, precisely for the sake of "controlling the state" (301).

To gain or maintain control over the state, political elites in oil-exporting states beyond the MENA have themselves employed particular sorts of narratives, often of an identarian nature or related to a moral order. As Ecuador's Rafael Correa negotiated new "sovereign" contracts with foreign oil companies, upon assuming the presidency in 2007 (until 2017), he defended his policies with assertions about the systematic corruption those companies had generated in the oil sector. The "corruption narratives" and colorful public relations campaigns that accompanied them proved to be particularly effective when the new contractual arrangements, in an environment of high oil prices (2008–14), resulted in a threefold increase in state revenues (Lyall 2018, 5). However, the discourse about the moral superiority of nationalist elites was used against Correa when oil prices collapsed in mid-2014. Then, the conservative political opposition re-appropriated the corruption narrative – not unlike Tunisia's Islamist opposition did with Bourguiba's *hijab* narrative – and used it to discredit Correa and his policies (6).

At different historical moments in oil-exporting states in Latin America, racial and/or ethnic differences have been constructed and instrumentalized by ruling elites (or their opponents) as a means to retain (or capture) control over and privileged access to oil, or simply for the ruler to legitimize his power and authority. In Venezuela, for example, the Vicente Gomez regime (1908–35) exploited the foreign oil companies' practice of racializing labor in the oil fields and labor camps to narrate an inclusive state, even though the latter manifested a distinct racial and ethnic hierarchy (Tinker Salas 2009). And in Ecuador in 2008–09, ruling elites pushed back against an initiative to create an indigenous-owned oil company in the northern Amazon by exploiting stereotypes of ethnic difference. With a discourse that contrasted "modernizing mestizo authority" with "anti-modern indigenous alterity," they cultivated popular expectations of a superior distribution of resources under ongoing elite control; thus, they managed to quash the initiative (Lyall 2018).[23]

Interestingly, narratives regarding modernity and its embodiment in ruling elites can be found in both (oil-rich) Latin American states and Gulf monarchies. Fernando Coronil (1997) referred to Colonel Perez Jimenez' dictatorship (1948–58) as the "fetishization of modernity" since Jimenez spent oil rents lavishly on dazzling projects and gave Venezuela,

---

[23] For the instrumentalization of indigeneity to capture state power and control over resources, see the case of Bolivia (Perrault 2012, 75–102).

thereby, the appearance of a modern state (rather than it actually becoming one). The same has been said of Gulf monarchies.[24] Moreover, as purveyors of modernity in the form of development, ruling elites controlling vast hydrocarbon rents, among other sources of wealth, present themselves as the font of progress and hence, the rightful rulers (Menoret 2014, 99–101, 114–16; Lyall 2018, 12). In Oman, for example, "royalist culture was centred on the constant narration and representation … of one major story: the 'launch of the age of renaissance, development, and construction under the leadership of His Majesty the Sultan the builder of Modern Oman'" (Takriti 2013, 256). Yet "modernization" has turned out to be another means of social control.

Elaboration of the Argument

Despite the insinuations of the "first wave" of research on the rentier state – that oil causes this or that phenomenon – in fact, the effects of oil (and natural gas), like those of any resource or commodity, result from how it is exploited and how it is utilized (which are, themselves, a function of human decision).[25] Of course, the same is true for the revenues that accrue from the sale of oil. Similarly, Islam, like any belief system or ideology, has no agency. It is interpreted and practiced by humans as they choose or are encouraged to. However, the ways it is elaborated and lived (or imposed) by its ideologues/adherents do have effects. Thus, agents make use of these resources – one, material and the other, ideational – to achieve certain ends. In Gulf monarchies, oil (revenues) and Islam (doctrine and/or practices), including the related notion of community (*umma*) are instrumentalized by ruling elites to advance their political (and economic) interests.

Islam, as with other religions, ideologies and identities, is neither fixed nor immutable; its principles and guidance can be interpreted variously. They can be understood in multiple ways by different actors and in different ways by the same actors at different times. Moreover, certain precepts can be accentuated and others downplayed in one place and time or another. Its variability, indeed malleability, has much to do with context and circumstance, and changes to them, in which actors locate themselves and which inform their interests and concerns. That is to say,

---

[24] For example, Kanna (2005, 2011); see, as well, Appendix, pp.175–76. Lowi (2016) refers to certain "pet" projects, such as the carbon neutral Masdar City in UAE, as representations of "modernity on steroids."

[25] For a review of the first and second waves of rentier state/resource curse research, see Lowi (2009, 30–9). For recent reviews of aspects of this body of literature with applications to the Gulf, see Herb (2017); Smith et al. (2021).

in the process of Islam's instrumentalization for the sake of achieving particular goals, some aspect of the normative framework, such as the notion of community (*umma*) or the payment of zakat, may be reinterpreted and the associated practice(s) revised, and in ways that would encourage the desired outcome(s). As Tabaar (2018, 12) notes: "Religious ideology is a strategic tool, crafted and deployed intentionally along with, if not before, behavioral change to advance the elites' interests at a given time and place." Thus, politics trumps religion and power trumps ideology/identity. Moreover, norms or belief systems are not merely secondary to the pursuit of power; like oil rents, they, along with repression, are part of its arsenal. Indeed, to varying degrees in the "royalist culture" that prevails in the Gulf, as Abdel Razzaq Takriti (2013, 260) has written with reference to Oman, "religion, tradition, and fear" are instrumentalized "in the service of monarchy."[26] In the particular case of Oman in the early years of the late Sultan Qaboos' rule, "religious motifs were constantly utilized to remind Omanis that his was the reign of justice on earth" – even going so far as to imply a strong resemblance between himself and the second caliph, Omar ibn al-Khattab, "traditionally associated with justice" (257).

It is important to note that while both oil (revenues) and Islam (principles and/or practices) are deployed for the purpose of goal attainment, their strategic instrumentalization is often intertwined. For example, in Gulf monarchies, oil rents are sometimes expended by rulers or their family members to showcase Islam: either the religion *per se*, a particular understanding of doctrine or an associated practice as in charitable giving. In so doing, a narrative of religiosity and authenticity is broadcast, and the political legitimacy of the family is asserted. Beyond that, alternate interpretations of doctrine – and the religious communities that adhere to them – are neutralized, denied or simply ignored. The conjoined instrumentalization of oil and Islam thus contributes to enforcing the submission of the people and consolidating the ruler's project of community, nation and state.

Furthermore, institutionalized practices that are financed at least in part by oil wealth and sanctioned, if not explicitly encouraged, by the normative tradition – such things as the distribution of government subsidies and Islamic banking – reflect the conjoined instrumentalization of oil and Islam. Detailed examination of these practices (in Chapters 3

---

[26] As for tradition, it is interesting that several recent anthropological studies of the heritage (*turath*) industry in the Gulf claim that the purpose is to encourage nation-building, an "exclusive citizenship," as envisioned by the ruler. They note that the hegemonic process has entailed revising history and eliding certain groups for the sake of privileging the elite. See, for example, Al-Nakib (2020); Sachedina (2021).

and 5–7) uncovers the various ways in which they fit within a strategy to advance regime priorities: specifically, to maintain and secure the monopolization of power, wealth and authority by the ruling family. How, though, do rulers pursue this goal? They do so, in large measure, via social management and social control.

To manage and control society, ruling elites often rely upon coercion and the threat of repression. They depend, as well, upon their ability to secure the support, and surely the submission of their subjects. To achieve this, they engage in behaviors, at times accompanied by the invocation or manipulation of religious principles, that appease particular social forces and enforce society's dependence on the state. Dependence is achieved through the well-nigh universal distribution of free or heavily subsidized goods and services, while appeasement is sought through the distribution of resources to some and the exclusion of others.[27] Given that distributions of these sorts are devised by ruling elites and are meant to achieve particular outcomes, they are, as Albertus et al. (2018) clarify, coercive in function. And given the centrality of distribution in the ruling elite's stratagem to manage and control society, consumption is a key organizing principle of the state. Hence, consumption is political.[28]

The ways in which the four oil-financed institutionalized practices explored in this book are carried out are infused with political purpose. Though they may incorporate religious rhetoric, brandish religious symbols or manipulate Islamic doctrine, they invariably favor some and deny others in access to resources while consistently prioritizing the ruler/ruling family and their closest associates. By reinforcing hierarchies of relative privilege, these practices contribute to the fashioning of community and the delineation of its boundaries. In so doing, they facilitate the management and control of society. Thus, they advance the ruler's agenda. In sum, the ruling strategy, the (intertwined) instrumentalization of oil revenues and Islamic doctrine, is pursued with the goal to protect and consolidate autocracy – its (more-or-less) absolute monopoly of power and wealth accumulation.

Cases, Contexts, Structural Particularities

Before the major transformations of the twentieth century, the tribal communities in the resource-scarce interior of the Arabian Peninsula

---

[27] For a seminal study on nation-building via the appeasement of some through the exclusion of others, see Marx (1998).
[28] Pascal Menoret (2014) writes the following about Saudi Arabia: "In the name of development and modernization, the royal family based the national economy of the kingdom almost exclusively on consumption" (121).

engaged primarily in oasis-based subsistence agriculture, animal husbandry and, where and when possible, the caravan trade. Along the eastern coast, they pursued maritime activities – pearling, boat-building and long-distance trading, eastward across the Indian Ocean and south along the East African coast – as well as land trade within the Gulf region and among major coastal settlements. Port cities of varying importance beckoned traders, laborers and administrators from foreign lands who engaged primarily with local merchants (Fuccaro 2014; Boodrookas and Keshavarzian 2019). Both in the interior and along the coast, tribal sheikhs (chieftains) functioned as the local authority within a more-or-less weakly delimited territory with "fluid and shifting" boundaries (Onley and Khalaf 2006, 191). By custom, they were considered as "first among equals." Typically, therefore, they administered their communities through consultation (*shura*) and depended on their members and especially, merchant families, for material support (Potter 2017, 16).

While imperial powers, beginning with the Portuguese and followed by the Ottomans, had intervened in the Gulf and exercised varying degrees of control in parts since the sixteenth century, it was arguably the British (from the late eighteenth/early nineteenth century) and later, the Americans (from the 1920s), whose interventions had the most profound effect on the region's political economy. Initially, British interests in the Gulf concerned trade with India and easy passage for both goods and people between Britain and the subcontinent. However, as economic activity along the coast and in the broader Gulf region increased in importance and profitability[29] while its imperial possessions in Asia and Africa needed to be secured, Britain sought to both extend its influence and gain easier access to high-value energy resources, first discovered in Persia in 1908. In doing so, it came up against Ottoman claims to parts of "eastern Arabia" (1871–1918) – most notably, Kuwait, Qatar and Hasa (an eastern province of present-day Saudi Arabia). The Ottomans already controlled the Hejaz in the western portion of the Peninsula.[30]

To establish its regional hegemony, Britain, through its political representatives "on the ground," worked on forming alliances with local forces. With promises of protection and financial support, it crafted

---

[29] In the late nineteenth century, British entities secured (short-lived) tobacco concessions, a monopoly over production, sale and export of tobacco from the Shah of Persia. Then, in 1901, exclusive rights were granted to an Englishman, William Knox D'Arcy, to search for, export and sell oil and natural gas from Persian territory.

[30] The Hejaz, home to Mecca and Medina and the important port city of Jiddah, was, in fact, controlled by the sherifian Hashemite family, but from the sixteenth century to World War I, it was under Ottoman "overlordship" (Ochsenwald 1984, 6).

preferential relationships with tribal sheikhs along the coast, recognizing a powerful sheikhly family as the legitimate ruler – or *emir*, effectively pushing aside other sheikhly families (Heard-Bey 2008, 28–9).[31] Eventually, these relationships were formalized through treaties – as with the well-established Al-Sabah in Kuwait in 1899 and 1914, and the less prominent Al-Thani in Qatar in 1916. Thus, the British succeeded in obtaining the support and dependence of these families, turning them into their local intermediaries who would contribute to the realization of British interests and reap some benefits from doing so (Onley and Khalaf 2006, 202). With this enhanced status, security and financial support, the *emirs* were further distinguished from their subjects; over time, they came to depend less on consultation (*shura*) in governance, exercising, rather, "unitary sheikhly authority" (Boodrookas and Keshavarzian 2019, 16). Furthermore, as power was consolidated in the hands of just a few families, the coastal sheikhdoms (chieftaincies), with crucial assistance from their British masters, gradually extended their influence into the interior of the peninsula and over other tribal confederations, incorporating the latter into their domain. In time, and to guarantee the imperial power's access to and control over increasingly valuable resources (through their oil companies), the emir's territory was delimited and his sovereignty, thereby confirmed.

The arrangements that were shaped and then formalized to varying degrees by the British imperial power in the nineteenth and early twentieth centuries laid the foundations for the emergence of tribal autocracy and eventually, tribal dynastic monarchies in which the extended families were included within the extended royal family and enjoyed privileges (Wright 2020, 350–51).[32] They also smoothed the way for the oil companies to conduct their exploratory activities from the 1930s. Indeed, explorations for and extractions of oil in the interior of the peninsula and along its shores by multiple (British- and American-owned) companies necessitated the precise demarcation of territory, not only to "delineate (particular) oil concessions and differentiate them from those of other companies" – that is, to keep others out – but also to facilitate the dealings between the company and a single, recognized ruler. In the cases of Kuwait and Qatar, the British authorities, in fact, were

---

[31] In fact, the preeminence of the Al-Sabah has been recognized from the 1750s when they were chosen by the leading merchants to govern Kuwait and to do so within the parameters established by the merchants (Tetreault 2011, 75).

[32] It is important to note, however, that Oman under the leadership of the late Sultan Qaboos (1970–2020) was somewhat different from the other Gulf monarchies in that a single individual dominated the political landscape while his family and tribe were more-or-less on the sidelines.

implicated as negotiators with neighboring rulers in fixing their borders (Heard-Bey 2008, 31–6, 38–41). Thus, not simply oil, but the interests of empire and international capital were endogenous to state formation along the coast, most notably in Kuwait and Qatar, and to the reconfiguration of the state in Oman and to an extent, in Saudi Arabia, as well. The export of oil began in earnest around mid-century. By 1971, Britain had terminated its treaty relationships with the Gulf sheikhdoms; Kuwait became independent in 1961 and Qatar, ten years later.

Of the four cases, Oman and Saudi Arabia are somewhat distinct from Kuwait and Qatar in their historical development. From the mid-eighteenth century, much of the area that came to be called the "Sultanate of Oman" was acknowledged as a political entity, albeit under divided sovereignty. The Omani coast, with its center in Muscat, was under the authority of the Al BuSaʿid clan, while the interior of the country was governed by an Ibaḍi *imam* (religious leader) and referred to as an Imamate with its capital in Nizwa. And in parts of the territory that would later become the modern "Kingdom of Saudi Arabia," there were two distinct periods of Saudi-Wahhabi statehood (1744–1818; 1824–91), in which an expansionist governing structure, formed by an alliance between the Al Saʿud clan and ʿulama of the local "Wahhabi" (Hanbali) tradition, ruled.[33] A third Saudi-Wahhabi state, the current one, emerged in 1913 (Vassiliev 1998; Steinberg 2006). Both Omani and Saudi-Wahhabi entities had functioned intermittently as regional powers, offering protection to or threatening Gulf sheikhdoms to the north, while coastal Oman, which for centuries had been actively engaged in Indian Ocean trade, ruled Zanzibar in the mid-nineteenth century (Onley and Khalaf 2006, 40–1). While in both cases, some degree of "stateness" preceded the inception of the oil economy, it is important to note that here too, imperial intervention was consequential. In a variety of ways, both legalistic (through treaties and agreements) and duplicitous (via palace coups, reneging on agreements),[34] the British played a key role in altering the political landscape and solidifying the borders of Oman, as we will see shortly, and in the expansion of the political authority of Ibn Saʿud (Abdulaziz bin Abdul Rahman Al Saʿud) and the borders of the third Saudi-Wahhabi state in the 1920s (Vassiliev 1998, 253–67). The Kingdom of Saudi Arabia was proclaimed in 1932, an oil concession agreement with the United States was signed in

---

[33] The term, Wahhabi, refers to the teachings of Mohamad ibn Abd Al-Wahhab (1703–92), a religious scholar and preacher from the Najd in central Arabia.
[34] See, for example, Britain's duplicitous dealings with Hussein bin Ali of the benu Hashem clan, Sharif of Mecca (Fromkin 1989; Vassiliev 1998, 235–50).

1933 and oil was discovered five years later (1938) (Vassiliev 1998, 312–20). But it was not until 1948 that, with US-owned ARAMCO (the Arabian-American Oil Company) at the helm, oil exports began.

The role played by imperial powers in fashioning the "modern" Sultanate of Oman – what Abdel Razzaq Takriti (2013) refers to as the construction of absolutism as an "imperial project" (312) – is especially noteworthy.[35] In 1937, the British-chartered Iraq Petroleum Company (IPC) secured a concession from the Sultan of Muscat to explore for oil in his territory (Valeri 2009).[36] Unsuccessful in its efforts, it then encouraged the Sultan to seize the territory of the Imamate in the interior, assuming that oil would be found there. With financial support provided by the IPC and backing from the British government that included military contingents, the Sultan proceeded to attack, beginning in 1954. By the end of the decade, the Imamate had essentially been crushed and the oil companies could at last conduct their explorations.[37] In 1962, oil was discovered in the interior, in former lands of the Imamate. Two years later, oil was also discovered in Dhofar in the south, a culturally distinct "dependency" of Muscat that had been mobilizing for political autonomy. To secure their (resource-driven) interests, the British then advocated for the "pacification" of Dhofar and its incorporation into a unified Omani state under a single, British-backed sultan. They orchestrated the coup that forced out Sultan Saʿid bin Taimur and replaced him, in 1970, with his British-educated son, Qaboos bin Saʿid. With crucial battlefield assistance from not only the British but the Shah of Iran and King Hussein of Jordan, as well, Qaboos worked to neutralize the Dhofari revolutionaries and bring them into an emergent, "modern" state in 1975 under his leadership as Sultan. The onset of oil production in Oman, in 1967, coincided with and precipitated these transformations.

Another important distinction between Kuwait and Qatar on the one hand, and Oman and Saudi Arabia on the other has to do with the place of Islam in governance. In the pre-oil Omani (Ibaḍi) Imamate and in the two Saudi-Wahhabi states, a close connection existed between religious

---

[35] Similar to Mitchell's argument (fn. 18), Takriti shows that absolutism took hold in Oman because of the particular ways in which Britain intervened and went about pursuing its interests.

[36] A multinational company, the IPC in the 1930s was a consortium of British, British-Dutch, American and French oil companies, as well as an individual (Armenian businessman) shareholder. On its formation and securing of the "Red Line Agreement," which allowed it to monopolize oil exploration within most of the former Ottoman territories of the Gulf region, see Yergin 1991.

[37] On the Imamate and its toppling, see Wilkinson 1987.

and political authority, such that the ruler enjoyed religious legitimacy either because he was himself an ʿālim or because he had the support of the ʿulama and was said to govern according to the precepts of the faith. In the small Gulf sheikhdoms, however, rulers did not claim religious authority, nor did their power depend on explicit support from the ʿulama. In all settings, however, Islam was practiced as a/the way of life.

It is worth noting, somewhat parenthetically, that just as they had promoted autocracy in the emergent states of the Gulf so as to advance their own interests, the British and the Americans encouraged the politicization of Islam, as well. As Tim Mitchell (2002) has argued, in the first decades of the twentieth century, the British, anxious for greater access to the interior of the peninsula, underwrote the alliance between the politically ambitious Ibn Saʿud and the deeply conservative Wahhabi (or rather, *muwaḥiddun*) forces. With critical logistical support from the Europeans, the politico-religious expansionist alliance eventually resulted in the formation of the Kingdom of Saudi Arabia in 1932 (and its opening up to foreign oil companies). Since then, the British, but especially the Americans, have continued to promote "Islamism" – indeed, the instrumentalization of Islam for political gain – by consistently supporting conservative religious forces in the region in their shared opposition to (anti-imperialist) Arab nationalists, communists and other leftists (Mitchell 2002). In so doing, they have been able to pursue their interests in the Gulf.

While the distinctive features noted suggest that Saudi and Omani rulers may have been somewhat better equipped than their counterparts in the small sheikhdoms to exercise authority and project power before oil, in both environments similar "state-society" relations and patterns of behavior prevailed. Rulers of the four more-or-less embryonic states exploited as their own whatever resources they could tap and activities they could tax,[38] as well as the allowances and eventually, oil concession payments they received from their foreign patrons. There was no clear distinction between the resources of the "state" and of the ruler (or ruling family). For example, when he abdicated in 1949, Qatar's emir, Sheikh Abdallah, made off with the state funds as well as advances on an oil concession agreement with an American company (Crystal 1990, 118–21). And in Oman, through the 1960s at least, the oil concession was registered in the Sultan's name and oil revenues were transferred directly to his personal bank account (Valeri 2009, 92). By and large, what indigenous administrative systems existed were personalized

---

[38] For pre-oil Qatar, see Fromherz 2012, 118–19.

arrangements fashioned by the ruler along kinship and clientelist lines and to serve his interest in political survival and personal comfort. Social elements which the ruler depended on, or felt threatened by, had to be appeased. The ruler, referred to as sheikh, emir or sultan, distributed money, land, gifts and positions as he chose among family members and allies, and beyond them to whichever social forces – tribes, merchants, minorities – and for whatever pursuits he deemed necessary; he expected loyalty, or at least obedience, in return (Crystal 1995; Kamrava 2013, 130; Al-Rasheed 2002; Valeri 2009). The patrimonial nature of rule would persist over time and with the expansion of resources. Society was constructed hierarchically, allegiance was accorded to a particular family and rulers' reliance on foreign protection and patronage, and their deference to the policies and plans of the British or Americans, were routine (Onley and Khalaf 2006).

Since their independence, tribal dynastic monarchy exhibiting varying degrees of authoritarianism characterizes these states. Political parties are illegal in all six GCC states, but political blocs are tolerated in Kuwait and they campaign for seats in parliament. Indeed, Kuwait is unique in that its 1962 constitution provides for an elected representative assembly with legislative authority; it has had a functioning, fully elected parliament for decades. Nonetheless, from its inception in 1963 until spring 2023, Kuwait's National Assembly has been dissolved by royal decree eleven times (Allarakia et al. 2021). In Oman, elected participation was introduced in the 1990s through its *majlis al-shura* (Consultative Assembly), while Qatar's *majlis al-shura* has been two-thirds elected since late 2021. As for Saudi Arabia, its 150-member *majlis* is appointed by the king and can only provide non-binding advice on legislation. Municipal councils, in place since 2005, are only partially elected (Freer 2019, 92). Thus, in the four states, insofar as sovereignty and political authority are concerned, the ruler remains supreme.

With the discoveries of oil in Kuwait and Saudi Arabia in 1938, Qatar in 1940 and Oman in 1964, the British and the Americans concentrated their investments in the Gulf on whatever was required locally to facilitate the extraction and export of oil and the importation of goods and services for the oil industry. Scant attention was paid to the development of local industries or other economic activities, or to addressing local needs (Commins 2012; Fuccaro 2022; Al-Nakib 2016; Takriti 2013, 151–52; Vitalis 2006). In no time, laborers, who had arrived from near and far to work for the oil companies, complained about their conditions and treatment, while local populations reacted to the foreign-induced transformations underway. Meanwhile, Gulf rulers, who had been receiving a minor share of the profits from the oil companies' extractions and sales, were anxious for a greater share of the pie, both for their own personal enjoyment and protection, and to quell popular demands via distributions of various sorts. Furthermore, once the oil companies recognized the extent of the subterranean endowment and the likelihood of untold enrichment from its exploitation for decades to come, Euro-American businesses followed on their heels into the Gulf to share in the bonanza . They did so by "fabricating need" and peddling their goods and services to what Abdelrahman Munif, in his masterful work, *Cities of Salt* (1984/1988), depicts as gullible, if not besotted, local rulers.[39] Thus, as Laleh Khalili (2020, 58–69, 123–34) describes, all-out development in the Gulf – no matter how unsuitable, extravagant, exploitative – began with "colonial decision-making" to buttress oil extraction. It was quickly manipulated by European and American companies, their home governments and "experts" to nurture their national economies and enhance capitalist profits. And it was "sold" to Gulf rulers in the form of endless imports of commodities, infrastructures, expertise and plans, to satisfy their demands and quell popular discontent.

Since the explosive growth in oil revenues on the heels of the Arab oil embargo of 1973[40] and the nationalizations of their oil and gas industries (1975–80),[41] unbounded development in the Gulf monarchies has persisted despite periodic economic downturns, and rulers' distributive activities, described in Chapter 3, have proliferated. With rampant consumption, indeed, an "energy-intensive consumerist lifestyle" at its core, so-called modernization, that had initially been imposed by Euro-Americans in order to advance their pecuniary interests, has become, in the embrace of Gulf rulers, not simply a reflection, but rather a tool of modern authoritarianism (Hammoudi 2006, 114–15). It is noteworthy that since the 1970s, these same governments have been championing Islamic values, at least discursively, in their national development programs. Routinely, these plans refer to safeguarding the ethical principles of Islam as a key objective and criterion of their implementation. For example, Saudi Arabia's Second Development Plan (1975–79) cites its first goal thus: to "maintain the religious and moral values of Islam"

---

[39] Mitchell (2009; 2011, 39–42) observes that big oil companies "manufacture(d) scarcity" to maintain their profits. They did so in a variety of ways, among them, by encouraging an "energy-intensive consumerist lifestyle."
[40] In response to the United States' and several other countries' support for Israel during the October 1973 war, oil-producing Arab states temporarily ceased shipments of oil to those countries. With the imposition of the embargo and the supply disruptions that ensued, the price of the barrel of oil quadrupled.
[41] Oman's oil industry is not fully nationalized; the Omani government owns 60 percent and foreign entities, principally Royal Dutch Shell, own the rest.

(Jones 2010, 84–5). And in its summary of Kuwait Vision 2035, Kuwait's Ministry of Foreign Affairs reports that one of the strategic goals of the national development plans is to "preserve the values of the Arab-Islamic identity."[42]

Finally, the Gulf monarchies are dependent states. To carry out the imperatives of modern states, they have depended, until recently, almost exclusively upon their hydrocarbon sectors and securing revenues that derive, either directly or indirectly, from the sale of oil and natural gas.[43] To be sure, these regimes' staying power has depended upon their ability to sell their hydrocarbon resources to meet both external demand via exports and, as Jim Krane (2019, 67–79) illustrates, internal demand – for (energy-intensive) development and the associated consumerist lifestyle – via imports from abroad, as well as distributions at home.[44]

In addition to depending on states in the international system as buyers of their oil and natural gas and producers of all that they import, the Gulf monarchies rely on foreign powers for (military) protection. Britain, as noted, was the guarantor of their security and that of their predecessors from the late nineteenth century, while the United States has assumed leadership of that role since the 1980s. For example, in response to Iraq's invasion and occupation of Kuwait in 1990/91, about 700,000 foreign troops from the United States and its partners were deployed to the Gulf whence they routed Iraqi forces.[45] Currently, the Al-Udeid base in Qatar is the largest U.S. military base in the Middle East and has been the headquarters of the US Air Forces Central Command since 2003, while Bahrain houses the US Fifth Fleet and Naval Forces Central Command. Both countries host several thousand foreign (mostly American) military personnel, as do Kuwait and the UAE (Wallin 2018).

Let us not forget that the Gulf monarchies are also deeply dependent on foreigners to not only draw up plans, but also work with the imported materials and build the countries. Indeed, labor and expertise are the most basic, most critical, the *sine qua non* of (hydrocarbon-financed)

---

[42] www.mofa.gov.kw/en/kuwait-state/kuwait-vision-2035. See, as well, the government of Qatar's discussion of its national development strategy for 2011–16: "Despite rapid socioeconomic change over a relatively short period, Qatari society has maintained the essence of its culture and continuity with the past. This continuity includes observing the fundamental principles of Islam, maintaining the inherited status and prestige of the leading families and preserving the family unit as the core of society" (GSDP 2011, 20).
[43] Increasingly, sovereign wealth funds and returns on lucrative international investments are important sources of government revenues, as noted, pp. 6–7.
[44] Krane goes on to say, referring to subsidized utilities – oil, gasoline, desalinated water – that "regimes stay in power not just by distributing oil rents, but also by distributing oil itself."
[45] On the Gulf War see, Gause (2010, 88–135). See, as well, Chapter 4, pp. 84–6.

Table 1.4 *Foreign nationals in Gulf monarchies, 2020*

	For. Nationals as % of Tot. Pop.	For. Nationals as % of Lab. Force
Bahrain	52%	78%
Kuwait	70	85
Oman	41	77
Qatar	88	95
Saudi Arabia	39	58
UAE	87	85–90

Source: Gulf Research Center (GRC): Gulf Labor Markets, Migration and Population Programme, Demographic & Economic Data Base, www.gulfmigration.grc.net

imports; without them, there would, no doubt, be development of a very different sort. It has been estimated that in 1975, 1.4 million foreign nationals were employed in the six states; by 1985 their numbers had increased to 4.4 million. In that ten-year period, the proportion of foreigners in the combined labor force of Kuwait, Qatar, Oman and Saudi Arabia increased from 57 to 75 percent (Baldwin-Edwards 2011, 8–9). In 2019, foreign nationals in the six Gulf monarchies combined constituted 48 percent of the total population of 49 million. They made up 56–82 percent of the employed in Saudi Arabia, Oman and Kuwait, and 93–94 percent in Qatar (Hanieh 2020, 112) (Table 1.4). As we will see in Chapter 5, the peculiarities of the labor force are integral not only to the construction of these states and nations but also to a better understanding of politics: the politics of appeasement and exclusion, of social management and social control.[46]

Structure of the Book

To respond to the questions that inform this study, I proceed as follows: I begin in Chapter 2 with a brief overview of elements of the Islamic normative tradition. I consider three key concepts – justice, the common good and community – and discuss interpretations thereof and ambiguities of their contemporary application. What constitutes justice and to whom does it apply? What constitutes the common good and who has the authority to make that determination? And who are members of the community which benefits from, lives and is governed by the normative

---

[46] As Michael Herb (2017, 17) points out, the peculiarities of the labor market in the Gulf are a function of them being very rich rentier states.

tradition? I then turn my attention to resources and wealth – their attribution, distribution and circulation. In broad strokes, I outline how the relationship between Muslims and their resources is conceived, and how, according to religious norms, resources ought to be utilized and managed for the sake of the common good. The purpose of this discussion is to provide a framework that facilitates a deeper understanding of the extent to which religious norms have been instrumentalized and at times, reformulated in the conduct of the four oil-financed institutionalized practices, explored in subsequent chapters.[47]

In Chapters 3–7, I probe the mechanics of what I identify as a ruling strategy – the actual repurposing of (oil) wealth and religious norms, and their intersection. With evidence from Kuwait, Qatar, Oman and Saudi Arabia primarily, I examine four institutionalized practices associated with welfare and/or development, financed by oil and gas revenues and sanctioned, either implicitly or explicitly, by Islam. The first two, government distributions and the employment of foreign labor, are indirectly sanctioned by Islam and distinctly associated with reshaping community as a community of privilege while at the same time managing and controlling society. The latter two, charitable giving and Islamic banking and finance, embody Islamic norms and thus, are directly connected to demonstrating, if not bolstering Islamic credentials. As they are performed, these practices also promote privilege on the one hand and enrichment on the other, while shaping community and managing and controlling society. I consider the four practices in terms of their (stated or implied) objectives and their effects, as well as society's evaluations of them. I explicate how, in fact, through these practices oil revenues and Islamic norms are mobilized to enforce submission, appease particular social categories, cultivate and reinforce an idea of the nation and thereby reinforce dynastic authority and related regime priorities.

I begin in Chapter 3 with attention to government distributions to society in the form of transfers and subsidies. I describe various types of transfers (universal, particularist and idiosyncratic), their recipients and rationale, and explore matters of equity and exclusion. I show how the variation in access to resources and the related hierarchization of society are both integral to the shaping of the national community, a key regime priority, and a means for the state to exercise control. Then, on the basis of interviews with scholars, economists, dissidents, bankers, (current and former) members of government, representatives or members of public

---

[47] It is not meant to provide the superstructure against which to evaluate the state-directed practices in order to demonstrate how far the Gulf monarchies have strayed from the religious tradition.

and private foundations and NGOs, and official and independent 'ulama, I probe, in Chapter 4, their responses in order to understand how Gulf Arabs appraise government behavior relative to the circulation of wealth. I note the extent to which my interlocutors criticize their rulers in ethical terms, especially insofar as their commitment to justice, equity and inclusion is concerned. Finally, I segue into a brief discussion of religiously inflected movements and individual clerics in the Gulf and their own instrumentalization of Islam to push back against ruling elites and influence politics. The purpose is to demonstrate that ruling elites are not alone in the exploitation of Islam for political ends. In fact, they have shown themselves to be vulnerable to resistance from "specialists in religion" who challenge them, their policies and practices, on the basis of the Islamic normative tradition. It is this vulnerability that suggests the limits of the ruling strategy that I refer to in the final chapter.

For the remaining institutionalized practices, I describe the practice as I witnessed and understood it, as its practitioners explained it and as society, through my interlocutors, evaluated it. In Chapter 5, I build upon the earlier discussion of internal forms of social "tiering" and exclusion to further interrogate the politics of belonging (*intīma'*) in Gulf monarchies, this time through the importation of labor. I disentangle the ways in which foreign labor, the other tier of the bifurcated labor force, plays a role in the definition and consolidation of the national community. Additionally, I examine some of the peculiarities of the importation, organization and incorporation of foreign labor, and consider how they serve the ruler's objectives to appease particular social categories, encourage consumption and enrichment, and enforce submission.

Following that, I turn to the two institutionalized practices that embody Islamic norms: charitable giving and Islamic finance. In analyzing these practices, I highlight the ways in which Islam is invoked and religious edicts are purposefully revised to accord with overriding secular objectives. In Chapter 6, I examine how charity is practiced in the four states. I consider the various kinds of entities that give, how they give, to whom they give or do not give and why they give as they do. In addressing the matter of access to charity, I offer an explanation for the exclusion of certain social categories. In Chapter 7, I investigate the actual goals and purposes of Islamic banking and finance (IBF) that in recent decades have undergone significant growth in both the Gulf and the global economy.[48] I do so through an examination of

---

[48] In 2019, one-third of all active banks in the GCC were Islamic banks. And in 2011, Islamic bank assets in Saudi Arabia, Kuwait and Qatar represented 23–43 percent of total bank assets (Hanieh 2020, 531–32).

some of the characteristic features of its form and substance in Gulf monarchies. The analysis shows that through this institution, Gulf regimes advance two aims: On the one hand, they try to appease those elements of their populations that seek a greater role for Islam in daily life. On the other hand, they uphold the acquisitive drives of a local elite – that includes royals, business associates and conformist religious scholars – and their interest in further integration in global capitalism. In the domain of Islamic banking and finance, ruling priorities related to accumulation and social management cohere; these are the principal purposes.

Finally, I conclude in Chapter 8 with an elucidation of the relationship between oil and Islam – two "strategic resources" – and what that relationship teaches us about politics in Gulf monarchies. The overwhelming message is that in this period of abundant wealth, not simply oil rents (and returns on associated investments) but also religious doctrine (and its interpretations) are exploited and repurposed by Gulf rulers to function as tools of social management and social control. Their aim is to bolster authoritarian ambitions: the capacity of ruling families to both dominate and shape their societies and retain their monopoly over resources. For the sake of maintaining and enriching dynastic states and constructing the nation, oil and Islam are their principal tools.

2 Islamic Norms, Interpretations, Applications

Introduction

As with other great religions, Islamic religious doctrine as presented in the sacred text is one, while interpretations of it are many. From the Prophet Mohamed's death in 632 until the present day, variations in understandings have emerged across the Muslim world and at different historical junctures as religious scholars have striven to both decode the messages of the Qur'an, supplemented by the Sunna (the sayings and example of the Prophet), and incorporate them into judicial decisions or rulings (*ḥukm*), appropriate for local application. Thus, the rich set of norms and principles presented in the Qur'an and Hadith has been adopted in various ways, a function of differing perspectives derivative of assumptions and subjectivities and the influence of space and time (al-Qaradawi 1969, xxxiv). On the basis of exegesis and commentary that engendered a vast jurisprudential literature (*fiqh*), religious scholars/legal experts (*fuqahā'*) would offer their opinions and thereby define the contours of what has come to be called "Islamic law" (*sharīʿa*).

No doubt, developments within the *umma*, as well as in non-Muslim societies with which the community came into contact, would contribute to understandings and opinions and thus exert influence on the transformation of norms and principles into rulings.[1] This being the case, the elaboration and application of *sharīʿa* varies with time, place and circumstance (Abou El Fadl 2001, 34). It is fair to assume, therefore, that the arrival and

---

[1] For example, Marshall Hodgson (1974), referring to the early Abbasid period (715–813), notes that "in law and ethics and popular lore ... both the ʿulama and the story-tellers of the mosque drew on the *dhimmi* background for their spirit and often for their materials" such that these older religious traditions contributed to the form which Islam took at a local level (307). Even a scholar like Sayyid Qutb not only acknowledged the influence on his thinking of developments elsewhere but also encouraged the deliberate incorporation of foreign influences into Islamic life. In his *Social Justice in Islam* (1953/2000), he wrote: "We should also incorporate discoveries, in terms of social legislation and systems, that have been made [elsewhere] that could advance social justice and welfare in Islamic society and that do not contravene the principles of Islam" (295–96).

Introduction 31

implantation of Euro-Americans in the Gulf region in the first decades of the twentieth century to explore for oil, and the resultant changes to local societies, impacted doctrinal interpretations and applications.

Further to the east, in fact, from the 1930s, the Indo-Pakistani *'ālim*, Abu al-A'la Mawdudi elaborated an "Islamic Economics" in which norms of behavior, as presented in the sacred texts, would govern economic decisions and transactions.[2] In his view, by adopting "Islamic economics" and leading an "Islamic way of life," the Muslim community would both reassert and protect its identity in the face of the onslaught of foreign influences and ideas that had, according to some, weakened the community. In the 1950s, several of Mawdudi's demands for the Islamization of life were integrated into *shari'a* rulings or incorporated into Pakistan's constitution (Nasr 2006, 117–18). And in the Gulf region in the 1970s, following the "first oil shock," Islamic economics was adopted by some institutions, as we will see in Chapter 7, to supposedly promote pan-Arab and pan-Islamic causes by "recycling petrodollars" in what was claimed to be an Islamic way.[3]

While diversity, debate and disagreement about ideas and interpretations have been very much a part of Islamic thought and Islamic history,[4] it is the case that in the majoritarian Sunni tradition, a mere four doctrinal schools of jurisprudence (*madhhab, madhāhib*), each with its distinctive features in terms of legal doctrine, methodology and assumptions, have survived since the eleventh century; they are the Hanafi, Maliki, Shafi'i and Hanbali. The four schools share the view that the purpose of the *shari'a* is to "serve the best interests of human beings" (*tahqīq maṣāliḥ al-'ibād*), but differences of opinion abound about how to meet or even interpret that principle (Abou El Fadl 2005, 157).

In the Shi'i tradition, two doctrinal schools, the Ja'fari and the Zaydi, persist, and a single Ibaḍi school exists among descendants of a subsect of the Khariji movement (mid-seventh century). In the Gulf today, Qatar and Saudi Arabia are officially doctrinally aligned to the Hanbali *madhhab*, Kuwait follows the Maliki, and Oman, the Ibaḍi. Nonetheless, from the 1970s and the explosion in their oil revenues, "Wahhabism," the Hanbali-derived creed and politico-ideological arm of the Saudi state, gained in force

---

[2] See Mawdudi's, *First Principles of Islamic Economics*, edited by Khurshid Ahmed, translated by A.I.S. Hashemi, UK: The Islamic Foundation, 2011. Mawdudi's compatriot, Syed Nawab Haider Naqvi (1994, 2003), who was an important *'ālim* as well, also wrote extensively about the Islamic economy.
[3] Yet as we will see, Islamic banking and finance has proven to be yet another way to accumulate capital.
[4] On the plurality of views and its challenges in the contemporary period see, al-Qaradawi (2001).

and influence. Characterized by a rigid, religious conservatism, Wahhabi thought shuns diversity of opinion and thus, insists upon conformity and obedience. It is these latter features that have been incorporated into governance, to varying degrees, by the other ruling families as well.[5]

Be that as it may, the foundational texts of Islam comprise a set of guidelines regarding devotion to God and ethical living. Islam has been described as a total system (Chapra 1992; Naqvi 1994), one that "deals with the whole field of human life" (Qutb 1953/2000, 37),[6] or as an overarching moral-legal order to which the political and economic spheres are bound (Hallaq 2013). Indeed, guidelines encompass a broad range of concerns and activities, including prayer, social relations, protections of various sorts, governance and accountability, crime and punishment, rights to and use of property, distribution of wealth, trade and market behavior. Reflecting a total system, all activities are meant to be suffused with the moral principles at the core of the religious tradition.

This chapter provides a brief synthesis of Islamic norms, including, where appropriate, challenges to and ambiguities of their various interpretations and contemporary application. The primary focus relates to resources – their attribution, distribution and circulation. How do Muslims conceive of their relationship to wealth, property and resources? To whom do wealth and resources belong, and what are their responsibilities? How, by whom and for what purposes are wealth and resources to be distributed, and who has the authority to make such determinations? While the topic is vast, I present a synthesis that most scholars and knowledgeable interpreters would find broadly accurate, and that reflects mainstream understandings of the contemporary Arabian Peninsula.[7] By providing this framework prior to the discussion of the empirical material in subsequent chapters, the aim is to facilitate a deeper understanding of how, in the conduct of oil-financed, state-directed institutionalized practices, religious norms have been manipulated and at times, reformulated.

---

[5] An 'ālim and incisive critic, Khaled Abou El Fadl states that present-day Saudi Wahhabism has defied the classical *fiqh* methodology insofar as it treats its own assumptions as sacrosanct, rather than it being open to examination and debate, and has, in this and other ways, closed the interpretive process. As such, it exemplifies, in his view, an authoritarian approach to Islamic law (2001, 158). He goes on to say that Saudi Wahhabism is not focused, in its determinations, on "Qur'anic morality" – not even on basic understandings of fairness and human dignity (269).

[6] "Because this religion is essentially a unity, worship and work, political and economic theory, legal demands and spiritual exhortations, faith and conduct, this world and the world to come, all these are related parts of one comprehensive whole" (Qutb 1953/2000, 113).

[7] Note that some generalizations are made where variations do exist across localities, sects, social classes and the like.

I begin with a discussion of the purposes and goals of the normative tradition. In doing so, I consider four key concepts: justice, equity, the common good and community. I then address the matters of distribution, circulation and poverty alleviation, with attention to rights and responsibilities but also to exclusions. Following that, I turn to the specific case of natural resources: to whom they belong, how and by whom they should be exploited. I conclude with some enduring questions relative to the normative tradition and its interpretation and application in the Arabian Peninsula in the contemporary period – most notably, the thorny issue regarding exclusions from access to wealth and resources.

Goals and Purposes: The Pursuit of Justice, Equity and the Actualization of Goodness

In the Islamic tradition, belief in God (*īmān*) implies acceptance of a set of moral principles enunciated in the Qur'an and the sunna and applied in the shari'a, and the commitment to live according to those principles. The basic objective of the moral principles is to promote good and prevent evil (*al-amr bil-ma'rūf w'al-nahy 'an al-munkar*) and to do so for the purpose of getting close to God (*qurba*) by adhering to that which is foremost among norms: the pursuit of justice ('*adl*). Indeed, as "God commands justice and the actualization of goodness (*iḥsān*)" (16:90), justice is the principal intention [*niyya*] – that which should guide behavior. Hence, believers' general conduct, as well as the good works (*ṣāliḥāt*) they are expected to perform as evidence of their devotion, must be morally motivated for the sake of justice (Hallaq 2013, 86–8). Justice is understood as equity (*qisṭ*), fairness and rectitude; and justice is served by attending to what is best for the community.[8] Furthermore, as Islam is considered an overarching moral order encompassing all spheres of life, justice is meant to pervade all spheres. Thus, it incorporates what we refer to today as social justice, distributive justice or environmental justice, alongside the more commonplace legalistic notions of justice, including such notions as just war and just rule.[9]

---

[8] For a thoughtful discussion of the evolution of the concept of justice and in different traditions, see Bishara (2013). See, as well, al-Khatib (2015).

[9] These are, indeed, twentieth-century concepts. In his 1994 volume, Naqvi employed the term "distributive justice," while Qutb wrote a book entitled *Social Justice in Islam* (1953). For Naqvi, distributive justice implies "a superior distribution of income and wealth, in accordance with the universally accepted norms of fairness" (89); it also implies equality of opportunity but not necessarily equality of result (90). For an illuminating discussion, see Tripp (2006), who points out that the term "social justice," as it relates to the

Equity (*qisṭ*) may be considered synonymous with justice (*'adāla*); indeed, the two terms seem to be used interchangeably in the Qur'an. But equity does not necessarily imply equality, even though many scholars insist on the "pervasive egalitarianism" of the Qur'an: "As believers ... (Muslims are) equal to each other in value and thus stand undifferentiated before God" (Hallaq 2013, 49).[10] As Louise Marlow (1997) notes, at its inception, Islam as ideology was indeed egalitarian, even though in practice there existed inequalities in the distribution of power, wealth and social status. Over time, however, inequalities grew as new peoples and new ways were incorporated into Islamic society, and political leaders typically assumed entitlements which they associated with power over larger numbers. Hierarchy and social divisions of various sorts prevailed, initially with the superior status of the Arab. And privilege turned out to be neither a function of merit nor even chiefly of birth, but rather, of what Marlow terms "the emperor's favour" (42). Furthermore, the scholars of Islam, the *'ulama,* were themselves complicit in the "progressive watering down of the egalitarian impulse" in that, for the sake of preserving domestic peace and warding off *fitna* (disorder), they were inclined to assert the legitimacy and therefore, uphold the behaviors of those who were unfitting rulers. In so doing, they retained their honored station as religious authority (Marlow 1997, 93). Thus, equality remained in force only as ideal, as expressed in Quranic assertions regarding believing men before God: that there was "no superiority except in piety" (Qutb 1953/2000, 70–1), and that all would be judged in the end according to how they lived their lives and fulfilled their responsibilities.

Alongside the real limitations of the egalitarian principle, justice and equity as ultimate goals of the faith are themselves fundamentally imperfect. As Abou El Fadl (2001, 27–8) indicates, both are highly subjective in that they "endow the agent with a considerable amount of discretion" in how they perceive what is just and equitable and what they can do and demand in their pursuit. This is the case whether the agent is an individual member or the leader of the community. The risks of subjectivity and broad discretion are supposed to be mitigated by the expected moral integrity of believing Muslims, but the reality of assuming such risks,

---

narrowing of social gaps, reflects a more modern perspective whereby human behavior is assessed on the basis of its social outcomes. However, what produces justice for the community is a reflection of justice as commanded by God (69).

[10] Besides, for Ibn Taymiyyah, the prominent thirteenth/fourteenth-century theologian, justice cannot be equivalent to equality since justice requires inequality between Muslims and non-Muslims, even *dhimmi*. See, Bishara (2013, 16).

Abou El Fadl insists, brings to the fore the possibilities for "moral transgressions" of various sorts.

As noted, justice is served by promoting good and preventing evil, and attending to what is best for the community. While the term *al-maṣlaḥa al-ʿamma* (the "public interest" or "common good") does not appear in the Qurʾan, preserving it is, according to jurists (*fuqahāʾ*), constitutive of justice; as such, it is central to the normative tradition. Abdelhamid Ghazali, the eleventh-century theologian, insisted that it was not enough to promote good and prevent evil, but rather, in order to uphold the common good, the purposes of the shariʿa [*maqāṣid al-shariʿa*] which, after all, had been elaborated for the benefit of the community, must be preserved. And for Ghazali, the shariʿa's purposes amounted to promoting and protecting religion, life, progeny, property and rationality.[11] In the contemporary period, the late Yusuf al-Qaradawi built upon and broadened Ghazali's definition of *maṣlaḥa* by expanding upon the domains that shariʿa would seek to advance and preserve; they include "honor, peace, rights and freedoms, the institution of justice and shared responsibility in what ought to be a model community, and everything else that makes life easier for them, removes oppression, perfects their character, and guides them to what is best in manners and customs, in social arrangements and in interactions" (Zaman 2012, 115).[12]

While allowing for flexibility and context-specificity, the *maṣlaḥa* principle, by virtue of its ambiguity, lends itself, as with justice and equity, to subjectivity; and subjectivity, as noted, can prompt manipulation and other forms of abuse (Salvatore 2007, 162). To be sure, the *maṣlaḥa* principle implies universality in the sense that the "interests of the Muslim community at large, and not only a limited segment of it, are served" (Hallaq 1997, 112). As such, it opposes personal and particularistic preferences. Furthermore, such consequential matters as what precisely constitutes the "common good" and who has the authority to make that determination have evoked differing opinions. Insofar as the latter is concerned, responsibility lies with the somewhat indistinct *ahl al-ḥal wʾal-ʿaqd* – the "people who loosen and bind": the problem-solvers and contract-makers. This is a reference to the six individuals whom the caliph ʿUmar ibn al-Khattab chose before his death in the seventh century to decide among themselves on his successor. Hence, it signifies those scholars who are qualified to name, give allegiance (*bayʿa*) to or depose (by rescinding allegiance from) the *khalifa*/leader, and to do so

---

[11] For an elaboration of Ghazali's thinking regarding *maṣlaḥa*, see Laoust (1970, 166–77).
[12] For rich discussions of *maṣlaḥa*, see, *inter alia*, Kamali (1988, 287–303), Khadduri (2013), Tripp (2006, 68–76), Zaman (2004, 129–55).

through consensus, on behalf of the community. Furthermore, this select group constitutes the bulwark against the possible abuse of the *maṣlaḥa* principle by the leader of the community in that they are in a position to rescind the *bayʿa* (Zaman 2012, 111–12). These individuals not only have expertise and moral-legal authority, but they are supposed to represent the community. Hence, they are best placed to define the common good. Indeed, as they alone decide what can be done in the name of *maṣlaḥa*, they enjoy enormous powers and privileges (Carré 1992, 56–7). But who are these people?

In interviews in 2012, Sheikhs Abdallah Bin Bayyah and Yusuf al-Qaradawi (d. 9/2022), two of the then most prominent living Sunni religious scholars, gave striking responses to the question of the identity, in this day and age, of *ahl al-ḥal w'al-ʿaqd*. Bin Bayyah began by admitting that there is disagreement on this matter. He stated that in principle, it is the (political) leadership – the state, in fact – which, in the contemporary period, represents *ahl al-ḥal w'al-ʿaqd* and decides on what constitutes the "common good." He noted that other scholars claim that the *ʿulama'* assume this identity and responsibility, but he disagrees.[13] Interestingly, Bin Bayyah's position does not allow for the withdrawal of support for the political leadership by another recognized entity in society. Moreover, it appears to allow the political leadership virtually free rein in determining what is right for the community and how to go about achieving that. Nonetheless, Bin Bayyah went on to say that in a globalized world such as ours, we should detach ourselves from strict doctrine and leave this matter open to *ijtihād* (interpretation through reasoning) and adaptation to the current environment.[14] In contrast, al-Qaradawi, equivocated: In his writings, he suggests that the *ʿulama'* are best placed to both determine what constitutes the "common good" and rein in the ruler if he wavers in governing "according to sharīʿa norms." Nonetheless, he acknowledges the rights of the ruler and prefers to contemplate him as imbued with moral authority and therefore, legitimate (Zaman 2004, 136–37). In the interview, however, al-Qaradawi side-stepped the debate over *ʿulama'* versus (political) leadership and offered the following anodyne response: "Each nation has people whom scholars call the problem solvers and those who bring people together and make binding decisions. The peoples' assembly, parliament, the

---

[13] Salvatore (2007, 153–55) writes that historically, the rulers were not responsible for caring for the common good, although they were expected to create conditions via public order for its pursuit. In contrast, the *ʿulama'* not only defined the common good, but were responsible for its management, as demonstrated by *waqf* arrangements, for example.

[14] Jeddah, 19 April 2012.

house of representatives, and the *shura* assembly represent the nation, and are supposed to represent the nation."[15]

No doubt, the responses of these most learned scholars reflect the current condition: In states of the Arabian Peninsula today, the common good has been subordinated to the authority of the ruler (*wāli al-'amr*), and the primacy of the prince's say is confirmed by 'ulama' and jurists.[16] Far from remaining independent voices, "official" 'ulama' and jurists are state employees and thus, beholden to the paymaster. Hence, the state has assumed the identity, or rather, the responsibility of *ahl al-ḥal w'al-'aqd* insofar as the *maṣlaḥa* principle is concerned.

Also ambiguous and problematic in the contemporary period is the notion of community (*umma*). Does it refer to the "totality of believers," wherever they are, as was the case in pre-modern times? (Hallaq 2013, 49) Does it remain a de-territorialized community of believers? Or, in the current era, characterized geopolitically by national states, does it refer, rather: to the territorial state ruled by Muslims and populated mostly, but not exclusively by Muslims; to Muslims, of whatever national origin or citizenship, within a particular state; or, to Muslim nationals of the state in which Muslim co-nationals govern? In the oil-rich, dynastic states of the Gulf with their very large numbers of expatriates, many of whom are Muslim, the definition of community is indeed consequential: It impacts, among other things, the breadth of social responsibility and the distribution of resources, establishing thereby the parameters of the common good.

Distribution for the Sake of Justice, Equity, Etcetera

For the purpose of advancing justice and the common good, the religious texts and commentaries are replete with directives regarding wealth (*tharwa*), property (*māl*) and resources (*mawārid*): their ownership, circulation and utilization.[17] To begin, the Qur'anic conception is that all wealth, property and resources belong to God, and humans are the trustees of God on earth. Hence, Muslims are enjoined to use God's property justly and ethically in accordance with God's laws for the good of the community (al-Khuli 1981, 61–3). These directives are

---

[15] Doha, 5 March 2012.
[16] Besides, these two prominent individuals are/were guests in their respective countries of residence, Saudi Arabia and Qatar, and are/were obligated to the local ruler for their (continued) hospitality.
[17] For rich discussions, see Bin Bayyah (2010); al-Khuli (1981); Baqir al-Ṣadr (1982). See, as well, Wohidul Islam (1999, 361–68). For an application to hydrocarbons, Farouk-El-Adé (1999a, 3–15; 1999b, 148–58).

understood in a variety of ways (Bin Bayyah 2010, 37–46). For one, private ownership is acknowledged as a right, as long as the owner – themself, a trustee – exploits the property judiciously: they cannot abuse, waste or be stingy with it; rather, they must work it to make it productive so as to meet their own needs, as well as the needs of others (Baqir al-Sadr 1982 II-2, 122–26). In this regard, the individual who, via their initiative and effort, revives fallow or unexploited land, gains possession of that land and for as long as they keep it productive.[18] And given the primacy of the community's interest and the state's responsibility for ensuring it, the ruler may expropriate property from private hands if doing so serves the community's welfare and the property was not being exploited appropriately (Hallaq 2009, 301). As for public property, it is held by the state in trusteeship to meet the needs of the community. In other words, wealth has no intrinsic value and ownership is not an end in itself. Rather, the good which the owner accomplishes with their property is what matters (Baqir al-Sadr 1982 II-1, 177). This being the case, working to increase wealth is incumbent upon all able Muslims. In fact, Qutb (1953/2000, 149–50) insists that lawful gain derives from hard work alone. (Thus, it is unlawful to live off and enrich oneself from the efforts of others.) Besides, the objective of expending effort to increase wealth is to enhance distribution. Hence, landed property, for example, must not remain unused; it must be worked and exploited so that it contributes to the sustenance of the proprietor, laborers and others.

Exploiting property and resources appropriately, therefore, achieves two (linked) core purposes: It facilitates the circulation of wealth in ways that address the needs of the community and promote good. In doing so, it makes the owner a better – that is, a more appropriately observant – Muslim and thus, brings them closer to God (Bonner 2005, 397–98). Hence, the modern interpretation expounded by Muslim scholars, and reflecting the influence of secular concepts of social welfare, is that wealth/property and resources, in the public domain or private hands, have a social function (*al-waẓifat al-ijtima'iyya*) (Tripp 2006, 56–67, 83–8).[19] Thus, piety (*taqwa*) and social responsibility (*al-takāful al-ijtimā'iy*), like belief (*īmān*) and good works (*ṣāliḥāt*), go hand in hand (Qutb 1953/2000, 89; al-Khuli 1981, 211–49).

---

[18] Referred to as the *iḥyā' al-mawāt* (revivification of dead land) stipulation, this has been discussed by several modern scholars of Islam; see Chapter 3, fn. 45.

[19] In Qutb's words: "Whatever belongs to the individual in the last analysis belongs to the community when it has need of it" (quoted in, Carré (2003, 209–11). See Baqir al-Sadr (1982 II-1, 96); al-Bahi al-Khuli (1981, 69–78); al-Ghazali (2005, 71–4).

Embedded in the understanding of wealth/property are two related notions with, as we will see shortly, contemporary significance: that of surplus (*faḍl*) and of right or entitlement (*haqq*) (Bonner 2003, 24). *Faḍl* suggests that whatever remains after an individual has fulfilled their needs is considered excess, and those who enjoy excess have a duty to share it with others. *Haqq* builds upon *faḍl*: It suggests that the needy are entitled to a portion of the surplus of those who are better off. Moreover, realizing both the right to wealth and the duty to share supports the circulation of resources, as opposed to their concentration (Qutb 1953/ 2000, 132–34). In turn, circulation may foster equity when it reduces wealth disparities which can themselves be divisive insofar as they inhibit social solidarity (*al-taḍāmun al-ijtimā 'iy*) (Tripp 2006, 51–6).

In the normative tradition, there exists, as Bonner (2005) discusses, the idea of "positive" circulation – in the form of, for example, charitable giving and fixed inheritance distributions – which is encouraged as it conforms to core values and objectives (397–98). There is, likewise, the idea of "negative" circulation which includes such things as monopoly (*iḥtikār*) and lending with financial interest (*ribā*) (397–98).[20] Such practices are repeatedly condemned in the religious texts and juridical interpretations, as are hoarding, greed, waste and ostentation – by no means uncommon over the course of Islamic history (al-Ghazali 2005, 146–73). As they deny the needy and create social divisions while distracting individuals from God and the moral precepts of the faith, they impede the pursuit of justice and the common good (Bonner 2001, 417–19). Hence, poverty, when it exists, is not a function of scarcity, but rather, of the inequitable distribution of wealth. And the latter results from the prioritization of personal interest at the expense of others. That is to say, the poor are poor because others are greedy.

Giving to others is an individual obligation to be performed with the appropriate *niyya* (intention) and a key instrument for the advancement of not merely distributive justice but social justice, as well.[21] Giving includes both the requisite zakat (alms "tax"), the third of the five pillars of Islam, and elective *ṣadaqa*.[22] Equivalent to 2.5 percent, zakat is levied on the growth of the individual's wealth over the course of one year – what might be referred to today as "capital gains" – minus *niṣāb*, a

---

[20] See Qutb's discussion of monopoly and usury as illicit (1953/2000, 147–53). There remain differences of opinion regarding the prohibition of any type of financial interest or only what would be deemed exploitative rates of interest. See, *inter alia*, Ghazali (2005, 146–51); Hallaq (2009, 525–26); Zaman (2012, 120–29).
[21] It is also considered a means to purify the self insofar as giving "removes the moral burden that accompanies the garnering of wealth" (Hallaq 2013, 123).
[22] For rich discussions, see al-Qaradawi (1969); al-Khuli (1981, 192–200); Zysow (2013).

minimum pre-determined monetary value deemed sufficient for subsistence, similar to a poverty threshold. Those Muslims whose assets are less than *niṣāb* are excused from the obligation to pay. Following the example of the early Muslim community, zakat contributions are to be collected by agents of the "state" and transferred to the Public Treasury (*beyt al-māl*). They are then distributed by the authorities among the poor and needy and other appropriate recipients, as stipulated in the Qur'an.[23]

While both anonymous and identified giving are permitted, the Qur'an is explicit that the former is preferable: "If you give charity openly, it is good, but if you keep it secret and give to the needy in private, this is better for you, and it will atone for some of your bad deeds: God is well aware of all that you do" (*surat al-Baqara* 2:271).[24] Nonetheless, some 'ulama' suggest that zakat should be given openly, as long as doing so is not a function of conceit, since by modeling good behavior it may encourage others to give. Even so, it is the intention (*niyya*) that matters, more than its manner (al-Qaradawi 1969, 290–94). Moreover, as the wherewithal for giving derives from earnings, and earnings result from productive activity, Muslims, as pointed out, are enjoined to work hard to produce wealth, to provide for themselves and help others (Kahlut 1982, 21–7; Bonner 2001, 412–17). Thus, charitable giving serves multiple purposes. Since the emergence of modern states and the influence of secular ideologies, it is thought to advance justice by reducing inequalities while connecting people to each other; this promotes social stability and thus, the common good.

As an individual act, therefore, zakat is a demonstration of piety as well as social accountability and responsibility. At the level of the community and the state, it is intended to be a principal instrument for discouraging hoarding, combating poverty and reducing inequalities, thus enhancing "social balance" and social solidarity.[25] Hence, zakat is an important financial resource of the state with which to achieve the aforementioned purposes (al-Qaradawi 1969, 116). The collection of zakat is a method for raising funds for the state. Furthermore, given his responsibility for

---

[23] These include travelers on foot, insolvent debtors, zakat collectors, slaves seeking to pay for their freedom, "those whose hearts need winning over" and "for the advancement of God's cause" (Qur'an 9:60). See Benthall (1999, 30–2) for a provocative discussion of these recipients.

[24] See, as well, al-Ghazali (1966, 77–87).

[25] On the notion of social balance, see *inter alia*, Baqir al-Sadr (1982 2:2, 134–43). Mohamad al-Ghazali (2005) notes that the leader has the right to determine the ways to achieve social balance. For the purpose of alleviating poverty, it was thought that the collection of zakat, plus the related injunctions regarding the exploitation of wealth and resources, ought to be sufficient. If not, though, it was incumbent upon the state to draw upon its own resources and those in the public domain to meet social needs (94).

the community's welfare, the ruler has the right to decide on appropriate ways to achieve it (al-Ghazali 2005, 94). According to some scholars, he may impose zakat payment, even with force; he may also insist on additional payments from the community to the extent that that would be necessary for preserving *maṣlaḥa* (Qutb 1953/2000, 127–28). Moreover, in view of the stipulation that lawful recipients of zakat include zakat collectors and those engaged in "the advancement of God's cause," zakat funds could be spent not only on such things as public works but also remuneration for state agents and even military campaigns and the expansion of territory. Sheikh al-Qaradawi insists, however, that the latter are legitimate only when the aim is to promote or defend Islam (1969, 66–70). Alas, how to ascertain such an aim incontrovertibly remains ambiguous.

In his discussion of the consolidation of political authority in the nascent Saudi state under Abd al-Aziz ibn Abd al-Rahman Al Saʿud (or, Ibn Saʿud), Anthony Toth (2012, 57–79) shows how zakat was a primary mechanism in the establishment of sovereignty. In the years preceding the exploitation of oil, funds from zakat and the pilgrimage constituted the main sources of state revenues. As such, they financed the ruler's campaigns for expanding and solidifying his political domain while maintaining him and his family and compensating his agents – among them the *muṭawwaʿu*,[26] who were responsible not only for collecting zakat but for imposing conformity to Wahhabi rules of behavior. When collected, often by force, from disparate tribes across Arabia, zakat was a "token of (their) political submission" to the ruler who would come to recognize them as (loyal) subjects with expectations for his protection (Al-Rasheed 2002, 20). Furthermore, zakat collected from one group could then be distributed to others as rewards for good work or payoffs to win them over. Whether or not zakat payment was imposed on a tribe or the broader "national" community and collected by force was, according to Toth (2012), a reflection of how confident, secure, and financially comfortable the ruler felt vis-à-vis the particular group and/or the broader society. He goes on to suggest that from the 1950s, with the Al Saʿud enjoying access to oil revenues of increasing importance, the zakat regime in Saudi Arabia was relaxed. Oil rents replaced zakat and

---

[26] Often referred to as the "religious police," this body, whose official name is the Committee for the Promotion of Virtue and the Prevention of Vice (*hayʾat al-ʾamr bil-maʿrūf wʾal-nahī ʿan al-munkar*) is charged by the government with supervising and ensuring the upholding of Islamic morals in social life and economic activity. On its origins and the changes to its responsibilities in the three Saudi-Wahhabi states, see *inter alia*, Cook (2001); Commins (2009).

other sources of state revenues as the instrument of choice for rewarding some, co-opting others, and neutralizing forces of opposition (78–9).

In sum, the story of its collection in the Arabian Peninsula demonstrates that zakat is by no means merely a simple act of religious duty (imposed by the "state" on believing Muslims) – which it never was, in fact – or even an economic activity with a social welfare function. Rather, as we will see in Chapter 6, across the Gulf states, it also is an instrument for consolidating relationships of power and authority. Indeed, exploring zakat practice may uncover complexities of domination and social control.

Natural Resources: Their Exploitation, Utilization, Distribution

As for natural resources, they constitute, according to most interpretations of Islamic doctrine, "public wealth" (*tharwa 'umumiyya*), referring to the common wealth of humanity, or "communal wealth" (*tharwat al-umma*), the shared wealth of the community (al-Khuli 1981, 91–100). Reflecting a well-known hadith in which the Prophet Mohamed said that people are partners in water, pastureland and fire (sources of energy), the notion is that resources considered to provide the primary necessities of life, on which the common good depends, should come under communal ownership for the benefit of all, without exclusion (Naqvi 1994, 91). Furthermore, the shared wealth should be managed, protected and exploited by governing authorities in trusteeship for the community. In the modern period, therefore, the state, as trustee and overseer, must preserve and develop the resources, and make them and that which they yield available to the community so as to meet its needs.[27]

Insofar as mineral resources are concerned, a distinction is sometimes made between those that are apparent (*al-ẓāhir*) and those that are hidden (*al-bāṭin*). According to Baqir al-Sadr (1982, 114), the prevailing opinion is that so-called apparent minerals, such as oil, for example, which are found in their natural state, constitute common property not specifically for Muslims but for all peoples living under the banner of Islam. Hidden minerals, such as gold, which require additional labor for their "true nature" to be revealed, are considered common property only if they are found close to the surface of the earth. As for hidden minerals that are far from the surface of the earth, there is a difference of opinion.

---

[27] Al-Khuli (1981, 94–104) provides a rich explication of water, pastureland and fire and their contemporary application, as well as a discussion of the role of the state relative to resources that belong to the people.

The minority view is that the individual(s) who have expended effort to reach, extract and refine the minerals have a special right to them. In contrast, the majority view is that they fall under the category of state property or public property and so, they too must be managed by the authorities for the sake of the public welfare.[28]

As with other forms of property, when there is a surplus – of oil, for example, or rather, revenues from its sale – it should be shared with those outside the community who have need for it. The dominant view today, as expressed by Sheikh al-Qaradawi, among others, is that other Muslim communities should be the first recipients from the surplus, followed by non-Muslims.[29] Furthermore, a portion of the resource or, in the case of oil, revenues from its sale, should be allocated for future generations so that they too may enjoy its benefits.[30]

According to the normative tradition, therefore, the leader of the community – the state, in contemporary parlance – is the custodian (*khalifa*), responsible for both preserving the common wealth, as well as exploiting and distributing it justly for the benefit of all, without preference or injury.[31] He must not take from it for himself, except what is due to meet his needs, and he must make known the standard upon which his distributions are based.[32] And if something remains after the leader has provided appropriately for the common good, it should be distributed among the people "because it is their right, or their property" (al-Khuli 1981,104). Moreover, the leader, whose legitimacy derives from his moral accountability, provides the model of behavior, attentive at all times to justice and equity in addressing the needs of the community (Zaman 2012, 251). Nonetheless, straying from the attributes of leadership, as outlined in the normative tradition, has not been uncommon over the course of Islamic history.

---

[28] For a detailed discussion, see Baqir al-Sadr (1982 2:1, 111–20). In his controversial book, *Ain al-Khiṭa'?: taṣḥīḥ mafāhīm wa'naẓra tajdīd* (1978), Sheikh Abdullah al-'Alayli (1914-96) denounced the monopolization of oil wealth in the hands of a few. He argued that the hadith regarding water, pastureland and fire implies that the wealth that derives from oil found in Muslim countries rightfully belongs to, and therefore must be for the benefit of, all Muslims and not only the residents of those particular countries.
[29] Interview: Doha, 5 March 2012.
[30] Interview with the late Dr. Mohamed Kamal Imam, Professor of Shari'a, Law School, University of Alexandria, Egypt; Cairo, 20 Jan. 2012.
[31] As Bahi al-Khuli (1981, 101–3) notes, the state assumes two roles in this regard: On the one hand, it serves as the storehouse (*khizāna*) of public wealth, responsible for its preservation; on the other hand, it spends from it for the well-being of the collective (*infāq fī maṣāliḥ al-jamā'a*).
[32] Interview with a Ṣaḥwa sheikh, Riyadh, 3 May 2012. On the Ṣaḥwa movement, see chapter 4, footnote 5.

Be that as it may, as designator of *al-maṣlaḥa al-ʿamma*, the leadership can claim that whatever they do is for the common good. Furthermore, the twelfth century Hanbali view, that openly contesting the political leader must be resisted for it could create disorder (*fitna*), came to dominate Sunni orthodoxy, informing customary practice, as well. This condition has persisted to the present in Arabian Gulf states and beyond, no matter the prevailing school of thought and with profound effects.[33] The ruler remains unchallenged in his beliefs and behaviors.

Enduring Questions: The Matter of Inclusion

In the contemporary period, to whom does justice apply and who are entitled to resources, distributions and protections? In the Islamic as in the Biblical tradition, justice applies to the believers of that tradition – hence, the *umma*, in the case of Islam (Bishara 2013, 18). Entitlements – or rights, a modern concept – may be thought of as associated with, indeed a privilege of belonging (*intīmaʾ*), in this case to the community of believing Muslims. Hence, any Muslim – regardless of their origin, place of birth or permanent residence – who lives in an "Islamic land" enjoys the same rights and duties as Muslims who are native to the place (Parolin 2009, 113).

It is important to remember that membership in the *umma* derives either from religious affiliation as a Muslim, or from the special status extended to non-Muslims, or *dhimmī*. In theory and in practice, the non-Muslim was incorporated into *dar al-Islam*, where Muslims live and rule, via a contractual relationship which accorded them particular rights and obligations.[34] The relationship endured for as long as the non-Muslim remained in *dar al-Islam* and abided by the stipulations of the contract. Provided that they submitted to Muslim power and authority and accepted its conditions in the form of supporting the state materially and politically, they received protection from the religious and political authorities, as well as the Muslim population, and could retain their religious allegiance and practice their faith (Abou El Fadl 2003, 189).

---

[33] See al-Rasheed (2013, 724–26) for what she refers to as a "theology of obedience" to the ruler/regime, disseminated by the religious authorities and critical in the consolidation of the Saudi state.

[34] While in simplest terms *dar al-Islam* refers to where Muslims live and shariʿa is in force, as a notion, it "connotes a commitment to a moral community not necessarily bounded by space or territory" (Abou El Fadl 2003, 194). As for "dhimmitude," traditionally it applied to *ahl al-kitāb* – that is, Jews and Christians at least, but also, Zoroastrians. According to some scholars, Hindus and Buddhists could be included, as well. See in this regard, Abou El Fadl (2003, 206 fn. 55).

Nonetheless, as non-Muslims, these protected subjects were prevented from acceding to political power and governance.[35]

Note, however, that "dhimmitude" did not imply equality in status with Muslims. Recall Louise Marlow's (1997) thesis that despite the pervasive egalitarianism of the Qur'an, hierarchy has been a feature of Muslim society virtually from the start, with not only religious affiliation but also ethnicity as markers of privilege: Muslims have always enjoyed superior rank to non-Muslims and in the early years at least, Arabs to non-Arabs (Hodgson 1974, 222–29, 242–43). Indeed, discrimination against *dhimmī* was by no means uncommon, depending on place, time and context, with occasional and sometimes quite vigorous persecution (Hodgson 1975, 537–38; Hourani 1991, 117–19; Sachedina 2001, 97). Moreover, rules stipulating how Muslims were to deal with non-Muslims were not necessarily fixed, nor abided by without fail. As Abou El Fadl (2003) points out, context-specific special arrangements were possible for the sake of "practical necessity and public interest" (190–91). Nonetheless, what is most significant about "dhimmitude" for my purposes is that according to Islamic jurisprudence and over the course of Islamic history, these non-Muslims were not only included in, but also considered to be a part of the state where Muslims ruled. As such, they enjoyed some rights, assumed obligations and received some protection and recognition.

In addition to *dhimmī*, another category of non-Muslim is recognized by *fiqh* as enjoying rights when in *dar al-Islam*. Irrespective of whether they are monotheist or polytheist, a non-Muslim living in *dar al-harb/al-kufr*, who travels to *dar al-Islam* with the intention to stay for a short period, is both subject to Muslim rule and has the right to protection of their person and their property while there and for the duration of their stay (Hallaq 2009, 332–33). Referred to as *musta'amin*, since they are the beneficiary of *'amān*, a contract of security and safe conduct, they can live in *dar al-Islam* for, in most cases, up to one year – although specifics vary from one *madhhab* to another – with their spouse and children (*al-mawsū'a al-fiqhīa* 1997, 168–79). If they stay longer, they can be naturalized as *dhimmī*, and from that moment on they will be subject to the rules of *dhimma*. Furthermore, the *'amān* can be extended either by the "state" – that is, the political or religious authorities – or by any Muslim member of the community (*al-mawsū'a al-fiqhīa* 1997, 169). As this migrant's status allows them to engage in productive economic activities that would benefit

---

[35] Indeed, in 1904, the Egyptian *'ālim*, Mohamed Abdu (1849-1905) issued a fatwa stating that the Muslim non-citizen resident was equal to the citizens of the national state except insofar as working in government was concerned; this latter domain was reserved for citizens alone (Abu Sahlieh 1996, 52).

themself and *dar al-Islam*, cooperative relations between their homeland and place of temporary residence could result (Abu-Sahlieh 1996, 42).[36]

To be sure, Muslim society would undergo fundamental changes over time with the introduction and intensification of capitalist relations of production, the rise of regionalism and localism, the intervention of European imperialism and colonialism and the emergence of the modern nation-state. These external forces would combine with critical internal developments – among them, increased power and authority of central power, loss of autonomy and (religious) authority of the 'ulama' and growing distance between the state and society. An important result of these transformations would be the fraying of the attachment to, or at least the practical application of the teachings relative to the status and treatment of the non-Muslim. Indeed, as legal categories, *dhimmī* and *musta'amin* were abandoned (Mednicoff 2011, 146–49). Nonetheless, these teachings and practices remain a template against which Muslim communities can be compared. In fact, the question of the foreigner, and their rights and status in Muslim countries, re-emerged in the twentieth century and was taken up by some Muslim scholars.[37]

For the Gulf monarchies with their very large numbers of foreigners, constituting between 30 percent and 88 percent of the population (2020) and between 50 percent and 94 percent of the labor force, the question of the status and entitlements of foreign nationals, whether Muslim or non-Muslim, temporary or longer-term residents, and their access to resources is, as we will see in Chapters 3 and 5, especially pertinent. It has everything to do with the practical application of justice in the contemporary period as well as with the notion of community – hence, the ruler's project of community, nation and state.

As I explore four state-directed, oil-financed institutionalized practices and how they contribute to advancing regime priorities in the chapters that follow, we should reflect upon the normative tradition, as outlined in this chapter, and ponder its interpretations and applications today. I turn first to a general discussion of distributive practices of the governments of Kuwait, Qatar, Oman and Saudi Arabia and their implications, and highlight matters of equity, preference and exclusion.

---

[36] Kemal Karpat (1996) refers to an "ethical-religious code of migration" in Islam, derivative of the central role played by *hijra* (flight, from Mecca to Medina) in the emergence of Islam in the Arabian Peninsula in the seventh century. Given the hospitality of the *Anṣār* (the Helpers), the local inhabitants of Medina, on the arrival of the *muhajirun* after their flight from Mecca, the Muslim community was required henceforth to accept and protect refugees and migrants, no matter their faith, but also others who were temporarily outside their place of residence and in *dar al-Islam* (79–81).

[37] See, *inter alia*, al-Bishri (1998, 34–6), al-Ghazali (1960, 72), al-Ghannouchi (1993, 66), Kamali (2009, 132–39).

3 The State and the Political Economy of Distribution

Introduction

The pursuit of justice and the commitment to goodness lie at the very core of the normative tradition. That being the case, advancing social justice through such things as sharing, caring for the needy and extending compassion are supposed to guide behavior. For the sake of attending to the common good (*maṣlaḥa*) and alleviating hardship and gross inequalities, resources and wealth must circulate. Thus, distributive activities play a central role in the Muslim community (*umma*).

In the political economy literature, the rentier state has been identified as the quintessential distributive state (and contrasted to the "productive state"). State revenues derive largely from external sources and, in the original typology, elaborated by Hossein Mahdavy (1970), via the sale of a resource that is extracted and then exported in the absence of domestic productive activities of note. Revenues of this sort are expended to carry out the many tasks of the modern state – among them, social, economic and infrastructural development, including the extension of goods and services to the population. Hence, distribution is not only a principal activity of rule; it is, for the rentier state especially, key to its legitimacy. In effect, in the oil-rich Gulf monarchies, resource rents are conjoined, at least discursively, with Islamic norms: Oil revenues are expended on distributive activities and through them, on enhancing the welfare of society.

In the Gulf, the important growth in state revenues from the sale of oil from the 1950s and their explosive growth from the 1970s prompted the proliferation of rulers' distributive activities. They encouraged, as well, the persistence, indeed intensification of the patrimonial nature of rule and the consolidation of royal privilege. A portion of state revenues has been distributed to the citizen population in the form of free social services (for example, health care and education), heavily subsidized goods and household utilities (e.g., water, electricity, gasoline), access to financial facilities (e.g., allowances, low-interest loans) and to public sector employment. Mass distributions of this sort ensure the citizenry's dependence upon the state.

While in the contemporary period there is universal dependence upon state largesse, access to some types of largesse remains determined largely on the basis of proximity and utility to the state, rather than on criteria related primarily to personal and productive capacities. This being the case, social forces, in their quest for social and material advantages and advancement, compete to improve their positionality. Indeed, well-placed individuals and families have received lucrative government contracts and exclusive licenses. As for positions in government and other state institutions, nepotism, proximity to rule and the political interests of the ruler have been key to determining their distribution, although some room for meritocratic placements exists, especially in strategic sectors (Hertog 2010, 103–5). They have tended to be allocated first among royals, followed by close allies from within tribal, merchant, and in the cases of Oman and Saudi Arabia, regional forces. Furthermore, by hierarchizing its distributions and fixing relative privilege, the state excludes some and appeases others; in fact, it appeases some by excluding others. In so doing, it shapes community and builds the nation. As with mass distributions, the goal is to enhance the state's monopolization of power and control of society.

In the petro-monarchies of the Gulf, it is not simply that distribution is a principal activity of rule and key to political survival. These regimes insinuate, through their public pronouncements and promotional blitzes, that their legitimacy since 1973 and in the post-1990s environment in particular, emanates, in large measure, from their being the purveyors of spectacular (oil-financed) development, indeed, of hyper-modernization.[1] In Saudi Arabia, for example, "its infrastructural and industrialization projects are branded as milestones on the path to inexorable progress" (Haykel et al. 2015, 4). (Incidentally, this suggestion does not appear to challenge rulers' long-standing claim that adherence to Islam is a source of their legitimacy.) Beyond that, not only does distribution stimulate consumption, but in Gulf monarchies, the latter has become an indisputable, albeit unstated organizing principle of the domestic political economy. Unbridled consumption, financed by the ruler and modeled by his example and extravagant projects, fosters submission. It does so in conjunction with the enduring threat of repression. Moreover, absolute royal privilege, combined with patronage practices and hierarchized distributions that elicit varying degrees of

---

[1] See Chapter 1, pp. 14–15.

incorporation and exclusion, facilitate the state's management and control of society while contributing to the definition of community.

In this chapter, I offer a cursory overview of oil-financed government distributions, the first of four institutionalized practices in Kuwait, Qatar, Oman and Saudi Arabia examined in this book. The aim is to clarify their scope and method, as well as to suggest some of the objectives and effects.[2] I focus on government transfers and subsidies of various sorts – universal, particular, idiosyncratic – to different social categories and changes to them, including during periods of economic malaise. I also explore matters of equity, belonging and exclusion. I elucidate how, through variable access to government distributions, both submission and relative privilege are imposed, hierarchy is reinforced and community is shaped to meet the ruler's goals.

Universal Subsidies and Transfers

Since the 1950s in Kuwait and Saudi Arabia, and the 1970s in Qatar and Oman, governments have invested increasingly large sums in infrastructure and social services. Given the preponderance of petroleum rents in state budgets and the expectation that important rents, as well as returns on lucrative international investments would continue to accrue, there was, until very recently, no perceived need to extract from the citizenry through taxation.[3] Rather, channeling revenues to the population and in so doing, encouraging consumption alongside socioeconomic development, have figured prominently in state agendas. However, as the price of oil fell precipitously in the summer of 2014 and remained relatively low through 2021, several extractive, or at least "belt-tightening" measures were introduced in the region, as I describe in the pages that follow.

Nationals have come to enjoy important financial transfers and an array of free or heavily subsidized goods and services. They are guaranteed free

---

[2] While I refer to "oil-financed" distribution, I acknowledge that since the new millennium especially, a growing proportion of government revenues derives from international investments. No doubt, the original driver for those investments was oil and natural gas exports.

[3] However, all businesses in Oman and Saudi Arabia, and non-GCC-owned businesses in Qatar and Kuwait, pay corporate taxes. Since 2018, the tax rate in Qatar, for example, excluding the petroleum sector has been 10 percent; it was 5–7 percent from 2009 (Deloitte, International Tax: Qatar Highlights 2019, June 2019). www2.deloitte.com/content/dam/Deloitte/global/Documents/Tax/dttl-tax-qatarhighlights-2019.pdf.
In Kuwait, the tax rate on the foreign ownership component of businesses has been 15 percent since 2008 (PWC, "Doing Business in Kuwait: A Tax and Legal Guide" 2015, 12pp). www.pwc.com/m1/en/tax/documents/doing-business-guides/doing-business-guide-kuwait.pdf; updated Jan. 2022: https://taxsummaries.pwc.com/kuwait/corporate/taxes-on-corporate-income.

Table 3.1 *Price of gasoline (/gal.), select countries, select years*

	2000 (avg.)	Winter 2013	Summer 2017	Summer 2020
Kuwait	$0.79	$0.89	$1.17	$1.30
Qatar	0.61 (1998)	NA	1.70	1.25
Oman	1.17 (2000-04)	NA	1.89	1.97
KSA	0.91	0.61	0.83	1.45
USA	1.5	3.70	2.40	2.26
UK	5.36	6.42	5.44	6.00

Sources: IMF 2018, 13; Kuwait Times 2013; www.globalpetrolprices.com

access to public education and health care; are entitled, in principle, to a plot of land; and until recently, many, if not most, could secure public sector employment fairly easily. In addition, transportation, gasoline, water and electricity have been heavily subsidized by the state, while in Kuwait, Qatar and Saudi Arabia staple food items have been subsidized as well (Woertz 2013, 13–14). Until very recently, water and electricity were absolutely free to citizens in Qatar, as were landline telephones. In Kuwait, Saudi Arabia and Oman, the cost to users has been minimal.[4] However, with the oil price downturn, all four states have raised the prices of fuel, electricity and water several times, beginning in 2015 (Krane 2019, 150–53). Nonetheless, in Gulf monarchies the price for subsidized fuel, for example, remains among the cheapest in the world (Table 3.1).[5]

The cost of these subsidies to the state is astronomic, even though precise details about expenditures and their composition are lacking in all four countries. According to the International Energy Agency (IEA), spending on subsidies on energy, utilities (gasoline, water and electricity) and food in 2010 represented more than 30 percent of total government expenditures in Saudi Arabia and Kuwait; 17 percent in Qatar; and just under 10 percent in Oman.[6] In the case of Kuwait, according to one analyst, the inclusion of the cost of health care, education and housing

---
[4] There are, however, variations among the three, with somewhat higher costs in Oman.
[5] It has been consistently cheaper in only a few countries, among them Venezuela, Iran and Angola.
[6] International Energy Agency (2010). World Energy Outlook. Online database available at www.iea.org/subsidy/index.html. Described in Espinoza (2012, 8). *The Kuwait Times* (3/11/2013) reported that in 2012, Kuwait, with a population of only 2.7 mill., of which 1.4 mill. were nationals, spent as much as $22 bill. – almost 20 percent of government revenues – on subsidies alone. According to another source, in 2014/15, government spending on subsidies, including such things as the marriage allowance and the contribution to private sector salaries of Kuwaiti nationals, represented 26 percent of Kuwait's budget (Al-Ojayan 2016, 23, 33).

would have brought the total of government transfers to as much as 40–50 percent of expenditures (El-Katiri et al. 2011, 11). As for spending on energy subsidies alone, Jim Krane (2019, 77) suggests that by 2014, it had reached 9.5 percent of GDP in Saudi Arabia, 9 percent in Oman and 5 percent in Kuwait.

In addition to their onerous cost to the state, subsidies of this type and extent have distortionary effects on the market insofar as they crowd out more productive spending. Moreover, they are subject to a variety of abuses, not least among them that they encourage wasteful consumption and discourage energy efficiency. Indeed, stories abound of Gulf residents leaving the air conditioning (A/C) on in their homes for weeks on end while they vacation outside the country. In some cases, subsidies encourage cross-border smuggling, as well. To take what is the most obvious example: Gasoline is so cheap in Saudi Arabia that, according to a high-ranking technocrat in the oil industry, domestic consumers turn a profit from it; large amounts are routinely smuggled out of the country where they are sold at higher prices.[7] To be sure, with prices at or close to zero, there is little incentive to exercise moderation and conserve.

Furthermore, such subsidies are regressive in effect. Although income inequality is thought to be great in Gulf states (Woertz 2013; Alvaredo et al. 2018), most consumer subsidies are universal, rather than targeted to those in need. While they provide a safety net for the poorest segments of the citizenry, they play a regressive role in fostering equity and distributive justice since high income groups benefit disproportionately from them (Askari and Arfaa 2007).[8] Take subsidized fuel, for example: It favors the rich as they are the ones who own vehicles, factories and businesses. Or consider students' allowances: In all four countries, university students receive a monthly allowance from the government. In 2012, according to my interlocutors, Kuwaiti students were receiving roughly $700 per month and Saudi students $300;[9] while the allowance for Omani students around the same time is unknown, it appears to have been a variable amount.[10] Apart from in Oman, every national, without

---

[7] Interview: Al-Khobar, 14 April 2012.
[8] Note that in Canada, for example, the regressive effect of universal health care and social security is mitigated somewhat by progressive income tax. Apparently, there has been some talk in Saudi Arabia about "rationalizing" energy subsidies so that the rich pay more while the poor do not suffer from higher prices (Krane and Hung 2016, 4).
[9] Interviews with: HADAS Member of Parliament, Kuwait City, 11 May 2012; Saudi lawyer, Riyadh, 28 March 2012. Menoret (2014, 43) claims that in 2002, Saudi students received a stipend of about $160.
[10] In February 2011, following the demonstrations in Sohar, the Sultan issued a decree announcing, among other reforms, a rise in monthly allowances for students by up to $234 ("Oman shuffles cabinet amid protests." *Al-Jazeera*, 26 Feb. 2011).

distinction, receives the (same) allowance – even if they are from a very wealthy family. Herein lies a major defect of such distributive practices and a hint to one of their underlying, yet undeclared purposes. Universal subsidies foster dependence and at the same time, they assure the continued loyalty of the wealthier strata. The latter is likely a far more pressing concern of the leadership than is some notion of distributive justice or even the declared aim, in national development plans especially, to "maintain and preserve the religious and moral values of Islam."[11]

As for public education and health care, while they are free to citizens in the four countries, they are considered to be of relatively poor quality and so, whoever can afford private alternatives chooses them instead.[12] This being the case, public health services, for example, tend to be utilized primarily, if not exclusively, by poor and vulnerable groups, including those living far from urban centers. They have to make do with services that are free but of inferior quality; higher quality care is available to those who can afford to pay for it. Indeed, the careful cultivation of hierarchy and difference triumphs behind the façade of uniformity. And the community of (relative) privilege is thus devised.

Public sector employment has remained another important channel, perhaps the most important channel after subsidies, of rent distribution. In the case of Kuwait, for example, government spending on wages and salaries in the first decade of the 2000s was the second largest budget item following subsidies and transfers, equivalent to about 20 percent of total expenditures (El-Katiri et al. 2011, 19); by the end of the second decade, it grew to about one-third of public expenditures (World Bank Group 2022, 23). In Qatar, more than 90 percent of employed citizens work in the public sector, although they make up less than half its workforce. In 2018, citizens comprised 86 percent of the public sector workforce in Oman, 84 percent in Kuwait and 94.7 percent in Saudi Arabia (Table 3.2).[13] Notwithstanding its apparent bloatedness, the public sector is most attractive for the job seeker as it offers job security and a comparatively high salary; in addition, the workday is short and the demands are few.[14] So important is it to regimes' interests that in Saudi Arabia, for example,

---

[11] Quoted from Saudi Arabia's "Second Development Plan for 1975–79" in Jones (2010, 85).

[12] Free access to public education may include, in addition to tuition and related fees, such things as books, school uniforms, meals and transportation. At Kuwaiti universities, for example, it has included free room and board, too (El-Katiri et al. 2011, 8).

[13] See, GLMM (Gulf Labour Markets and Migration (www.gulfmigration.org). For the proportion of the sector made up of Qatari nationals, see Table 3.2.

[14] According to Espinoza (2012, 18), the lowest paying public sector job in the Gulf in the first decade of the 2000s paid, on average, about 30 percent more than a private sector job.

Table 3.2 *Nationals as proportion of public sector, select GCC states, select years*

	2010	2022
Kuwait	71%	80%
Oman	86	85.5
Qatar	44	42.4
Saudi Arabia	95	90.6

Source: Gulf Research Center (GRC), Gulf Labour Markets, Migration & Population Programme database

the number of public employees and the share of public wages in government expenditure grew every year from 1970 to 2015, including, as noted by Hertog (2010, 121–24), during the bust period of the mid-1980s when oil income plummeted by 87 percent. And in response to the region-wide uprisings that began in 2010–11, the so-called Arab Spring, Gulf rulers not only raised public sector salaries but created new jobs – as many as 60,000 in Saudi Arabia and 41,000 in Oman – and this despite the persistent talk about the need for job creation in the private sector (Hvidt 2014, 28). However, the generalized commitment to provide public sector employment has come up against two important challenges: first, the persistent growth in numbers of job seekers as a result of high population growth rates and an enduring youth bulge; second, the extended period of relatively low oil prices (2014–2021) that has strained national coffers.[15] Nonetheless, Qatar, with one of the highest GDPs per capita in the world and the smallest citizen population of the four states, continues to guarantee civil service positions to all Qatari high school and university graduates, regardless of the oil price downturn since 2014.[16]

Like most other generalized subsidies and transfers, allocating public sector employment is regressive in effect. While in principle available to all, it favors particular segments of the population over others. At its inception, it was a mechanism for the nepotistic distribution of favors to family, friends and actual or sought-after allies. In Oman, for example, jobs were dispensed, through the 1990s, primarily on the basis of tribe

---

[15] To address the former and combat rising unemployment, both the Saudi and Kuwait governments began (in the 2000s) to incentivize their private sectors to hire more nationals in place of expatriates by, for example, partially subsidizing the national's salary.

[16] Kamrava (2009) noted that at the time of writing, the Qatari regime included with public sector employment "a generous housing allowance, which is doubled if the employee is married" (406).

and ethnicity (Valeri 2009, 158–59). Today, some Omanis insist that the *wasta* system (personal connections and preferential treatment that derives therefrom) continues to characterize public sector employment in that "jobs are handed out not on the basis of competencies but rather on who you are."[17] In general, public sector jobs favor educated segments of the population and hence, relatively comfortable urbanites. This being the case, they do little to promote equity and inclusion: In Saudi Arabia and Oman, for example, there remain important rural and (formerly) nomadic populations, and in Kuwait and Saudi Arabia, there are large numbers of undocumented residents (considered "stateless" – *bidūn*). Furthermore, as there tends to be insufficient matching of qualifications with tasks, there is, despite some notable exceptions,[18] inadequate attention paid to promoting productive activities within the sector or developing the requisite skills for performing such activities successfully. Although the practice of distributing jobs in the public sector remains more-or-less exclusionary while contributing little to human resource development or national productivity (outside the oil/gas sector), it is considered to be indispensable. Not only is it critical for cementing relationships of dependence on the state, but that dependence, combined with the various perks and protections that come with the job, make of the civil service what Valeri (2009) refers to as the "most reliable ... allies of the ruler" (89).

In all four countries, each national has, in principle, the right to a plot of land of a certain dimension and, for those who are credit-worthy, access to attractive loans of long duration to build on the land. For example, in 2012, Omanis could receive plots of at least 600 square meters and loans at roughly 4 percent interest, while Kuwaitis could hold loans of up to about $260,000 that were repayable, interest-free and in monthly instalments of no more than KD 100 ($350 in 2012) over a period of 65 years.[19] In 2008, Qataris were eligible for plots of 700–1,500 square meters and interest-free loans of about $235,000 (Kamrava 2009, 406).[20] However, it has been reported in each country

---

[17] Interview with oil industry engineer, Muscat, 8 Feb. 2012. See, as well, Valeri (2009, 206–7).

[18] See, for example, Steffen Hertog's (2010) rich discussion of "islands of efficiency" in Saudi Arabia and his (2010c) analysis of the creation of successful state-owned enterprises in the Gulf.

[19] Interviews with: oil industry engineer, Muscat, 3 Nov. 2013; former Member of Parliament, Kuwait City, 8 May 2012.

[20] Note the following statement: "Most Qataris have come to expect the state's generous allowances which in 2011–12 could reach as high as $7,000 a month, along with interest-free loans, free land and guaranteed civil service employment" (Kamrava 2013, 158).

that some nationals do not receive plots at all, while others have received several plots and of larger dimensions than the norm.[21] Mitchell and Gengler (2018, 78) note that to receive a plot of land in Qatar, citizens must go through a non-transparent application process that forces some to wait longer than others. And in Saudi Arabia in 2012, several of my interlocutors pointed out that nationals who had in recent years gone to the appropriate authorities to claim their plots were told either that there was no more land to distribute or that available plots were far from where they resided, in undesirable locations. I was also told that, at that time, only about 30 percent of Saudi nationals owned their homes – a circumstance that was considered indefensible, given the country's vast wealth and expansive territory, and nationals' avowed right to land.[22] Indeed, not all citizens are created equal.

There are, as well, a host of idiosyncratic financial transfers from the state to its citizens. For example, the Saudi and Kuwaiti governments provide funds to men to assist with their marriage expenses (Longva 2006, 180; Menoret 2020, 106), while in Qatar, Qatari men who marry Qatari women automatically become eligible for a regular government stipend (Kamrava 2009, 406).[23] In addition, a Qatari citizen in financial difficulty can request assistance from the *Amiri Diwan* (the sovereign body and administrative office of the Amir/ruler). It was reported to me in 2012 that such requests had to be made in writing and for a sum no less than QR 10,000 ($2,750 in 2012); they could be made once every six months, but, in the words of my interlocutor, "not more often than that."[24] Distributions akin to a bonus have been made to all citizens at times of particularly high oil prices, as in Kuwait in 2006/07, for example (El-Katiri et al. 2011, 12), or during oil-price downturns, to soften the blow of the austerity measures, as in Saudi Arabia at the beginning of Ramadan in 2015.

With the precipitous fall in oil prices beginning in summer 2014, from about $110/barrel in June to $60/barrel in December, and the persistent

---

[21] Interviews: Kuwait City, 5 May 2012; Doha, 4 March 2012; Muscat, 11 Feb. 2012. For what are essentially class-based discrepancies in access to land in Kuwait, and especially that between *hadhar* (settled) and *badu* (formerly nomadic), see, Al-Nakib (2014, 5–30). See, as well, Wells and Azoulay (2014).
[22] Interviews with a dissident, Riyadh, 2 April 2012; an economist, Riyadh, 6 April 2012. This point is also reported in Menoret (2014, 225, fn. 34). Derbal (2022, 288) suggests that in 2018, 42 percent of Saudis owned their homes.
[23] Jill Crystal (2020, 283) notes that in Kuwait, the financial allocation from the government to Kuwaiti men upon their marriage is conditioned upon their first wife being Kuwaiti.
[24] Interview with Professor of Economics, Qatar University, Doha, 4 March 2012.

low price environment through September 2021,[25] all Gulf monarchies have reduced their energy subsidies and raised fuel and electricity prices a few times, at least, in addition to introducing other government revenue-saving as well as extractive measures.[26] For example, in summer 2017, Saudi Arabia imposed an excise tax (of 50–100 percent) on certain products deemed unhealthy or not to be encouraged – such things as sweetened carbonated drinks, energy drinks, tobacco and tobacco products; Qatar and Oman followed suit in 2019.[27] Then in January 2018, Saudi Arabia (and the UAE) introduced a value added tax (VAT) of 5 percent on most goods and services, including energy and food;[28] in July 2020, it tripled the tax to 15 percent.[29] And Oman introduced a VAT of 5 percent in April 2021.[30]

Another effort to save government revenues has been through reducing disbursements for public sector employment. Oman, for example, initiated a hiring freeze in the public sector in 2016, while Saudi Arabia cut salaries and canceled bonuses and allowances for state employees in fall 2016 – but then reversed those measures six months later in response to popular discontent (Hanieh 2018, 223); it cut allowances again in summer 2020.[31] And all but Qatar, which has a citizen population of roughly 300,000, have been insisting on the need to nationalize the work force. With that in mind, Kuwait, Oman and Saudi Arabia have imposed a host of restrictions on the employment of foreign labor. For example, since 2015, the Saudi government has imposed an "expat" levy on Saudi employers, making it significantly more costly for them to hire non-Saudis. By summer 2017, in fact, more than 2 million workers had been

---

[25] The price of oil hovered between $40 and $60/barrel in 2015 through 2017 and then between $42 and $75/barrel in 2018 and 2019 before plummeting to $20–30/barrel in the first half of 2020. The price gently climbed to $47–75/barrel in the first half of 2021.
[26] See Krane (2019, 152) for a useful illustration of changes to energy subsidies and oil and gas prices.
[27] www.arabianbusiness.com/saudi-arabia-become-first-gcc-country-impose-sin-tax-675875.html.
[28] www.thenational.ae/business/economy/all-in-the-details-for-value-added-tax-in-the-gcc.
[29] "Saudi Arabia Triples VAT to Support Coronavirus-Hit Economy." BBC, 11 May 2020 www.bbc.com/news/business-52612785.
[30] www.thenationalnews.com/business/economy/oman-introduces-5-vat-on-goods-and-services-1.1204907. By summer 2023, neither Kuwait nor Qatar had imposed a VAT, although both continue to refer to plans to do so.
[31] "Saudi Arabia's King Salman Reverses Public Sector Pay Cuts."*BBC*, 23 April 2017 www.bbc.com/news/world-middle-east-39683592. Riad Hamade, Zaid Sabah and Vivian Nereim, "KSA Triples VAT, Cuts State Allowances Amid Crisis." *Bloomberg*, May 10, 2020. www.bloomberg.com/news/articles/2020-05-11/saudi-arabia-plans-26-6-billion-austerity-cuts-triples-vat-ka1uss4c.

Universal Subsidies and Transfers 57

forced out of the kingdom, having lost their jobs (Hanieh 2018, 221). In January 2021, a revised residency law came into effect in Kuwait, with the aim to radically reduce the non-citizen labor force in part by setting a limit to the number of foreigners that businesses could recruit each year. Nonetheless, special dispensations have been made to retain higher paid and highly skilled expatriates.[32]

In the wake of citizens' rumblings, some of these measures have been modified, and in significant ways. For example, in September 2016, when the Kuwaiti government reduced subsidies on water, electricity and fuel, there was strong opposition in Parliament. Not only did the government eventually scale back the price hikes, but it went after the non-citizen population, imposing new fees on them (Freer 2016; Weiner 2017). While all four states have targeted foreign nationals in their efforts to curb the drain on national reserves, the differential treatment of citizen and non-citizen in this regard has turned out to be the principal strategy of both Kuwait and Qatar, given their significantly smaller citizen populations and higher per capita incomes (Hanieh 2018, 225–27).[33] Oman and Saudi Arabia have initiated targeted welfare measures, as well. Shortly after removing fuel subsidies in 2016, the Omani government revived a small gasoline subsidy through its newly created National Subsidy System, restricting it to low-income Omanis who owned a vehicle (Asl 2018); in 2020, it added an electricity subsidy. And in a midterm economic plan made public in fall 2020, it was reported that Oman would not only redirect state subsidies to those in need but would also impose an income tax on high earners in 2022; the latter decision has since been postponed to 2024.[34] As for Saudi Arabia, in late 2017, it instituted, through its Ministry of Human Resources and Social Development (MHRSD), the Citizen Account Program, a cash transfer program of monthly payments of variable amounts to eligible low- and middle-income Saudi households (Nereim 2017; Ramady 2018, 76–7; Derbal 2022, 288).

---

[32] https://english.alarabiya.net/News/gulf/2020/07/06/Kuwait-to-reduce-expats-with-new-residency-law-within-months-Officials.

[33] In 2016, per capita income in Qatar was $120,000 – the highest in the world. Excluding those residents who did not hold Qatari citizenship, per capita income was close to a whopping $700,000 (Mitchell and Gengler 2018, 75).

[34] "Oman Income Tax Expected in 2022 in Fiscal Shake-Up." *Reuters*, 2 Nov. 2020. www.reuters.com/article/oman-economy-int/oman-income-tax-expected-in-2022-in-fiscal-shake-up-idUSKBN27I0XZ; "Oman Sticks to Target of Implementing Income Tax by 2024." 20 Sept. 2022. www.zawya.com/en/economy/gcc/oman-sticks-to-target-of-implementing-income-tax-by-2024-e39vy7t6.

Particularist Subsidies and Transfers

To Royals

In Kuwait, Qatar, Oman and Saudi Arabia, the royal family has consistently enjoyed preferential access to financial resources, landed property and leadership positions. On the eve of oil production, as noted in Chapter 1, the ruler was in the habit of treating the resources available to him as his own, to distribute as he saw fit and as evidence of his magnanimity. Typically, he favored his kin, as well as whomever he sought to keep close to him. With the onset of oil exports, part of the associated revenues was allocated for "development" and eventually, social services; a proportion was retained for the personal use of the ruler and in most cases, the royal family, as well. It has been suggested that in Qatar, for example, that proportion was as much as 42 percent between 1953 and 1970.[35] Alshehabi (2017, 16–22) claims that this basic pattern persisted in the Gulf monarchies, in broad strokes and to varying degrees, until the mid-1970s. In Kuwait, however, since independence in 1961 and according to its constitution, the Emir receives a fixed annual sum, decided upon by Parliament. The allowance is for his own personal use and to distribute to whomever and however he pleases. In 1963, the Emir's allowance was set at KD 10 mill. (equivalent to $28 mill./year in 1970 and $32.6 mill. in 2000); in February 2006, Parliament increased it to KD 50 mill. ($166 mill. in 2006 and $178 mill. in 2012).[36]

Since the mid-1970s and the explosion in state revenues, whatever transparency existed regarding royal allocations has disappeared in all Gulf monarchies excluding Kuwait (al-Ojayan 2016, 32; Alshehabi 2017, 22). Neither detailed state budgets nor information regarding royal allocations are available to the public.[37] Qatari scholar and former oil industry employee, Ali Khalifa al-Kuwari, suggests that from 2002 to 2011, one-fifth to one-half of the total value of hydrocarbon exports from

---

[35] Alshehabi (2017), based on Al-Kuwari (1974, 186), writes that in Qatar, 35.1 percent of oil revenues went to the ruler and royal family, "complemented by a further 6.6 percent for land purchases, which in large part went to high-ranking individuals from the royal family" (19).

[36] Interview with former member of Parliament, Kuwait City, 8 May 2012.

[37] Alshehabi (2017) suggests that in most cases, parts of state budgets are not even available to the *majlis al-shura*, the Consultative Council (7–8). In contrast, Kuwait's constitution not only includes an article specifying the allocation to the ruler but also stipulates the creation of an independent and transparent State Audit Bureau (6–7).

the six GCC states were unaccounted for.[38] The ruler takes from state revenues an undisclosed sum to use as he chooses while members of the (extended) royal family receive allowances from the national coffer.[39] In Qatar, the size of the allowance, according to Kamrava (2009, 414) – who refers to it as "salary" – was determined by a Royal Family Council, whose members were hand-picked by the former Emir Hamad, who had created the institution in 2000 and headed it until his abdication in 2013. It has been suggested that in Saudi Arabia and Oman, where the exact numbers of Al Saʿud and Al BuSaʿid family members are unknown (by the public), the size of the allowance(s) – also not publicized – depends on genealogical proximity to the throne.[40]

Apart from their privileged access to financial resources, royals have been the principal landowners in the region. In the early years of state formation, rulers across the Gulf appropriated for themselves whatever land was not *mulk* (personal property) and then distributed from it to family members (Crystal 1990, 63–77; Jones 2010, 233). The practice of distributing land primarily among royals continued, evolving into a lucrative trade, embracing tribal leaders and "commoner clients," as well. The real estate market, in which land is transferred, redistributed, sold and re-sold among royals and non-royal business elites is especially noteworthy in Kuwait, Qatar and Saudi Arabia. It is a major and oftentimes opaque source of enrichment for the most privileged, although again, precise details are often difficult to acquire (al-Nakib 2016, 93–158; Crystal 1990, 148–49; Hertog 2010, 94–111; Kamrava 2009,

---

[38] Specifically, Saudi Arabia (18 percent), Oman (32 percent) and Qatar (56 percent). His calculations are based on the difference between the total value of oil and gas exports, provided by the Institute of International Finance (IIF) and the total officially declared public oil and gas revenues, provided by GCC governments (Alshehabi 2017, 24–7, based on al-Kuwari 2009). See, as well, Seznec (2012, 86) who estimates that 4 percent of oil revenues were going to Saudi royals. Alshehabi (2017, 9–12) adds that most likely, portions go to undisclosed foreign transfers and military expenditures, as had been the case in the past. He notes that in Saudi Arabia's budget for 1960/61, available in the British archives, the king and family were allocated 14.4 percent of total expenditures, while in the 1970/71 budget, the royal allocation was equivalent to 2.7 percent and defense 28.5 percent. Payments to Egypt and to Jordan were 10 percent of revenues (20–1).

[39] Alshehabi (2017) quotes from Wikileaks' 2013 US Embassy cables referencing estimates by US Embassy staff regarding royal allocations in Saudi Arabia in 1996: "Monthly stipends for all members of the Al Saud, managed by the Ministry of Finance's 'Office of Decisions and Rules.' The stipends range from $270,000 per month ... to $800 per month for the lowliest member of the most remote branch of the family ... The Embassy estimates that the stipends system puts an annual drain of about $2 bill. on the $40 bill. government budget" (13). For citizens' reactions to such privileges, see Chapter 4.

[40] Interviews with: former member of *majlis al-shura*, Riyadh, 28 March 2012; former member of *majlis al-shura*, Muscat, 4 Nov. 2013; technocrat in the oil industry, Muscat, 3 Nov. 2013.

406).[41] From the outset, land has been not merely an important source of income, but also a means for the regime to manipulate the population through its distribution to key social categories and exclusion of others. Land ownership and allocation practices create and consolidate state clienteles; in the process, they contribute to shaping the community.[42]

It is claimed that in Kuwait, for example, from 1952 to 1970, land purchases by the state from private owners, and primarily for distribution among royals, accounted for more than 20 percent of oil revenues (Alshehabi 2017, 22, referencing Al-Kuwari 1974, 186). Despite its important cost, the land purchases program resulted in the state owning as much as 90 percent of the land since the 1990s. Thus, royals have enriched themselves markedly.[43] And in Saudi Arabia in 2012, I was privy to anecdotal reports that about 40 percent of real estate in Riyadh belonged to Saudi princes who had received land as gifts, while 70 percent of the Saudi coastline had been given to five princes by former King Fahd.[44] Furthermore, numerous properties on the periphery of cities remain undeveloped, despite the *iḥyāʾ al-mawāt* (revival of dead land) stipulation in the normative tradition and its decreed implementation in Saudi Arabia. "Land whales" (*hawamīr al-ʾarāḍiy*), the term used to describe very rich, well-connected, land-owning nationals, maintain them thus as long-term, speculative investments.[45] Hence, the Islamic injunction, meant to encourage production, has been ignored for the sake of the further enrichment of the most privileged. However, in November 2015, new legislation was passed, aimed at addressing this problem by taxing the so-called white lands (al-ʿUwaisheg 2015).

Key positions in government have been distributed to royals, as well. In Kuwait, for example, reflecting a pattern put in place by the Al Sabah ruler in 1938, family members hold all of the most important portfolios including the Ministries of Defense, Interior and Foreign Affairs, as well as senior posts throughout the bureaucracy and military. As Sean Yom

---

[41] Menoret (2020) quotes a French expert working with Saudi authorities in urban development in the late 1970s: "All lands are the king's property ... Moreover, all lands that did not have a clear owner in 1978 ... became municipal property. The king gives away gigantic properties to princes and collaborators. These are sold by chunks, progressively, to citizens or real estate agencies" (62).
[42] For a fascinating discussion about land distribution in Saudi Arabia as a political resource see, Menoret (2014, 87–94, 105–9).
[43] On the evolution of land ownership in Kuwait, see Herb (2014, 150–61).
[44] Interview with former member of *majlis al-shura*, Riyadh, 28 March 2012. Menoret (2014, 106) refers to this phenomenon without providing percentages.
[45] On *iḥyāʾ al-mawāt*, see Carré (1992, 57) and Chapter 2 (p. **38**). Menoret (2014, 83) points to a 1968 decree in Saudi Arabia enacting the Islamic notion of land revitalization and notes its relative neglect in urban peripheries.

(2011, 230) notes, the Al Sabah had fashioned a ruling "familial cartel" that would persist, while, at the same time, they have consistently rewarded important merchant families with cabinet positions.[46] Qatar, according to one survey, is said to have had, during the reign of the former emir, Hamad bin Khalifa, the highest number of royals as cabinet ministers compared to the other Gulf monarchies. Moreover, the most important state institutions were distributed among loyal members of the Emir's branch of the family (Kamrava 2009, 412–14; Kamrava 2013, 110–21). In recent years, with Sheikh Tamim bin Hamad at the helm, the prime minister and ministers of Interior and of Foreign Affairs are al-Thanis. As for Oman during the reign of the late Sultan Qaboos, cabinet positions were distributed primarily among members of three groups: the Sultan's family, other branches of the Al BuSa'id, and families that had been closely connected to Qaboos' father, Sa'id bin Taymur, either as merchant elites or political allies (Valeri 2009, 94–5). In fact, it was suggested to me in 2012 by one of my Omani interlocutors that eight to twelve families dominated government, and the system had been shaped, in part, to cater to those families and their interests.[47]

In the case of Saudi Arabia, since the mid-1960s, the most important portfolios have remained in the hands of close family members of the ruler, while other cabinet posts have been extended to members of important families – for example, the Al Sheikh, descendants of Mohamad ibn Abd al-Wahhab – and other well-placed, more or less meritocratic commoners. Until the reign of King Salman (2015–present), senior posts in government filled by royals became well-nigh hereditary, reserved for and remaining within particular branches of the family (Hertog 2010, 47). Moreover, with access to important budgets and other resources, and enjoying some autonomy free from oversight, at least until the elevation of Mohamad bin Salman to Crown Prince in 2017, princes fashioned what are described so meticulously by Hertog (2010) as functional "fiefdoms": They used their position and the publicly funded budgets of the ministries or foundations they controlled to not only bolster their influence and enrich themselves but also embrace the patrimonial/rentier model of the ruler. Through the targeted extension of favors including positions, land and contracts, they too have been able to build and nurture an entourage of clients, dependents and business partners (42– 8, 64– 7). Nonetheless, in November 2017, mass

---

[46] Pete Moore (2004, 144–45) indicates that coordination between the state and business increased from the 1990s, largely in response to the growing economic and political prominence of the Islamist opposition. See, as well, Chapter 7.
[47] Interview with oil industry technocrat, Muscat, 11 Feb. 2012.

arrests of several prominent princes (as well as government ministers and business people) ordered by the Crown Prince, were allegedly meant to purge the state of corruption or at least chasten several important (rival) actors (Nakhoul et al. 2017).

Across the region, royals – those within and outside the governing bureaucracy – have found their way into the private sector as owners or co-owners of businesses, or board members thereof, where they enjoy most favorable facilities such as privileged access to state-funded contracts and/or to land; others have secured directorships of banks or of peculiarly private-public companies, as described in rich detail by Hanieh (2018, 67–70, 110).[48] Of recent note, Haitham bin Tariq, confirmed as Sultan of Oman in January 2020, is said to be among the first Omani royals to have gotten involved in business. Among several interests, he has a controlling stake in the National Trading Company (NTC), a diversified conglomerate involved in many areas of the sultanate's economy (Valeri 2013, 32). Interestingly, the Kuwait Projects Company (KIPCO) is a holding company that is essentially an Al-Sabah enterprise. In fact, the positions of chairperson, vice chairperson, C.E.O., and chief strategic projects officer are held by royals. Of the four Gulf monarchies, however, Qatar may stand out in this regard since the Al-Thanis are especially prominent in both business and governance. It is common to find members of the family engaged in private sector businesses of their own while holding important paid positions in state enterprises (Kamrava 2013, 123). In fact, Hanieh (2018) points out that "eighty percent of all firms listed on the Qatar Stock Exchange have at least one al-Thani family member sitting on their boards … in a private capacity, not as representatives of state institutions" (101). Whether public or private, companies controlled by royals – like Qatar Petroleum, Qatar Mining, Aspire Katara Investment and Commercial Bank – dominate the economy (Kamrava et al. 2016, 5).

To Tribes

As noted in Chapter 1, the ruler, in the pre-oil era, invested resources in the co-optation of select social categories in an effort to bring to heel other real or potential power centers and consolidate his authority. Such allocations have been maintained in the modern state when they were perceived as likely to cultivate and strengthen allegiance, keep opposition at bay and secure additional resources that would contribute to

---

[48] For variations among the four states in relation to royals' involvement in business, see Kamrava et al. (2016).

leadership survival. Historically, and because of their strength, geographic distribution and presumed ʿaṣabiyya (group feeling, social solidarity/cohesion), the loyalty of tribes was crucial for rulers, for the purposes of ensuring political "reach" and controlling territory. In fact, tribes were the principal contributors to rulers' guardsmen and fighting forces (Onley and Khalaf 2006, 195–96). In the modern state, the assertion of tribalism, as in Saudi Arabia when it introduced tribal names on identity cards in 1969 (Samin 2015, 185), is a tool for demonstrating belonging. By distinguishing between those members of society with a tribal affiliation and those without, tribalism is also a means for establishing social hierarchy and distributing resources selectively while depriving the unaffiliated.[49]

In the early years of Saudi King Faisal's rule (1964–75), the distribution of tribal stipends was formalized. Tribes had to be appeased: With state formation and the new oil-driven economy, they had gradually lost their regional command, as well as their economic autonomy as pastoralists (Hertog 2010, 80). Similarly in Oman, precisely because of their relative strength, politico-economic interests and their having been sidelined by the Al BuSaʿid, local tribes have remained recipients of uninterrupted personal patronage (Valeri 2009, 152). In fact, it was suggested to me, in 2013, that tribal leaders, estimated to number around 2,000, received a monthly stipend from the state in addition to, depending on their influence, an annual gift from the (former) Sultan Qaboos.[50] This is the case even though, officially, the Omani government does not acknowledge tribal identities (Valeri 2013, 152). Furthermore, most government ministers who are not royals, are members of sheikhly, tribal families.[51] In Qatar, as well, prominent tribal families, such as the al-Attiyah and al-Kuwari, secure important positions in government.

As for the Kuwaiti regime, it has remained beholden to tribes since historically, they formed the Al Sabah's traditional base of support and became an important counterweight to the powerful merchants. To retain their allegiance, the ruler extends socio-economic and political patronage in a variety of ways. For example, since the 1950s, the Al Sabah has provided subsidized housing for sedentarized tribal groups and has spent lavishly on development in tribal areas (Yom 2011, 230,

---

[49] On tribalism in Gulf monarchies, see Peterson 2020/21; Samin 2015; al-Sharekh and Freer 2023. The Emirati researcher and member of the Sharjah ruling family, Sultan al-Qassemi (2012), writes the following: "Tribalism effectively sidelines non-tribal and naturalized citizens ... [It] is a sort of elite club that outsiders can never truly belong to."
[50] Interview with policy advisor, Muscat, 4 Nov. 2013.
[51] Interview with oil industry technocrat, Muscat, 3 Nov. 2013.

236). In the early years of state-building, members of tribes were wooed into the civil service, and into the security sectors especially. In the political sphere, the emir makes sure that electoral laws, including redistricting, favor tribal representation so that the Al Sabah's "most loyal allies" would be assured "a real sense of proximity to power" (Yom 2011, 230). This is the case even though, over time, some tribal representatives have become "the most coherent and consistent members of the parliamentary opposition" (Tetreault 2011, 91). Indeed, in all four states, the relative importance of the tribe, within the hierarchy of tribes, determines its access to state resources.

To Private Sector

Across the region, the indigenous private sector is fairly small. It is characterized by a select group of commoner families, many of whom gained prominence, largely through rent-seeking and patronage, in the early years of state-building and through (traditional) mercantile activities that may have originated in the pre-oil era (Kamrava et al. 2016).[52] (Recall that, to varying degrees, merchants provided crucial material support to the local authority prior to oil.) Over time, trading companies created by these well-placed families diversified their activities, benefiting from connections to the royal family and therefore, to lucrative state-funded contracts for development projects and privileged access to land.[53] And as royals have become increasingly involved in business, often in collaboration with merchant families, ensuring that the latter continue to accumulate while remaining unquestioningly loyal and politically quiescent has gained in importance.

With the massive development "push" in Gulf monarchies flush with oil wealth, private sector businesses have enjoyed an array of subsidies on utilities, inputs and other financial facilities such as interest-free loans. For example, the Saudi government, through the Saudi Industrial Development Fund (SIDF), has been contributing up to 50 percent of the funding of new industrial projects in major cities proposed by private

---

[52] Notable business families in Saudi Arabia include, among others, Alireza, Juffali, Khashoggi, Rajhi; in Oman, Bahwan, Barwani, al-Shanfari, Zawawi; in Qatar, Jaidah, Attiyah, Mannai, Al-Fardan; in Kuwait, Behbehani, al-Ghanim, Kharafi, al-Sagar.
[53] See, for example, Rosie Bsheer's fascinating discussion about the close and tremendously profitable collaboration between prominent family business groups and Saudi royals in the destruction and re-development of sections of Mecca as part of the state's efforts to create a new national narrative (2015; 2020, 24–6). For instructive analyses of the relationship between the state and merchants in Gulf monarchies, see Azoulay 2013, Hodson 2013, Kamrava et al. 2016, Moore 2004, Valeri 2013.

sector firms; the associated loans are repayable over fifteen years or more.[54] Moreover, the governments of Saudi Arabia and Kuwait have been extending subsidies to their private sectors to facilitate the hiring of more nationals, rather than expatriates. Through its Human Resources Development Fund (HRDF), the Saudi state pays up to one-half the salary of its nationals, recruited into the private sector, for the first two years of their employment.[55] As for Kuwait, the national budget for 2014/15 registers that, of the total allocation for subsidies (6.2 bill. KD or $24 bill.), just under 9 percent (558 mill. KD or $1.84 bill.) went to support national labor in the private sector (al-Ojayan 2016, 33); in 2022, the expenditure was similar (538 mill. KD or $1.75 bill.).[56]

In the Gulf monarchies, scores of private sector businesses have become multi-faceted conglomerates overseen by a holding company. And as noted, many of these business groups are peculiarly private in that they have incorporated royals in different capacities. For example, it is not uncommon for private companies to invest jointly with state-owned companies in which royals are ever-present, or for "prominent business people" who are commoners to appear on the boards of state-owned firms (Hanieh 2018, 67, 110). Furthermore, in all four states, successful private sector elites with strong business connections may be awarded ministerial posts. In that way, they can exercise some influence over decision-making in governance and continue to prosper. In Kuwait, for example, the late Jassim al-Khorafi, former director of the Khorafi Group, was speaker of the Kuwaiti Parliament from 1999 to 2011 and Minister of Finance before that (Kamrava et al. 2016, 7). And of the Zamil brothers, of the multi-faceted Zamil Group in Saudi Arabia, one had been Minister of Commerce, another Minister of Industry.[57] In Oman, where several of the prominent merchant families are of South Asian origin, Qays al-Zawawi, of the Al-Zawawi family conglomerate, was Foreign Minister (1973–82) and then Deputy Prime Minister

---

[54] Interview with member of the prominent Zamil Group, Riyadh, 11 April 2012. For further details, see www.sidf.gov.sa/en/ServicesforInvestors/Sectors/Pages/industry.aspx.
[55] Interview with member of Supreme Economic Council, Riyadh, 2 April 2012. See the website of the HRDF: www.hrdf.org.sa. On the nitaqat (Zones) program, introduced in 2011 and revised in 2021, which establishes quotas on the hiring of Saudis in the private sector by rewarding or punishing firms on the basis of their performance, see Peck (2017).
[56] "Kuwaitis' Private Sector Allowance Will Not Stop," *Kuwait Times*, 4 Aug. 2022. www.kuwaittimes.com/kuwaitis-private-sector-allowance-will-not-stop. It is interesting to note that a portion of the zakat payment required of Kuwaiti companies (see Chapter 6) goes into a fund for the government's contribution to the salaries of Kuwaiti private sector employees. Interview with prominent economist, Kuwait City, 10 May 2012.
[57] Interview with Abdelrahman al-Zamil, Riyadh, 11 April 2012.

for Finance and Economy until 1995. Maqbool al-Sultan, a Lawati businessman from the Al-Sultan family conglomerate (WJ Towell), was Minister of Commerce and Industry (1991–2011) until his removal from office in response to the popular protests of 2011 (Valeri 2013, 20–1).[58] According to Marc Valeri (2009), the late Sultan Qaboos favored this kind of mixing of public and private sector activity since it was, in his view, an effective means of winning over the "politically most threatening social categories" (117). In short, by intertwining public and private, governance and business, the private sector is effectively co-opted. Its dependence on the state is enhanced and its loyalty assured as ruling elites reinforce their power to shape community, control society and accumulate.

Poverty Alleviation

That poverty persists in Gulf monarchies, despite spectacular national revenues, has to do, fundamentally, with the vastly inequitable allocation of resources.[59] Although these governments provide no reliable data on the topic, there is considerable anecdotal information about economic hardship among their citizens (and/or other residents). For example, a prominent Saudi economist, former member of the *majlis al-shura* (consultative council), told me in 2008 that real poverty affected as much as 25 percent of the Saudi population and that roughly 550,000 families were registered in welfare programs at that time. And recall that in 2012, as noted, it was said that only about 30 percent of Saudis owned their homes – or 42 percent in 2018, according to Derbal (2022, 288) – and this was considered a sign of poverty.[60]

Insofar as distribution for the specific purpose of poverty alleviation is concerned, it is said to be provided in Kuwait and Qatar primarily by charitable organizations since poverty among the acknowledged nationals today is considered to be negligible. As for those who are poor but not recognized as citizens or even legal residents, such as stateless or undocumented populations, their material conditions are not of concern to the state. In Oman, according to one of my interlocutors, the government

---

[58] The protesters had denounced corruption in government. In response, the sultan removed several ministers from their posts. The Lawatiya are a small Shi'i community, originally from Hyderabad, and known historically as merchants and traders. It is fascinating to learn from J. E. Peterson (2020/21, 511) that the Omani state appoints a shaykh for the Lawati, "who is responsible for the community as if it were an Arab tribe" (highlighting, my own). Thus, the community's belonging is affirmed.
[59] See Chapter 4 for a discussion of how my interviewees explained this phenomenon.
[60] Interview: Riyadh, 6 April 2008; *supra* fn. 22. See, as well, Bsheer 2010.

was providing some low-income housing and supplemental social security payments to eligible families, and distributing school supplies and supplemental monthly allowances to needy students.[61] Since 2011, a monthly allowance has been made available to unemployed job seekers (Valeri 2015, 11); this evolved into a more formal Employment Security Scheme as part of a multi-faceted social assistance program in 2019/2020.[62] And Asl (2018) notes in passing that the government was subsidizing "the basic living costs of around 84,000 low-income households, or roughly one-third of its citizens."

In Saudi Arabia, where the late King Abdallah acknowledged publicly in 2002 that poverty in the kingdom impacted about 30 percent of the population and had to be addressed, a well-endowed anti-poverty campaign, referred to as the National Strategy to Eradicate Poverty, was launched by him in 2005.[63] Along with an increase in allocations to charity organizations to encourage their engagement, various social welfare programs have been in place since then. They include the extension of low-income housing and monthly allowances to unemployed nationals who numbered roughly 1.2 million in 2012[64] and the Citizen Action Program, a cash transfer scheme created in 2017 (Derbal 2022, 288). However, "Vision 2030," the long-term socio-economic development strategy inaugurated in 2016 by King Salman's government, does little to tackle the problem of poverty.[65] Indeed, the structural features at the source of the persistence of poverty in Gulf monarchies – such things as the concentration of wealth in the hands of the royal family, the inequitable development of regions, multiple labor market distortions (most notably the preference for foreigners in the private sector and, in Saudi Arabia especially, constraints upon women's participation) – have neither been effectively dealt with, nor even, in some cases, acknowledged.

---

[61] Interview with representative of Oman charity, Muscat, 29 Oct. 2013.
[62] "Job Security Fund Benefits over 10,000 Omanis who Lost Jobs," *Zawya*, 19 Oct. 2021. www.zawya.com/en/economy/job-security-fund-benefits-over-10-000-omanis-who-lost-jobs-en81syy0. See, as well, Oman, Ministry of Social Development, www.portal.mosd.gov.om
[63] For details of its various elements, including an analysis of its implications, see Derbal (2022, 146–49).
[64] Interviews with: economist, former member of *majlis al-shura*, Riyadh, 1 April 2012; representative from King Abdullah Foundation for Development Housing, Riyadh, 28 March 2012.
[65] For a thoughtful critique of Vision 2030 in this regard, see Ihsaan bu Haliqah, "*kayfa tabada'a al-ru'iyya fi mukāfaha al-faqr*? ("How Does the "Vision" Begin to Fight Poverty?), *Al-Arabiya*, 30 Oct. 2016. www.alarabiya.net/saudi-today/2016/10/30/كيف-تبدأ-الرؤية-في-مكافحة-الفقر؟

Who Is "In"? Who Is "Out"?

In Gulf monarchies, with their considerable wealth, vast welfare systems and large expatriate communities, citizenship (*jinsiyya*) is the primary determinant of access to government distributions. In these autocratic if not absolutist environments, where political rights are at best minimal and civil rights uncertain, citizenship signifies the legal right to goods and services provided by the state. However, internal forms of exclusion, or at least relative discrimination, are practiced in the four countries. To reiterate, not all citizens are created equal.

"Originals," those citizens who have proven that they (or their ancestors) were settled on the territory of the future state at the specific time designated by the national government as critical for establishing belonging[66] – and among them, preferred tribes and families – enjoy greater privileges in the form of access to resources than all others. Those citizens who are non-"original," non-tribal or naturalized and those who were nomadic (*badu*) enjoy second, or even third tier status.[67] Throughout the region, in fact, *ḥaḍar* (sedentary populations) are favored over *badu* (Fahad 2004). In Kuwait and Saudi Arabia, this is evident, most distinctly, in their spatial separation via urban planning and housing policies; *badu* and (other) migrants from rural zones tend to live away from urban centers and on the outskirts of cities (Wells and Azoulay 2014, 44–5; al-Nakib 2016, 204; Menoret 2014, 82–3). To varying degrees, women, Shiʿa and Afro-Arabs encounter relative discrimination, as well.[68]

In Kuwait, Qatar and especially, Oman, Sunni-Shiʿi differences are far less politicized than they are in Saudi Arabia (and of course, Bahrain).[69] In the former, wealthy Shiʿi families are prominent in the business and financial sectors, and members of some of those families have held positions in government – even, in Kuwait and Oman, in strategic

---

[66] In Kuwait, for example, according to the Nationality Law of 1959, the "original" national was from the settled (*ḥaḍar*) population that had lived there in 1920 (Longva 2000, 185–88). In Qatar, they had lived there in 1930 (Babar 2014, 411).

[67] In his discussion of the elections in Qatar in September 2021 for two-thirds of the seats on the *majlis al-shura*, Marzooq (2021) writes that the Kuwaiti and Qatari governments adopt policies that discriminate against naturalized or non-original citizens, allowing them "only a fragile and marginal status in the country."

[68] For details see, *inter alia*, Lysa and Leber 2018; Maktabi 2016; Menoret 2020, 137, 155–56; Louer 2014, 117–42. On religious and ethnic minorities in the Omani citizenry and their relative incorporation, see Peterson (2004).

[69] Valeri (2010) describes a long-standing "peaceful" relationship in Oman between the Shiʿi communities, which constitute less than 5 percent of the population of the sultanate, and the late Sultan Qaboos.

ministries or as advisors to the ruler (Azoulay 2013; Kamrava 2013; Moore 2004, 144; Valeri 2010). In comparison, Saudi Shiʿa, who constitute 10–15 percent of the citizen population, are subjected to (considerably more) religious discrimination and political exclusion, in addition to more-or-less routine repression.[70] Furthermore, since the early 1980s, they have typically been denied access to employment in government ministries, defense and security services, and the education sector. Indeed, it is exceedingly rare to find a Shiʿi in a position of influence in the government bureaucracy or ARAMCO.[71] For the most part, Saudi Shiʿa need to find work in the private sector.

The tiering, or hierarchization of citizenship and the related variation in access to resources are basic state- and nation-building practices. They are both integral to the shaping of the national community and a means for the state to exercise control insofar as key social categories are appeased via the relative marginalization of others. These practices are replicated with and among non-citizen populations, as we will see in Chapter 5. Since the mid-1970s and the tremendous growth in oil revenues and imported labor, Gulf monarchies have demonstrated an unwillingness to expand community. For example, it has become increasingly difficult to acquire the local citizenship for those who are not descendants of males who were considered citizens at the time of independence. Hence, those born in GCC states to foreign parents – even, in most cases, to foreign fathers and "national" mothers – cannot, with few exceptions, become citizens (Parolin 2009, 99). Naturalization laws, stringent throughout the Middle East and North Africa, are particularly so in the Gulf, and the extent of naturalization, in comparison with other countries with large migrant populations, is extremely low (Fargues 2013, 29).[72] That being said, the ruler reserves the right to confer citizenship to non-nationals whom he judges meritorious (Babar 2014, 411–12) or when deemed political expedient (Ulrichsen 2016, 180) – as in the case of Egyptian national, Sheikh Youssef al-Qaradawi, naturalized by the Qatari emir in 1968. In Kuwait, for example,

---

[70] For example, punishments for the "crimes" of Saudi Shiʿa can be draconian, as in the 34-year prison sentence in 2022 of a female student for her social media activity while at university in the UK or the death sentence of Shiʿi youth for engaging in public protest. See Kirschgaessner (2022); Amnesty International (2023).
[71] However, see the exceptional case of Nadhmi al-Nasr, former Executive Vice President for Administration and Finance at King Abdullah University of Science and Technology (2008–18) and CEO, since 2018, of Crown Prince Mohamad bin Salman's NEOM City project. Al-Nasr began his career as an engineer with ARAMCO and remained with the company for many years. For more on the Saudi Shiʿa, see Matthiesen 2015; Jones 2007; Freer 2019a.
[72] For details on prerequisites for naturalization, see Lowi (2018, 406–7).

citizenship was granted in the 1970s and 1980s to roughly 200,000 Sunni Arabs so as to "balance the influence of the Shi'a" citizens (Crystal 2020, 282). And in 2021, the UAE announced that it would offer citizenship to select foreign nationals – "investors, doctors, specialists, inventors, scientists, talents, intellectuals, artists and their families" – nominated by an Emirati royal or government official (Turak 2021). (Similarly, the ruler may strip citizenship, as has happened on occasion for (suspected) political positions or for "reasons ... rooted in sectarianism.") However, the naturalized either does not enjoy the few civil rights that accompany citizenship, or else such rights are accessible after some delay; the same is true for social rights. Typically, the naturalized is a second- or third-class citizen (Babar 2014, 414; Parolin 2009, 105).

In short, the notion of community (*umma*) has been both constricted and refined such that a "community of privilege" is configured. Stringent citizenship and naturalization laws, as well as marriage practices by which citizens are discouraged from marrying foreign nationals, and non-GCC nationals especially, are effective means for keeping others out.[73] Gulf rulers have been anxious to preserve the oil rent for themselves and for their relations with their subjects; this has remained a regime priority.

As for non-nationals, they are typically excluded from the states' manifold distribution schemes. Non-nationals include (juridically) stateless, long-time residents such as Palestinian refugees and the so-called *bidūn*, short for *bidūn jinsiyya* (without citizenship), and others who do not carry the local citizenship. This latter category includes the imported labor which constitutes the majority of the work force in each country – roughly 95 percent in Qatar, 80 percent in Kuwait, 70–75 percent in Oman, and 60–70 percent in Saudi Arabia – and has built these countries virtually from scratch. They, too, as we will see in Chapter 5, are vertically differentiated but on the basis of ethnicity and occupation – indeed, race and class, and they face varying degrees of discrimination. For the unskilled among them, precarity defines their experience.[74]

---

[73] In Kuwait, Qatar and until very recently, Oman, permission from the government is required of a national to marry a non-national. If the citizen seeking to marry a non-national is female, she knows that her children will not carry her citizenship, although in most cases, they may apply for it at the age of 18, and her foreign husband will, likely, be denied her citizenship, as well (Babar 2014, 412–13; Limbert 2007, 172–74; Longva 2005, 131; Parolin 2009). By Royal Decree on 16 April 2023, Omanis no longer need such permission. "Oman's Sultan Introduces Changes to Laws Regulating Marriage of Omanis to Foreigners," *Gulf News*, 16 April 2023. https://gulfnews.com/world/gulf/oman/omans-sultan-introduces-changes-to-laws-regulating-marriage-of-omani-citizens-to-foreigners-1.1681675027709.

[74] See, *inter alia*, Kamrava and Babar (2012); Gardner et al. (2013); Ahmad (2017).

While there are *bidūn* in Qatar and Saudi Arabia, we know far more about their condition in Kuwait. There, they are thought to number between 100,000 and 150,000, equivalent to about 10 percent of the (citizen) population of 1.4 million.[75] Of tribal background from the peripheries of Kuwait or the interior of the Arabian Peninsula, many of them entered Kuwait between the 1950s and 1980s in search of employment, and many have served in the Kuwaiti military or police force. As noted by a prominent Kuwaiti personality and multi-term member of Parliament, "although some of the *bidūn* were born here and some have served in the army, they cannot marry nor work legally outside the military or security sectors; they have no rights since they have no documents."[76] While they used to receive many of the same benefits as Kuwaiti citizens – and those who worked for the state do receive benefits and pensions for the years they were employed – they have been progressively excluded from the welfare state provisions since the mid-1980s (Kareem 2012; Beaugrand 2018; Weiner 2017). As for *bidūn* in Saudi Arabia, Menoret (2020, 106–7) notes that many, but not all are of nomadic background. He suggests that they are stateless because they failed to apply for citizenship when the state was granting it, most likely because they lived far from administrative centers and were unaware of or unfamiliar with the procedure. However, the Saudi government provides them with a *bidūn*-specific, "Arab migrant" ID that distinguishes them from the typical labor migrants in that it allows them to work without a visa or a sponsor. Interestingly, in this context, Arabness incurs marginally superior benefits. Nonetheless, the *bidūn* of Saudi Arabia tend to work poorly paid, menial jobs and face extraordinary hurdles accessing such things as higher education and other opportunities that would enhance their quality of life.

Another stateless/undocumented population in Saudi Arabia are Muslim refugees from Myanmar (formerly, Burma), predominantly of the Rohingya ethnicity and referred to by Saudis as *burmawiyya*. Estimates of their numbers range from 250,000 to 600,000. It is said that a portion of them are members or descendants of the Rohingya who, facing persecution at home, had been granted asylum in the mid-1970s by King Faisal, while the others had entered the kingdom as pilgrims to perform the hajj and remained. Not only are they excluded from the

---

[75] According to my interlocutors, they numbered between 250,000 and 300,000 in the 1980s, representing close to one-third the size of the citizen population. However, roughly half left the country after the Iraqi invasion in 1990. (Interviews with: former Secretary-General of Kuwaiti Human Rights Society, 8 May 2012; prominent Arab nationalist, Kuwait City, 6 May 2012).

[76] Interview, Kuwait City, 6 May 2012.

well-heeled government distributions, but their status and living conditions are dismal and the threat of arrest and deportation is constant (Naffee 2011; Aziz 2019; Derbal 2022, 224; Lysa 2023, 14–19). That they, the *bidūn*, and several million foreign workers are Muslim appears irrelevant. In Gulf monarchies, these populations enjoy neither inclusion nor even empathy, for they do not belong to the community that actually matters.

Conclusion

While the social welfare function of government distributions is obvious, their strategic purpose requires some clarification. Government transfers, whether universal or particularist, are infused with political intent. They enhance the legitimacy of the ruling elite at the same time as they ensure society's dependence on the state. Thus, they encourage submission while frustrating (possible) dissent. Beyond that, preferential dispensations to specific social categories – such as royal (and other leading) families,[77] (select) tribes and business elites – contribute to their social and material interests. In doing so, favors of this sort appease them for whatever they may have lost or believe they are entitled to and keep them close to the regime. Furthermore, the combination of generalized distributions with the variation in access to resources is integral to the structuring of the (national) community. Hence, while Islam is a resource that can be used to delineate boundaries, as in the community of believing Muslims (*umma*), other frameworks such as nationalism, classism, and periodic deference to tribalism (or to Arabness) have become important for maintaining power, placating society and shaping the nation.

In examining government allocations, it is evident that distributive practices have not only favored the concentration of wealth within ruling elites and their closest allies, but at the same time, they have systematically encouraged, modeled and financed hyper-materialism among subjects, and among some subjects more than others. By underwriting consumption in this manner, these practices are meant to broadcast the "good life," assuage strategic social categories and reinforce both relative privilege and the limits of the hegemonic notion of community. The purposes and effects of these practices are by no means lost on Gulf subjects – many of whom, as we will see in Chapter 4, criticize their rulers' behavior in ethical terms. To be sure, absolute royal privilege,

---

[77] For example, the Al Sheikh of Saudi Arabia. Descendants of Mohamad ibn ʿAbd al-Wahhab, who formed a politico–religious alliance with Mohamad Al Saʿud in the eighteenth century, the Al Sheikh remain the leading religious family in the kingdom.

combined with both comprehensive and hierarchized distributions that elicit varying degrees of incorporation and exclusion while cultivating and reinforcing dependence, facilitate the state's management and control of society. Indeed, distributive practices of this sort are not only coercive in function and intent (Albertus et al. 2018), they are integral to the ruling project of community, nation and state.

4 Society Responds

As the so-called Arab Spring mobilizations of 2011 and the wave of popular protests (in Sudan, Algeria, Lebanon and Iraq) from 2019 to 2021 demonstrated, (predominantly) Muslim publics across the Middle East and North Africa contest the legitimacy of governing institutions and reproach their rulers for failing to make ethical choices relative to governance, distribution and welfare. In oil-rich and oil-poor countries alike, they complain about hoarding, nepotism, inequity and opacity. In the more traditionally repressive Gulf monarchies, via social media and other less overt means, they rail against government behavior regarding wealth circulation, resource management and the constriction of rights. In my discussions with scholars, economists, dissidents, members of official bodies and independent ʿulamaʾ, criticism was profuse but rarely expressed in religious terms. This is noteworthy for it suggests that Gulf nationals, like their rulers, may not be as pious as they are often portrayed (or as rulers seek to appear). It may also suggest that they view (their) government as a secular entity in which religion – specifically, the precepts of the faith – plays no role *per se*, and this despite the regime's narrative and mythology. For whatever reasons, they tend to assume a secular subjectivity at least insofar as they relegate matters of state to a non-spiritual sphere. Thus, governance, as practiced today, is understood to be disconnected from Islam (as a set of beliefs).

In the Gulf environment of autocratic, if not absolutist rule, creative forms of expressing dissent abound. Saudis have been especially prolific in this regard, with YouTube as a favored vehicle for some time.[1] Two independent satirical comedy series, ʿala al-ṭāyir (loosely translated as "On the Fly") and *La Yekthar* ("Don't Overdo It!"), appeared in 2010 and were immensely popular for as long as they lasted. Focused on social criticism, they addressed a host of issues impacting Saudi society: among them, corruption, unemployment, consumerism, constraints on

---

[1] For a novel method of expressing dissent, see Menoret (2014).

women, mistreatment of foreign laborers and even the transformation of Mecca.[2] In September 2011, an independent film described as a "mockumentary" and entitled *Monopoly – A Short Film* was released on YouTube.[3] The sardonic comedy, created by a group of young Saudi men, explores the controversial land question in the kingdom (referred to in Chapter 3) and links the persistent housing crisis to the monopoly over land ownership and the "white lands" (*al-arāḍi al-beyḍaʾ*) phenomenon. Interspersed with recitations of Quranic verses about justice and goodness (*al-ʿadl w'al-iḥsān*) and current economic data highlighting the reality of inequality, the film insinuates that constraints on social welfare in the kingdom derive from the greed of ruling elites.[4]

The prominent Saudi Sheikh Salman al-Aouda, a towering figure of the *Ṣaḥwa* movement of the 1980s and 1990s, in prison since September 2017, also turned to YouTube to voice criticism of ruling elites.[5] In a video posted in 2012, he framed his censure against the backdrop of the reported practice of Umar bin Khattab, the second caliph of Islam who is said to have repeatedly asked local governors about the sources of their possessions: "*min ʿayna laka hadha?*" ("From where did you get this?").[6] Throughout, al-Aouda posed questions regarding the corruption of ruling elites, their enrichment via illegitimate means including the routine pilfering of public resources and opaque spending in the absence of legal scrutiny and oversight, their assumption of privileges irrespective of merit and at the expense of others, and their arrogance and complacency.

Poetry/music is another popular form for the expression of dissent. In a poem referred to as "Tunisian Jasmine," for which he was imprisoned

---

[2] www.mashallahnews.com/made-in-ksa-3al6ayer-the-saudi-youtube-comedy. While most of the episodes are no longer available on YouTube, see www.youtube.com/watch?v=6tDYt9Qe5Uo. See, as well, the parody music video, "No Woman, No Drive." www.youtube.com/watch?v=aZMbTFNp4wI.

[3] www.youtube.com/watch?v=NMvCURQEhpM.

[4] The economic analysis is provided by Essam al-Zamil, a young Saudi economist and entrepreneur who was detained in fall 2017 and sentenced in October 2020 to fifteen years in prison. https://english.alaraby.co.uk/english/news/2020/10/6/prominent-saudi-economist-sentenced-to-15-year-imprisonment-report. See, as well: "Saudis Arrested for Criticising King Abdullah on YouTube," *The Observers*, France24, 1 April 2014, https://observers.france24.com/en/20140401-saudis-chastise-king-abdullah-youtube-get-arrested.

[5] The *Ṣaḥwa*, short for *al-ṣaḥwa al-islamiyya* (Islamic Awakening), refers to a movement initiated by Saudi *ʿulama'* who, in the 1990s, criticized government policies and via petitions demanded reforms (Lacroix 2010). Al-Rasheed (2007) locates the origins of the *Ṣaḥwa* in the 1960s and 1970s. She describes it as a movement made up of both *salafi* and Muslim Brotherhood tendencies that sought to "re-enchant" public life by combining living according to the tenets of Islam with activism for the purpose of advancing social justice (65–72). Menoret (2020) refers to it as a "movement of movements" (27).

[6] www.youtube.com/watch?v=InqD2edqb4U&feature=youtu.be. As of January 2024, the video is no longer available.

(November 2011–March 2016), the Qatari poet, Mohammad ibn al-Dheeb al-Ajami, disparages ruling elites with the following lines:

> The Arab regimes and those who rule them
> are all, without exception,
> without a single exception,
> shameful, thieves.
> ...
> Why, why do these regimes
> import everything from the West—
> everything but the rule of law, that is,
> and everything but freedom?[7]

Another Qatari, Soad al-Kuwari, offers veiled rebuke of Gulf ruling elites – their phoniness, mendacity and deference to the West:

> We talk of many things we don't understand.
> Modernity in the desert! The latest
> joke in a world full of jokes.
> But this is the desert,
> where the dust hovers in the air like butterflies
> in a graveyard.[8]

Menoret and Samin (2013) introduce us to *kasrat*, a musical form of Bedouin origin popular among marginalized Saudi youth, and the, at times, illicit sentiments they broach. In one particular *kasra*, the poet refers to a "paternalistic culture that pretends to be based on generosity when in reality it is based on self-interest, ostentation, and exclusion: 'Whatever shit people give you, they brag like it's a gift'" (223).

Indeed, among the most prominent sentiments conveyed by my interlocutors was scorn for their rulers as leaders with a commitment to the community and its welfare. And to them, "community" is implicitly understood as the territorial nation-state or more appropriately as the ruler's subjects; it does not refer to the de-territorialized Islamic *umma*. To varying degrees, interviewees identified self-preservation, personal enrichment and pandering to Western powers as rulers' primary motivations, not the prescribed intention (*niyya*), discussed in Chapter 2, to pursue justice (*'adl*) and the common good (*maṣlaḥa*). A Kuwaiti Arab nationalist activist proposed that "these countries are run like investment

---

[7] Al-Ajami spent 4.5 years in prison on state security charges: insulting the former Emir Hamad bin Khalifa and "inciting to overthrow the ruling system" through his poems. https://arablit.org/2016/03/16/qatari-poet-muhammad-al-ajami-in-jail-on-15-year-sentence-pardoned-by-emir.

[8] From "Modernity in the Desert" (*Ḥadathiyun f'il Ṣaḥara*), published in Lodge et al. (2012, 167).

companies."[9] A Qatari, once prominent in the Muslim Brotherhood, elaborated: "Our rulers are puppets of the colonial powers. Our governments try to modernize and westernize, but also show the West that they are obedient and just like them. As evidence we find corruption and concentration of wealth at the top, and poverty in the community ... These oil states are small businesses; they're not countries."[10] Furthermore, according to a Saudi ṣaḥwa sheikh: "There are no strong institutions, no models of proper behavior, and no regulations about proper behavior except, ridiculously, to some extent, in the religious domain."[11] Elaborating on the weakness of institutions, a prominent Saudi (Shiʿa) intellectual explains, "there is no legal system; the Government is the law: it has the laws and violates the laws."[12]

A recurrent complaint concerned the state's mismanagement of resources. In Kuwait, for example, "there's a crisis of leadership and of management, and so, a total waste of wealth and possibilities."[13] In Saudi Arabia, according to a former member of *majlis al-shura* (consultative council), "wealth management is a total mess, characterized by corruption, nepotism, tremendous waste." The kingdom "has enough resources to take care of Oman, Bahrain, Yemen, and Jordan, but wealth is concentrated in the hands of royals and squandered by them ... At the same time, poverty in the kingdom is greater than you imagine ... The system is rotten."[14]

How, though, can poverty still exist in the Gulf after more than fifty years of oil wealth?[15] According to a Saudi social scientist and columnist, "corruption, nepotism, and the concentration of wealth explain why there is poverty in the region. But these behaviors are manifestations of the way the state is organized. And in the Gulf countries, the state belongs to a particular group, and this is what affects the distribution of wealth."[16] In the words of an Omani, formerly in leadership positions in the *majlis al-shura* and the *majlis al-dowla* (state council), "the explanation derives from the fact that the state owns the resources.[17] Then there

---

[9] Kuwait City, 6 May 2012.   [10] Doha, 22 Feb. 2012.   [11] Riyadh, 3 April 2012.
[12] Qatif, 14 April 2008. In taunting verse, Saudi poet, Hissa Hillal ("The Chaos of Fatwas") denounces leaders and official ʿulamaʾ for their abuse of legal and Islamic norms of behavior: "I have seen evil from the eyes of the subversive fatwas/in a time when what is permitted is confused with what is forbidden" (emphasis my own). "Saudi Woman Poet Lashes Out at Clerics in 'Arabic Idol.'" *The Independent*, 24 March 2010. www.independent.co.uk/news/world/middle-east/saudi-woman-poet-lashes-out-at-clerics-in-arabic-idol-1926176.html
[13] Interview with prominent philanthropist, Kuwait City, 15 May 2012.
[14] Riyadh, 28 March 2012.   [15] See Chapter 3 p. 66.   [16] Riyadh, 28 April 2012.
[17] Does the state own the resources, or does it not? In response to my question about whether zakat should be taken from oil revenues in the hands of the state, Sheikh

is the matter of how the government spends." He went on to ask rhetorical questions: "Does the government have a clear vision of how the country should be in twenty years? Is there wise planning? Is there precise implementation of plans? Is there accountability that is strict and consistent? Are policies routinely evaluated and revised on the basis of new knowledge?"[18] A Ṣaḥwa sheikh elaborated:

> The most important reasons for the persistence of poverty in Gulf monarchies are first, that wealth is concentrated in the hands of the state, and the state uses that wealth according to the "logic of state authority" – that is, to enhance its own authority. Second, clarity and transparency in the standards followed in the distribution of public wealth are lacking, such that wealth does not reach those who are (most) deserving and in (greatest) need; rather, it circulates among the wealthy and mostly bypasses the poor. Third, development projects are often ill-conceived, understudied, poorly realized, and ill-suited for contributing to social welfare.[19]

A senior researcher at the Islamic Development Bank in Jeddah stressed the absence of vision and accountability. As a result, oil revenues are distributed in ways that enrich only some people, rather than all. Corruption flourishes, as does unsustainable development.[20] A Saudi economist, a former Secretary-General of the now defunct Supreme Economic Council, agreed that poverty persists because of a maldistribution of income, and suggested that most egregious were such things as the unequal development of regions, women's exclusion from certain sectors of employment and the wage gap between nationals and non-nationals.[21] A prominent ʿālim, formerly in a leadership position in the International Union of Muslim Scholars (al-ittiḥād al-ʿālimī li-ʿulamāʾi al-muslimīn), was more guarded in his response: "Poverty persists in these lands because of human weakness that produces such things as corruption, waste, mismanagement, inequitable distribution."[22]

Reflective of mismanagement is, indeed, the manner in which resources are allocated. Distribution is determined not on the basis of analysis of indicators but in accordance with what the regime considers

---

al-Qaradawi (Doha, 5 March 2012) said the following: "Zakat cannot be taken from oil. Zakat is taken from those who own wealth. The government does not own wealth; it does not own the oil. Revenue from oil does not belong to the government. It is public wealth and oil revenues, in their entirety, must be spent for the benefit of the *umma*" (emphasis, my own).

[18] Muscat, 4 Nov. 2013.   [19] Riyadh, 3 May 2012.   [20] Jeddah, 16 April 2012.
[21] Riyadh, 2 April 2012. The Supreme Economic Council was established in 2005 by the late King Abdallah as an advisory body; it was disbanded by King Salman soon after coming to power in January 2015 when he created the Council of Economic and Development Affairs.
[22] Jeddah, 19 April 2012.

Society Responds 79

important at any particular time.[23] According to a Qatari sociologist and referring to the reign of the former king, Hamed bin Khalifa, "the Qatari state, centralized around three-to-four people, functions on impulse: when the Emir's personal taste changes, everything changes."[24] Besides, distribution is not only haphazard but inequitable, beginning with the state's pilfering of resources. National wealth has become royal wealth, and royals assume for themselves budgetary prerogatives which remain beyond the remit of society.[25] A Ṣaḥwa sheikh went on to say that "unfortunately, the leaders today deal with national wealth as if they own it. But leaders have no right to public money except what is due for their labor."[26] Recall, as noted in Chapter 3, that rulers in Saudi Arabia, Oman and Qatar take for themselves (and their families) from national revenues, and family members receive regular stipends; however, details regarding amounts and numbers of recipients are unavailable. Referring to the Saudi context in 2012, a former member of the Saudi *majlis al-shura* suggested that "there are roughly 15,000 princes who, from the day they were born, receive a monthly stipend, ranging from SR 100,000 ($25,000 in 2012) to SR 150,000 ($40,000), by virtue of being royals."[27]

In a rare evocation of religious norms, a prominent Saudi intellectual comments on the practice of opaque extractions thus: "According to the teachings of Islam, an *imām* (religious leader) who uses the common property or national treasury to promote his own personal interests would be called a *khā'in* (traitor). Today, though, our Government owns all this common wealth, disposes of it and distributes it as it wishes."[28] A Qatari scholar of Islam concludes that, "as long as there's a small group that takes the largest share, there is no justice in wealth distribution and in opportunities."[29] Reflecting on the peculiarities of distribution, a Kuwaiti philanthropist opined that, "those in charge do everything in a tribal way."[30] And an Omani, former member of the Council on Higher Education, suggested acerbically that, "the tremendous inequalities of wealth have been brought about by those who think they are our saviors."[31]

Indeed, there is neither transparency nor oversight in rent distribution, beginning with what royals take for themselves. In the words of a Saudi

---

[23] Interview with Saudi economist, formerly on *majlis al-shura*, Riyadh, 6 April 2008.
[24] Doha, 22 Feb. 2012.
[25] Kamrava (2009, 412) points out that three Qatari emirs, when forced from power (1949, 1960, 1995), took with them all or most of the national Treasury.
[26] Riyadh, 3 May 2012.
[27] Riyadh, 28 March 2012. However, see Chapter 3, p. 59, fn. 40.
[28] Qatif, 12 April 2012. *Supra* fn.18   [29] Doha, 27 Feb. 2012.
[30] Kuwait, 15 May 2012.   [31] Muscat, 7 Feb. 2012.

ṣaḥwa sheikh, "the lack of transparency (*shafafiyya*) allows for the concentration of wealth in the hands of the people of authority (*'aṣḥāb al-nufūdh*) rather than in the hands of those who work and are productive (*'aṣḥāb al-intāj*)."[32] Thus, fabulous fortunes are made and corruption persists. Of the Gulf monarchies, and as noted in Chapter 3, Kuwait is unique insofar as the ruler receives a precise annual allocation (KD50 mill.) that is approved by Parliament, written into law and publicized. He may spend and distribute this allotment as he chooses.[33] Furthermore, Kuwait's State Audit Bureau is independent and "answerable to the ... elected parliament" (Alshehabi 2017, 6).

Addressing some of the vexing effects of the undeclared and unacknowledged royal extractions, a prominent Saudi economist and former member of *majlis al-shura* exclaims:

> How can we evaluate the government's distributive activities when no one knows how much the royal family takes for itself from the national wealth before oil revenues enter the treasury? ... What comes to the state in the form of hydrocarbon rent and what goes into the national budget are two different amounts. The latter is what remains after the family has taken what it wants from the rent. But there is no line item in the budget that shows what goes to the family, and there is no way to check on this.[34]

This concern is echoed, indeed elaborated upon by a Qatari scholar and former employee in the country's oil and gas sector.[35] On the basis of figures provided by the Institute of International Finance in a 2008 report, he claims that while the value of Qatar's oil and natural gas exports in 2007 was US$40.7 billion, the country's general budget revenues for that year were $20.2 billion (al-Kuwari 2009, 84). With as much as 50 percent of hydrocarbon receipts unaccounted for, the implication is that they may have been appropriated by the royal family.[36]

Distribution favors proximity to rule and to the capital, the seat of power. Hence, important families and loyalists enjoy disproportionate benefits, merit is under-valued as a criterion for advancement and regions suffer from inequitable development. An Omani oil industry technocrat remarked: "Jobs are handed out not on the basis of competencies but rather on who you are. Ministers, for example, are tribal leaders, friends or relatives of tribal leaders, or heads of communities.

---

[32] Riyadh, 3 May 2012.
[33] Interview with former M.P. *tajama'a al-islamī al-salafī* (Salafi Islamic Gathering), Kuwait City, 8 May 2012.
[34] Riyadh, 1 April 2012.　　[35] Interview: Doha, 10 Nov. 2013.
[36] The analysis suggests, further, that 27.4 percent of Saudi, 17.3 percent of Emirati and 8.5 percent of Kuwaiti hydrocarbon revenues were unaccounted for, too. See, as well, Alshehabi (2017, 6–8).

Society Responds

In Oman, eight-to-twelve families dominate government; the system is based on pleasing those families, allowing them to get very rich. This is how legitimacy has been built."[37] A Kuwaiti oil industry engineer concurred: "We don't have the right people in the right places in Kuwait. People are not elected on their merits, but rather, for political purposes: to respond to family interests, favor one community/tribe/branch or another, return a favor."[38] Referring to Saudi Arabia and the phenomenon of inequitable development, a prominent economist offered the following insight: "What counts are the big, important towns with influential governors that together form the corridor from east to west: east (oil) → center (seat of power) → west (seat of Islam); outside this corridor, nothing matters."[39]

Governments are not inclined to address inequalities because that would oblige rulers to acknowledge their stranglehold over wealth and power. Verily, "insatiable greed, love of money, and total disregard for the common good characterize the state."[40] Besides, as an Omani former diplomat pointed out, "the concern for equity only becomes an issue if you are aware of and sensitive to inequity."[41] Equally oblique in his disparagement of the ruler's rectitude (and its impact on society), a Qatari scholar of Shariʿa noted that: "A man without *ikhlās* (sincerity, integrity, righteousness) cannot guide people in the way of *ikhlās*."[42] In other words, "the environment, beginning with the model provided by the leader, distorts incentives for ethical behavior."[43] Thus, the Omani former diplomat just quoted went on to say: "In the Gulf, when people complain about the disparity in income, for example, the focus is not between rich and poor, but between the self and those who are better off. Indeed, a major preoccupation is that 'there's so much wealth to be gained, so why don't I have more?'"[44] And the Qatari scholar of Shariʿa summarized, tongue in cheek: "We don't talk about or even care about *maslaḥa ʿamma* [common good]; we only care about *maslaḥa khaṣṣa*" (private interest or individual benefit).[45]

Governors shun real reform since their distributive activities are politically motivated. They encourage their subjects to consume, and

---

[37] Muscat, 11 Feb. 2012. [38] Kuwait City, 22 April 2008. [39] Riyadh, 6 April 2008.
[40] Interview with economist on shariʿa board of Islamic banks, Riyadh, 5 April 2012.
[41] Muscat, 1 Feb. 2012. [42] Doha, 27 Feb. 2012.
[43] Interview with economist at Islamic Development Bank, Jeddah, 18 April 2012.
[44] Muscat, 1 Feb. 2012. One of my interlocutors offered that in the Gulf monarchies, people consider (their) wealth as "bounty": a reward to which they are entitled, rather than a means of production (and certainly not a return on production). (Riyadh, 28 March 2012).
[45] Doha, 27 Feb. 2012.

consume extravagantly so that they remain complacent and steer clear of politics. Rulers extend universal subsidies and selective material incentives so as to placate those whose allegiance they depend upon. In effect, the emphasis on consumption is a principal tool of governance: It contributes to meeting the royal families' objectives to maintain themselves, consolidate their power and manage society. According to an outspoken Qatari 'ālim: "Gulf dynasties try to appease their populations by reducing fees, raising subsidies ... Overall, the policy is to increase the happiness of their subjects by enriching them."[46] At our first meeting, an Omani activist offered the following: "The objective of distribution is primarily the consolidation of loyalty." At a subsequent meeting, he suggested, more boldly: "Distribution is a coercive means to enforce complacency: you feed the mouth, you blind the eye."[47] Similarly, with regard to Saudi Arabia, "the most powerful element of the Al Saʿud system is its penetration of society through connections and gift-giving, and maintaining itself and the system thereby."[48] A Kuwaiti political-economic analyst summarized thus:

We have ruling projects, related to security, that involve corruption and the use of resources essentially for the purpose of maintaining the system. However, there are no "state projects" that would take care of education, encourage productivity, honor merit, etcetera. The problem is that the objective to improve the quality of life for all simply does not exist. Rather, those in power pay those who keep them in power.[49]

In short, interlocutors confirm that there is no genuine concern for equity in the distribution of resources, and no indication that religious norms are integrated into this domain, indeed most domains of governance, except perhaps in the encouragement of charitable giving. Rather, fairly narrow political and material interests prevail. A prominent Saudi businessperson insisted that "the government uses oil money to impose a certain understanding of Islam on society." Moreover, it "utilizes Islam to remain in power and consolidate its position. It does not care about incorporating Islam into policy."[50] A Kuwaiti former member of Parliament noted that "Islam is weakly adhered to; rather, it is commercialized and manipulated."[51] Waving the banner of Islam is a means to assert the legitimacy of rulers and identify them with justice and righteousness, while enforcing conformism and obedience. As evidence, in March 2011 in reference to the popular mobilizations in Tunisia and

---

[46] Doha, 27 Feb. 2012.   [47] Muscat, 5 Feb. 2012; 4 Nov. 2013.
[48] Interview with former member of majlis al-shūrā, Riyadh, 28 March 2012.
[49] Kuwait City, 10 May 2012.   [50] Al-Khobar, 13 April 2008.
[51] Kuwait City, 18 April 2008.

Egypt that led, just weeks before, to the fall of the regimes of Presidents Ben Ali and Mubarak, respectively, the Saudi Grand Mufti, Sheikh Abd al-Aziz Al Sheikh warned that, "Islam strictly prohibits protests in the kingdom because the ruler here rules by God's will" (Murphy 2011). To be sure, as noted by one of my interlocutors, "Islam is like a machine; it is certainly a tool in the hands of the state, used to pursue political and economic objectives."[52] A Saudi religious dissident elaborated as follows: "Policy makers have nothing to do with the Islamic point of view. They are focused on their personal interests and comforts, and on spending money to stabilize the situation in the country so as to maintain their rule and the status quo. Although they claim to incorporate Islam into governance, in reality this is not true."[53] Hence, insofar as governance is concerned, Islam in Gulf monarchies today is, according to an incisive Qatari intellectual, "a decoration."[54] Another Qatari, a scholar of Islam elaborated thus: "The soul of (Qur'anic) principles has been forgotten and the focus, instead, is on their outward manifestation."[55] What does it mean, then, that these states proclaim their adherence to Islam? It is "some sort of playing with words by those who feel they own the religion, in addition to everything else."[56]

★★★

While my interlocutors rarely expressed their criticisms of ruling elites in explicitly religious terms, they typically invoked concepts such as justice, equity, the public good or public interest – often employed by religious scholars and ordinary pious citizens to censure political leaders. To be sure, Gulf rulers have also experienced pushback from the religious field, on religio-moral grounds and expressed in religious terms. They are not alone in their instrumentalization of Islam for political ends. And given that Gulf rulers insist upon their commitment to the faith, the invocation of the normative tradition by their subjects precisely to criticize their policies and behaviors is an important source of their vulnerability. Indeed, the strategic use of Islamic discourse (and practice) has been intrinsic to the political capital of religiously inflected dissident movements in the Gulf in the past several decades.[57] While a close

---

[52] Interview with an economist, formerly in a leadership position in the Ministry of Finance, Riyadh, 1 May 2012.
[53] Riyadh, 2 April 2012.   [54] Doha, 22 Feb. 2012.   [55] Doha, 27 Feb. 2012.
[56] Interview with Qatari intellectual, a former member of Muslim Brotherhood, 10 Nov. 2013.
[57] Furthermore, what is often referred to as Wahhabism can be understood as a dissident Islamo-revolutionary movement in the mid-eighteenth, nineteenth and early twentieth centuries that rose up to challenge political rulers of the times.

examination of the latter's efforts in this regard would deviate from my focus on Islam as a tool of governance and statecraft, a brief foray into a few select moments of resistance and ruling elites' responses to them can offer some indication of both challenges to and the limits of what I refer to as a ruling strategy.

The occupation of the Grand Mosque of Mecca in November 1979 by Juhayman al-Utaibi and his *Ikhwān* followers is perhaps the most spectacular moment of resistance to Gulf rulers from the religious field (Vassiliev 1998; Hegghammer and Lacroix 2007; Menoret 2008). Through their leader, the *Ikhwan*, which was an offshoot of a broader pietist movement, *al-Jama'a al-Salafiyya al-Muhtasiba* (JSM) (The Salafi Group That Commands Right and Forbids Wrong), called for the end of Al Sa'ud rule and the strict application of shari'a. They insisted that for the Al Sa'ud, Islam was nothing more than a means to legitimize their rule. They noted, for example, that the ruler had forced the Saudi population to declare their allegiance (*bay'a*) to him, which is proscribed by the faith, rather than allow them to offer it freely of their own accord. They denounced the moral corruption of the princes and the regime's engagement with Western powers.

The government, under the leadership of King Khalid, chose to respond to the "Mecca insurgency" with force. To storm the mosque with armed personnel, they sought the approval of the Grand Mufti, the most senior religious authority (appointed by the king), so as not to defy the Qur'anic injunction forbidding the use of violence in the "most sacred space of Islam." Nonetheless, the regime relied upon first, American and then, French forces – the very nonbelievers that Juhayman had criticized it for consorting with – to capture the Saudi insurgents and end the occupation. No doubt, the conduct of the operation, with its use of Western expertise, brute force and poisonous gasses, and the severe repression that ensued were damaging to the legitimacy of the Al Sa'ud. Shortly thereafter, the regime aimed to restore its Islamic credentials by acknowledging the preferences of the more socially conservative 'ulama'. Thus, they extended the powers of the *mutawa'un*, the so-called religious police, and constrained further the mobility and opportunities of Saudi women and girls while at the same time stepping up surveillance of society and punishing dissent.

Iraq's invasion of Kuwait in August 1990 and its occupation of the emirate until mid-January 1991 provided another important moment of pushback to Gulf ruling elites from the religious field. In fact, in Kuwait and Saudi Arabia, religious forces of both the Muslim Brotherhood and various *salafi* persuasions criticized their governors' response to the invasion. And it is worth noting that in earlier decades, these very movements had been encouraged by Gulf rulers who at that time were engaged in efforts to counter the popularity of Arab nationalism and leftist ideologies at home.[58]

In Kuwait, the influence of organized religious forces has been longstanding. Indeed, the Muslim Brotherhood has been active there from the 1940s (Freer 2018, 45–55). Initially, its efforts focused mostly on Islamizing Kuwaiti society through the educational and cultural spheres, as well as the provision of charity. Its maneuverability grew from the 1960s as the Al Sabah, feeling threatened by the popular recognition of Arab nationalist mobilization in the emirate, bent to some of the Brotherhood's demands, as in the introduction of "Islamic banking," discussed in Chapter 7, and further incentivized it with various forms of support. Furthermore, in the post-Juhayman and post-Iranian Revolution environment of the 1980s, Islamist movements and activists across the region were invigorated. Thus, the Kuwaiti Muslim Brotherhood and *salafi* formations expanded their activities to impose their ideas about living according to Islam and to influence politics. In both domains they achieved considerable recognition, and this gave the ruling elite cause for concern (Freer 2018, 71–7).

It was, however, during the Iraqi invasion and occupation that the Brotherhood's acquired social and political capital in Kuwait was indisputably on display. With the emir and much of the ruling family having fled the emirate within hours of the invasion, it was the Brotherhood that both organized the resistance and distributed goods and services to the population. The religious institutions that it dominated – mosques, cooperatives and charitable organizations – became key sites for its functioning "like a state." With the return of the Al Sabah following the US-led routing of the Iraqi occupation forces, the Kuwaiti opposition, including the Brotherhood, demanded the re-convening of parliament and more representative government. The emir balked and sought to win them (and their supporters) over by extending broad-based financial handouts. Alas, he failed. By that time, as Courtney Freer (2018, 81) explains, "the Muslim Brotherhood offered the ideological inspiration that the government could not provide." Ever since, the Al Sabah have routinely had to contend with pushback from the Brotherhood and *salafi* formations. And because of the nature of politics in Kuwait, with its fairly vibrant parliamentary life, ruling elites are indeed expected to be responsive to them. Nonetheless, when he is unable to advance his agenda otherwise, the emir, like the rulers of the other Gulf monarchies, resorts

---

[58] See Chapter 5.

to repression. In his case, this takes the form of (repeated) unilateral dissolutions of parliament.

With Iraq's mobilization in the summer of 1990, Saudi Arabia's ruling elite feared that Saddam Hussein's forces would extend their military intervention southward into the kingdom. It was at this time that religious scholars affiliated with the *Sahwa* (Awakening) movement[59] – most notable among them, Sheikh Salman al-Aouda – came to the fore. Through their mediatic pronouncements, they mobilized a critical mass of disgruntled Saudis (Lacroix 2010; al-Rasheed 2007). First, they publicly criticized the Al Saʿud for seeking protection from Western powers. They categorically rejected the legitimacy of the *fatwa* (formal ruling or religious interpretation) issued by then Grand Mufti Ibn Baz (and sought by King Fahd) that it was acceptable to invite foreign troops to not only protect the kingdom but also to launch their war on Iraq from Saudi soil. Second, they issued petitions to the king in which they demanded the departure of Western forces and called for comprehensive reforms of the political system in line with the shariʿa. They denounced government corruption, insisted upon greater equity in economic matters and opposed un-Islamic financial practices, as in the collection of interest (*riba'*) . While the public criticism of ruling elites would result in repression of the *Sahwa*-led mobilization and prison sentences for many, the regime again felt obliged to appease its detractors and shore up its Islamic credentials. It announced the prompt departure of foreign forces and conceded greater moral authority to the religious establishment. It increased the prerogatives of the "religious police" and at last, accepted the creation of "Islamic banks," as I discuss in Chapter 6.

In short, when faced with resistance from the religious field, the ruler, with his vulnerabilities exposed, typically tries to restore his religious credentials. He does so by allowing the more conservative religious forces somewhat greater maneuverability and by accepting a larger role for Islam in daily life. At the same time, he tries to win over his subjects by extending financial disbursements and perhaps conceding to some of their demands, as in, for example, the availability of more employment opportunities. More often than not, his response also includes the resort to force. In broad strokes, this is the playbook that the late Sultan Qaboos followed when confronted with the protests in Oman in winter and spring of 2011. He gave orders to create 50,000 new public sector jobs and offer monthly allowances to registered job seekers (Valeri 2011). He removed from office several government ministers who were reputed

---

[59] See fn. 5.

to be corrupt, and accepted the introduction of Islamic banking and finance in the sultanate. At the same time, he both intensified the policing of society and stepped up repression with hundreds of arrests and prison sentences (Valeri 2011).

Departing only slightly from this "convention," Saudi Arabia's Crown Prince Mohamad bin Salman (MbS) has been more muscular in his response to pushback from religious forces, as well as to those whom he perceives as critics and/or (potential) competitors. In September 2017, for example, several prominent Saudi clerics, among them Sheikhs Salman al-Aouda and Awadh al-Qarni, were arrested, allegedly for their pronouncements; they remain in prison to this day (December 2023). In the case of al-Aouda, he was detained after having posted on Twitter a religiously laden text in which he obliquely criticized the Saudi-led blockade of Qatar (June 2017–January 2021) and recited a prayer for reconciliation among the Gulf states "for the good of their people(s)" (*limā fīhi khayru shuʿūbihim*).[60] Promoting what he refers to as "moderate" Islam, the Crown Prince has stripped the religious establishment of some of their prerogatives while "consolidating religious authority and discourse under the sole supervision of the royal palace" (Hoffman 2022).[61] The purpose is to control the narrative, neutralize other potential power centers and enhance his own authority. As for prominent *Saḥwa* sheikhs like al-Aouda and al-Qarni, he considers their influence and their independence a threat to his authority. Hence, they have to be silenced. But alongside the centralization of control and the repression of independent and/or dissenting (religious) voices, the Crown Prince coaxes the population to consume – and consume extravagantly. He does so by investing lavishly in entertainment of various sorts, long absent in the kingdom, and in futuristic development projects, among other things. Consumption provides an engrossing alternative to critical engagement and encourages complacency.

---

[60] www.hrw.org/news/2018/01/07/saudi-arabia-cleric-held-4-months-without-charge. The chief prosecutor has since asked for the death penalty for al-Aouda and other detained clerics (Qiblawi 2019). www.cnn.com/2019/07/25/middleeast/saudi-cleric-sheikh-salman-al-awda-intl/index.html.

[61] In an interview with Abdallah al-Mudaifer on *Al-Arabiyya* network (28 April 2021), Mohamad bin Salman (MbS) shared his views on religion and its place in Saudi society. www.youtube.com/watch?v=xqXl0L3lL8w.

5 Imported Labor
Building/Appeasing the Nation

Introduction

In Chapter 3, I began the examination of state-directed institutionalized practices with a discussion of the various ways in which Gulf rulers distribute oil wealth among their subjects and their purposes. In describing different types of allocations and addressing related matters having to do with privilege in and exclusion from access to resources, I highlighted gradations in citizenship and other internal forms of discrimination against particular social categories. And I connected the tiering of access to both the shaping of community as a community of (relative) privilege, and the ruler's efforts at social management and social control.

In this chapter, I build upon that earlier discussion to further interrogate the politics of belonging (*intīma'*) and the building of community within the broader ruling project of community, nation and state in the four Gulf monarchies. I do so through another government-sponsored, oil-financed institutionalized practice implicitly sanctioned by Islam – the employment of foreign labor. I explore the role of the foreigner – in this case, imported labor, referred to variously as expat(riate), temporary resident, contract worker, guest worker or migrant – in bringing together the citizenry as a distinctly national community and shaping its identity. In doing so, I address the confounding role of the Islamic normative tradition. Additionally, I examine some of the peculiarities of the importation, organization and incorporation of foreign labor, and consider how they, and the associated modes of management and control contribute to political-economic priorities of rule: ensuring sustained support for the regime and consolidating the power, wealth and authority of the ruling dynasty.[1]

Encounters

In *Mudun al-Malḥ* (Cities of Salt, 1988), a fictionalized account of the encounter between the local Gulf Arab and the prospecting

---
[1] This chapter builds upon Lowi (2018).

Euro-American on the eve of the discovery of oil, Abdelrahman Munif describes an awestruck society in the face of the "European," with their machines, manners and manipulation. Confronted with the overwhelming power and possibilities of European technology and authority, the Gulf Arab was made to feel inferior, inadequate and undeserving.

Franz Fanon reflects on similar encounters, the relations of domination and deference that ensue and their effect. In *Black Skin, White Mask* (1952), he suggests that to be acknowledged by the colonial master, the colonized subject dons the white master's masks. They try to be like the master and appropriate their culture, and the European encourages them in this regard. Alas, not only does the colonized fail ultimately to gain the recognition they seek, but they end up with a fractured personality.[2] Homi Bhabha (1984), elaborating on the ambiguity that results from what he refers to as "mimicry," claims that it produces in the colonized subject an uncomfortable and unsettling condition: that of being "almost the same, but not quite" (126).[3]

While there had been contact between Gulf society and the European well prior to the explorations for oil, as noted in Chapter 1, it was largely confined, during the period of British rule over the Indian subcontinent, to the Gulf coastline. It concerned Indian Ocean trade relations and the administration of the Trucial States[4] primarily, and engaged mainly local tribal sheikhs with whom the British had forged alliances (Onley 2007). There were, as well, other foreigners with whom Gulf Arabs had had regular contact: South Asian traders and merchants had lived in coastal towns along the Gulf for as long as there had been Indian Ocean trade, and enjoyed special privileges (Metcalf 2007), while Omanis, especially,

---

[2] In an interview in Doha (26 March 2015), a Qatari intellectual expressed this "divided self" or cultural ambiguity quite poignantly: "Culturally, we are defined by the camel and the Rolls Royce: sometimes we're the camel, sometimes the Rolls Royce ... less often we are in between."

[3] Ibn Khaldun, the fourteenth-century Arab social theorist, discussed in his *Al-Muqadimmah* (Book One, chapter 2, no. 22) the tendency toward imitation (*iqtidā'*) on the part of the defeated: "The vanquished always want to imitate the victor in his distinctive mark(s), his dress, his occupation, and all his other conditions and customs. The reason for this is that the soul always sees perfection in the person who is superior to it and to whom it is subservient. It considers him perfect, either because the respect it has for him impresses it, or because it erroneously assumes that its own subservience to him is not due to the nature of defeat but to the perfection of the victor. If that erroneous assumption fixes itself in the soul, it becomes a firm belief. The soul, then, adopts all the manners of the victor and assimilates itself to him. This, then, is imitation."

[4] This was the name given by the British to a group of sheikhdoms, or tribal confederations, roughly equivalent to present-day UAE, that had signed truces ("treaties of protection") with Britain in the nineteenth century.

had established trade links with East Africa, too. In fact, Oman has long been home to populations whose origins were further to the east, but also the south; and this accounts, in large measure, for its more diverse citizen population (Peterson 2004; al-Rasheed 2005, 104). As for Qatar, the bulk of its foreign population until the mid-twentieth century was comprised of Persians but also Africans, most of whom were or had been slaves (Fromherz 2012, 11). Through the 1960s, in fact, African slaves could be found among settled communities of the Arabian Peninsula and along the coastline.[5]

Despite a history of exposure and interactions of various sorts, the arrival of Euro-American oil companies – with their taskmasters, technicians and technology – to the Arabian Peninsula from the 1930s added a new dimension to the encounter with the foreigner. Along with the authority and privileged arrangements that had characterized the British presence, those prospecting for oil brought with them what their Gulf Arab interlocutors lacked, came to feel they needed and were quickly seduced by: the stuff of "modernity." Thus confronted, Gulf elites may have anticipated that with the export of oil, European power, wealth and authority would be transplanted to the Peninsula in the form of not only machines and consumption goods, but also, as Toby Jones (2010) notes, practices and plans. Oil would be exchanged for modernity – that is, for things European – and Gulf Arabs, having succeeded at bringing Europe to the desert and adopting its ways, would at last be acknowledged.[6]

Furthermore, the arrival of the oil companies prompted the migration of labor to the oil fields and surrounding areas. Initially, Arab *bedu* from other parts of the Peninsula moved into Bahrain and the east coast of Saudi Arabia to work for the British and the Americans. Eventually, Omanis, Yemenis, and even Iraqis found jobs in and around the oil fields; they were joined by Egyptians, Jordanians, Palestinians and Sudanese (Vitalis 2006, 92; Alzahrani 2014, 379). So great was demand that in Kuwait, for example, the proportion of foreigners in the workforce increased from 5 percent in 1945 to 68 percent in 1949 (Seccombe 1987, 20–1). And as had been the case in Iran and Iraq, the oil industry on the eastern shores of the Peninsula inspired the emergence of a nascent labor

---

[5] On the African diaspora in Arabia, see Hopper (2015).
[6] For a contemporary rendering of the aspiration to bring Europe to the desert, consider the Villagio Mall in Doha, Qatar, designed to represent Venice with its canals, gondolas, loggias, etc. (see Appendix, pp. 175–76). For a biting critique of such efforts, see excerpt from poem by Al-Kuwari, *supra* p. 76.

Table 5.1 *Foreigners as percentage of labor force, select years*

	1975	1985	1990	1999	2008	2019
KSA	42.9	64.9	59.8	55.8	50.6	56
Kwt	69.8	81.2	86.1	82	83.2	82
Oman	34.1	64.2	70.1	61.7	74.6	71
Qatar	80.6	89.7	91.6	87.1	94.3	94
Total	56.85	75	76.9	71.65	75.67	75.75

Source: adapted from Baldwin-Edwards (2011, 9) and Hanieh (2020, 117)

movement. Virtually from the outset, oil fields were sites of protest against the companies' discriminatory practices.[7]

While initially, labor migration followed the Euro-American oil companies, the importation of labor, both skilled and unskilled, from near and far, continued through independence and the intensification of state-building and "take-off" after the 1973 "price shock." According to one source, the number of migrant workers, including accompanying family members, in the six Gulf monarchies at the beginning of the 1970s is estimated to have been between 800,000 and 1.25 million (Winckler 2010, 9); by 1975, it more than doubled, reaching 2.76 million (Winckler 2009: 135). Of these, 1.4 million were in the labor force; their numbers increased to 4.4 million over the ensuing ten years. By 1985, foreigners constituted 85 percent of the combined labor force of the six Gulf monarchies, and 75 percent of Kuwait, Qatar, Oman and Saudi Arabia – up from 57 percent ten years earlier (Baldwin-Edwards 2011, 8–9). In 2019, they constituted 56 percent of the labor force in Saudi Arabia, 71 percent in Oman, 82 percent in Kuwait and 93–94 percent in Qatar (Hanieh 2020, 117) (Table 5.1). And as a proportion of the total population in the six states, foreigners made up only 9.7 percent in 1973 but increased to 36.6 percent in 1991 and 48 percent in 2019 (Fargues 2011, 278–80; Hanieh 2020, 117) (Table 5.2).

Given the pervasiveness of foreign nationals and indisputable dependence on their labor, it is worth considering how that earlier encounter with the (uninvited) newcomer of European descent may have influenced how the Gulf Arab – decades later and in a different context – confronted foreigners who, responding to demand, arrived to work and build their country.

---

[7] See Vitalis (2006, 92–5, 102–4, 145–62, 175–84, 263–64) on labor unrest at the ARAMCO camp in Saudi Arabia; for Bahrain, see Nakhleh (2011, 75–84).

Table 5.2 *Foreigners as percentage of total population, select years*

	1975	1985	1990	1999	2008	2019
KSA	25%	41%	37%	27.5%	27%	38%
Kwt	52.5	72	73	64	68	70
Oman	19.5	31	26.5	26	31	44
Qatar	62	72	78	62	87	89.5

Source: Gulf Research Center (GRC), Gulf Labour Markets, Migration, and Population Programme, database

The Argument and Its Underpinnings

The study of the foreigner, in the Gulf as elsewhere, is connected to the universal question of the "stranger" (Simmel 1908): who is both familiar and unfamiliar, who embodies the unknown even if we know them and who evinces hostility because they represent a (real or an imagined) danger. With all-out development in Gulf monarchies, fueled by oil-infused wealth, the ever-present foreigner elicits considerable fear and insecurity on the part of citizens relative to who they are – their self-identification – but also their access to resources; indeed, to their preservation (al-Najjar 2013, 17–19).[8] Such concerns can foster group cohesion. That is to say, while the endogenous feature of tribalism and the hierarchy of citizenship create sub-divisions among the citizenry, the prodigious foreign presence, perceived as a more-or-less threatening "external other," stimulates social bonding. Sub-national groups conjoin to secure, if not to form the nation, an overarching "collective subject" in reaction to the foreigner (Geertz 1973, 240).

Moreover, the combination of persistent existential concerns derivative of dynastic autocracies' uncertain durability, Gulf nationals' relatively weak numbers and considerable wealth, and the acute dependence on the foreigner has prompted the regimes' adoption of defensive, indeed divisive strategies. Since the 1970s, legislation regarding citizenship has inhibited the expansion of the boundaries of national community, as noted in Chapter 3, while exclusionary policies and practices have governed the incorporation of the foreigner into the Gulf state. No doubt, the absorption of vast numbers of foreigners, comprising, in most cases, the (overwhelming) majority of the labor force, and the

---

[8] Similar sentiments can be found in other countries experiencing large influxes of foreign populations. See, for example, Justin E. Smith, "Does Immigration Mean 'France Is Over?'" *New York Times*, 5 Jan. 2014.

distinctive ways thereof, contribute to shaping the country's identity as a unified community – a "national" community.[9]

Acknowledging the foreigner in Gulf identity is not particularly new. More than twenty years ago, the anthropologist Ahn Nga Longva (2000) noted a connection in her research on Kuwait: "Migrants are the foil in relation to which the Gulf nationals perceive and define themselves" (183). Since then, there has been a growing body of social scientific literature on foreign labor, although relatively little that is specifically about identity.[10] Besides, until recently, most scholars who study Gulf states through their foreigner communities have concerned themselves primarily with the unskilled and relatively poor, predominantly Asian and increasingly African workers.[11] However, I bring into the discussion whites of European descent – among them, non-indigenous North Americans, Australians, New Zealanders and South Africans[12] – and non-GCC Arabs, as well. I suggest that not only do the three different categories of foreigners – the "European," the non-GCC Arab and the predominantly Asian (and increasingly African) laborer – play important and distinct roles in shaping the identity of the national community, but there is a relationship among the three that is critical to the matter of belonging. If we consider the incorporation of foreign labor, enacted through policies and practices, we note variable degrees of distancing and privation depending on the category to which the foreigner belongs. This tiering, in which "Europeans" enjoy relative privilege, reveals the perceptions and/or aspirations of Gulf elites relative to their own status in the hierarchy of social and economic relations internationally. At the same time, the imposition of variable degrees of distancing may contribute to attenuating anxieties that derive from historical relationships with the "European" on the one hand, and the non-GCC Arab on the other prior to the "oil boom." More broadly, and insofar as statecraft is concerned, the practice advances the ruler's efforts to appease the citizen as part of his overall strategy to manage and control society.

---

[9] This is, of course, in addition to each country's distinguishing features and historical experience. On particularities that contribute to national identity, see, *inter alia*: for Bahrain, Alshehabi (2017); Kuwait, Tetreault (2000); Oman, Limbert (2010) and Sachedina (2021); Saudi Arabia, Doumato (1992) and Hertog (2015); United Arab Emirates, Samin (2016).

[10] However, see al-Najjar (2013). Fargues (2011) and Okruhlik (2011) suggest a relationship between national identity and the foreigner, as does Mednicoff (2012, 189–94) who elaborates somewhat with regard to Qatar and the UAE.

[11] Neha Vora studies middle- and upper-middle-class South Asians in the UAE (2008; 2011) and Euro-American "expats" in Qatar (2015).

[12] In what follows, I use the term "European" as shorthand for "whites of European descent," as previously described.

Indeed, the ranking of foreigners, relative to citizens and to each other, and the associated variations in access to resources serve the interests of rule. As autocracy and rentierism are essential features of the domestic political economy, rulers (and their families) exercise a seemingly immutable monopoly over power and wealth. To sustain that monopoly and ensure the regime's durability, they have been anxious to preserve the oil rent (and returns on the state's international investments) for themselves and for (their relations with) their subjects; this has remained a principal regime goal. Furthermore, rent-driven enrichment and development in a context of dependence, on imported labor and expertise, inflect the sense of entitlement of the citizen relative to the foreigner. And the citizen, who is, after all, a dependent subject, benefits in multiple ways from the marginalization of the foreigner. Thus, the importation and organization of foreign labor advances the ruler's agenda and his capacity to manage and control society. This institutionalized practice contributes to structuring the community of (relative) privilege and delineating its boundaries, constructing a national identity and securing the loyalty, or at least acquiescence of key social categories to the dynastic state.[13]

The Foreigner and ... the Foreigner

In the process of building modern states, the nature of the interaction with foreigners began to change as Gulf rulers assumed the role of employer, formerly occupied by the "European." In this new capacity, however, the rulers have remained beholden to the latter. Despite their numerical inferiority relative to Arab and eventually to Asian migrants, "Europeans" have exerted disproportionate influence through their employment as advisors but also as "designers, managers and executors" of Gulf rulers' projects (Alshehabi 2014, 22). As for Arab migrants, they made up as much as 85 percent of the foreign labor force in the Gulf between 1945 and 1973 (Khalaf 2014, 46–7). Palestinians, Jordanians and Egyptians especially filled the ranks of skilled manpower and the professional cadre in the new bureaucracies (Ulrichsen 2016, 174–75). And in the early 1970s, Arabs made up roughly 80 percent of the foreign population in Kuwait and 90 percent in Saudi Arabia (Birks 1980, 66–76).

---

[13] For a useful overview of national identity construction as a ruling project in Gulf monarchies – one that includes the recent focus on heritage (*turāth*) practices, see Crystal (2020).

With the spectacular growth in national revenues from the mid-1970s and the related increase in imported labor, foreigners were perceived increasingly as a security threat (Al-Najjar 2013, 17–19; Longva 2000, 122–25; Mednicoff 2011). Interestingly, Arabs from elsewhere in the MENA came to be considered a greater threat than others (Kapiszewski 2006, 6–8). No doubt, they represented a very particular sort of threat to increasingly rich, Arab-Muslim host societies. Not only had they stood with their Gulf cousins, resisting discriminatory treatment by the Euro-American oil companies in the 1940s through the 1960s, but the vast majority of Arab migrants were Muslims, as well. Given the Islamic notion of belonging (*intīma'*), described in Chapter 2, in which one's religious affiliation as a Muslim grants one full membership in the *umma*, it would not be unreasonable to assume that Arab migrants were entitled to greater rights and a larger "share of the pie." In fact, so destabilizing was their presence felt to be in Gulf monarchies that when the Lebanese *'ālim*, Sheikh 'Abd-allah al-'Alayli, published a study (1978) in which he argued that oil wealth belonged to all Muslims and not just to those in whose territory it was found, that book quickly became unavailable in Saudi Arabia. It eventually disappeared from the Gulf altogether until a second edition was published in 1992 (AbuKhalil 1992, 33).

It is often noted that Arab migrants were conduits for progressive ideologies sweeping the region from the 1950s through the1970s, and this was deeply threatening to conservative monarchies (al-Naqeeb 1990, 100–2; Kapiszewski 2006; Bsheer 2018). What may also have troubled Gulf elites was the possibility that given their shared ethnicity, language and in most cases, religion – principal markers of identity – Arabs would claim access to greater rights and resources.[14] In other words, cultural similarity, which initially worked in favor of Arab migrants, eventually became a liability as Gulf monarchies became increasingly wealthy, acquisitive and exclusionary, and fellow Arabs could not be denied as easily and to the same extent as others. To be sure, spreading entitlements beyond the narrow confines of Gulf citizens would threaten the community of privilege. Furthermore, Asians were unlikely to have as high expectations as Arabs, and Asian labor was considerably cheaper (Khalaf and Alkobaisi 1999, 296). Hence, since 1973/74, GCC states have undergone a move away from importing Arab labor (Roper 2014,

---

[14] For a different but related interpretation of the threat they represented, see Chalcraft (2010). For a rich treatment of the emergence and evolution of Arab nationalism in Kuwait and the broader Gulf region through a focus on the thought and practice of one of its leaders, see Takriti (2018).

Table 5.3 *Non-GCC Arabs as proportion of foreign population, select GCC states, select years*

	1975	1985	1995	2004	2020
KSA	91%	79%	30%	33%	N/A
Kuwait	80	69	33	30	27
Oman[1]	16	16	11	6	2
Qatar	33	33	21	19	13

[1] Owing to Oman's historical ties to the Indian subcontinent, Asians have comprised the bulk of the foreign labor population from the outset. And in 2017, according to one source, as much as 90 percent of Oman's foreign resident population were Asian and less than 5 percent, Arab.
Source: Kapiszewski 2006, 9; ILO database

40; Shah 2013, 44–6; Alzahrani 2014, 380–81) (Table 5.3). This new direction can be understood as part of the broader effort at distancing and dissociating particular populations for the sake of preserving the community as a geopolitically delimited and strictly "national" entity, asserting its (oil-driven) privilege and re-shaping its identity. Needless to say, the Islamic notion of belonging (*intīma'*), indeed, the very idea of the *umma*, is absent.

As foreigners came to be perceived increasingly as threats to Gulf wealth, restrictions of various sorts were imposed to keep them separate and distinct from citizens, first *de facto* and eventually, *de jure*, as well (Longva 2005, 122–24; Fargues 2011, 278; Mednicoff 2011, 151–53). Hierarchy, that ubiquitous feature of the national community, was extended and a bifurcated society alongside a segmented labor market was created. In the most basic sense, bifurcation is conveyed through physical separation. In terms of residence and lodging, for example, specific parts of town and/or types of accommodation may be reserved for non-nationals (Dresch 2006, 209–10; Nagy 2006, 122–26; Gardner 2010a, 55). Thus, urban space functions as "a mechanism of division and differentiation" (Boodrookas and Keshavarzian 2019, 20).[15] Other forms of segregation, if not exclusion, were gradually put into place. Apart from the introduction of more stringent naturalization requirements, mentioned in Chapter 3, some government-subsidized public services, including health care and education, were discontinued for foreign workers and their families from roughly the mid-1980s

[15] See fn. 17.

Table 5.4 *Labor force by nationality and employment sector, select GCC states, 2022*

Countries	Nationality	Public Sector	Private Sector	Domestic Sector	Total
Kuwait (2022)	National	366,238 (80.11%)	72,321 (4.96%)	0	438,559 (17.06%)
	Non-national	90,911 (19.89%)	1,386,395 (95.04%)	654,764 (100%)	2,132,070 (82.94%)
	Total	457,149	1,458,716	654,764	2,570,629
Oman (2017)	National	195,680 (84.3%)	238,688 (13.7%)	0	434,368 (19.17%)
	Non-national	36,383 (15.67%)	1,502,808 (86.3%)	292,881 (100%)	1,832,072 (80.83%)
	Total	232,063	1,741,496	292,881	2,266,440
Qatar (2022)	National	82,135 (52.03%)	9,555 (0.6%)	0	115,505 (5.71%)
	Non-national	76,734 (48.61%)	1,584,118 (99.4%)	160,786 (100%)	1,906,079 (94.29%
	Total	158,869	1,593,673	160,786	2,021,584
Saudi Arabia (2022)	National	1,544,301 (90.67%)	2,093,843 (23.06%)	0	3,638,144 (25.68%)
	Non-national	159,483 (9.36%)	6,985,067 (76.94%)	3,387,069 (100%)	10,531,619 (74.32%)
	Total	1,703,784	9,078,910	3,387,069	14,169,763

Sources: Gulf Research Center (GRC), Gulf Labor Markets, Migration, and Population programme (GLMM), database 2022; GLMM, Demographic and Economic Module 2019

(Winckler 2013, 461).[16] And with rare exceptions, foreigners, typically, could no longer own property or access certain jobs. A dual labor environment was fashioned such that the public sector, with its various perks, has remained the secure domain of Gulf nationals, while foreigners mostly populate the private sector and are subjected to a distinct labor regime (Baldwin-Edwards 2011,14–17) (Table 5.4).

Foreign labor is itself vertically differentiated in terms of not only occupation (and therefore, class) but also race and ethnicity. In this hierarchy, whites of European descent are at the very top, followed by

---

[16] However, it has not been uncommon for the employer to provide some health insurance for their foreign worker.

Arabs; Africans and most Asians, apart from the "talented" ones, are at the bottom. How, though, has this labor regime come about? And how does it impact identity construction and the consolidation of community in Gulf states, in keeping with regime priorities?

Hierarchy of this sort can be explained in multiple ways. First, it is a logical extension of the dual labor environment, as described. Second, it is a loose replication of what the "colonial masters" imposed in the 1940s, with the arrival of American oil company officials to Saudi Arabia's eastern shores. As Vitalis (2006) elucidates, racist laws that separated blacks from whites, then popular in the American South, were transplanted to the Arabian Peninsula. From the outset, Arabs were segregated from Euro-Americans and subjected to inferior conditions. A labor hierarchy, fashioned according to race and class, was put in place such that Euro-Americans (and a few Saudi elites) were privileged at the expense of poor Saudis, *bedu* and (other) migrants. Arguably, that system, of social management and social control elaborated to protect privilege, has been adapted throughout the region, with Gulf nationals followed by "Europeans" at the top, and – not Arabs, but – Africans and most Asians at the very bottom (Naithani 2010, 99–100).[17] Somewhat exceptional are middle-class Asians who, by virtue of their expertise, are treated like "brown Europeans." Third, as Gulf petro-monarchies with their vast wealth and lucrative foreign investments have become increasingly integrated into global capitalism, since the 1990s especially, the pool from which they draw labor is essentially the globe. Not surprisingly, therefore, as Dresch (2006, 208) notes, the labor regime reproduces the current hierarchy of economic and social relations on a global scale.

Incorporating Foreign Labor: Methods and Purposes

The bifurcation and hierarchization of society are central to the structuring of the national community and shaping its identity as a community of (relative) privilege, and to the broader ruling strategy of social management and social control. The same is true with the employment of foreign labor and the peculiarities of the incorporation of each category of foreigner. In fact, we can distinguish three overlapping features of the

---

[17] Building upon Vitalis (2006), Boodrookas and Keshavarzian (2019, 19) refer to oil company towns as segregated environments that "blended imperial strategies of governing through difference and corporate techniques of dividing workers, and reflected a strict racial and economic hierarchy." They added that urban environments in Gulf states today reflect practices followed in the company towns of yore.

system that incorporates foreign labor. They are: first, a racially and ethnically stratified structure of access to goods and services, akin to what Vitalis (2006) describes at the ARAMCO camp in Saudi Arabia from the 1940s and what Lori (2012), in her study of migrants in the UAE, refers to as a "hierarchy of labor value." This hierarchy, in which "Europeans" enjoy the highest rank, (most) Asians and Africans occupy the lowest rank and non-GCC Arabs are somewhere in between, gets expressed and reinforced through policies and practices. Its purpose is to set boundaries: to establish relative proximity to, but also difference and dissociation from the citizen, and in that way to insure the latter's status and privilege vis-à-vis the foreigner. Thus, fixing hierarchy contributes to the ruling elite's aim to appease the citizen relative to the state's overwhelming power and secure their loyalty.

The second feature includes the various constraints on the foreigner's personal autonomy and mobility – such things as having to relinquish their passport to their employer or secure permission to change jobs or leave the country, being denied legal appeal in the case of dismissal from their job or even, for some, denied entry into malls on Fridays (Bruslé 2012, 7). By imposing such constraints, the foreigner's vulnerability, their (insecure) status relative to the citizen as well as to other categories of foreigners, is underscored. Thus, the foreigner is deterred from making claims for access to rights or resources.

The third, and most discussed feature is the distinct labor regime, referred to, somewhat ironically, as *kafāla*, a term used in Islamic jurisprudence to describe a type of legal contract of an economic nature whereby a person acts as the guarantor for the person or property of another. In the Gulf monarchies, *kafāla* is a triangulated arrangement among the state, the citizen and the foreigner; it governs the employment of foreigners and does so via social management.[18] The purpose of the arrangement, whereby the foreigner is attached to and dependent upon a citizen or national entity that acts as their sponsor (*kafīl*) and usually, employer as well, is to both administer social control and protect privilege while building the country.[19] To that end, *kafāla* performs three key functions. First, it provides the frame for the implementation of the two features just noted: the racially and ethnically stratified structure of access to goods and services, and the array of constraints imposed on

---

[18] For descriptions see, *inter alia*, Longva (1999); Gardner (2010a); Ahmed (2010); Babar (2014).
[19] Khalaf (2014, 48) refers to *kafāla* and related migration management policies as mechanisms that enable rulers to both "shape their societies at the micro level, and to control the activities of all inhabitants within their territories – whether citizens, bidoons, or foreign migrants."

the foreigner. Second, it assists in fulfilling the ruler's objective to appease the citizen-subject, and it does so by contributing to their relative enrichment and empowerment. Not only can the citizen accrue vast sums via sponsorship-related practices,[20] but also they become an "agent of the state" in that the arrangement implicates them – as sponsor, employer and enforcer – between the ruler/government and the foreigner (Gardner 2010a; Shah and Fargues 2011, 268; Lori 2012, 12; Hanieh 2020, 117). In the case of business elites and royals engaged in private sector activity, their enrichment on the backs of foreign labor is especially noteworthy for they are the major employers. Third, *kafāla* creates dependencies, incentives and high stakes for all parties such that they are locked into an arrangement in which everyone is invested.

Kafāla includes a hierarchical incentivizing structure made up of a pre-eminent authority, the rentier state/patrimonial ruler, and dispersed, multiple enforcers who happen to be citizens. Each citizen-sponsor-enforcer becomes a kind of patrimonial authority vis-à-vis their client(s), the foreigner. They dispense favors in the form of a visa and a job; in turn, they both demand obedience and profit from the foreigner, from their labor and inferior status. To be sure, they benefit in multiple ways from the authority and privilege they derive through the foreigner.[21] With regard to semi-skilled and unskilled labor especially, it is typical for the citizen-sponsor-enforcer to introduce a slightly advantaged foreigner between themselves and their workers to act as their overseer "on the ground"; in other words, the functional authority and manager vis-à-vis the latter. In this way, with some supervising others, foreign workers are fractionalized at their workplace and thus neutralized, while the citizen-sponsor-enforcer is assured that the work gets done without them having to mingle and get directly involved (Vora 2011, 307). Accordingly, everyone has an important stake in the system and maintaining it. Relations of domination, control and dependence proliferate, the rentier-client arrangement is replicated at multiple levels of society, authority and privilege are protected and regime goals are advanced.

In addition to being an instrument of social management, *kafāla* is a core nation-building tool. By institutionalizing the protection of privilege

---

[20] For details, see, *inter alia*, Dito (2014); Hertog (2010b); Jureidini (2014); Khalaf (2014).
[21] For Dresch (2006, 202), citizens are "rentiers" insofar as they make a profit by "drawing surplus from the foreign presence" who do the work in their place. Alzahrani (2014, 383) adds that, like the ruler, the citizen-*kafīl* is, for all intents and purposes, accountable to no one. There is virtually no oversight of the latter's behavior toward their foreign employees. As Hanieh (2020, 117) explains, since the state has "subcontract(ed) power over migrant labor," citizens have become "intrinsic to the containment and disciplining of labor."

of Gulf nationals via their control and the marginalization of foreigners, it is a means not only to placate citizens relative to the overwhelming power of the state, but also to encourage recognition of their shared, albeit unequal interests vis-à-vis the foreigner. Thus, it strengthens the connection between the state and the private sector elites, the biggest employers. Indeed, both ruling elites and citizens mediate between labor and production, at minimal cost to themselves in terms of capital and effort, and maximum benefits, not least among them that they alone enjoy what is produced. Thus, *kafāla* fosters social cohesion around the issue of employment of foreign labor and the attitude toward the foreigner, *tout court*.[22] Furthermore, *kafāla* contributes to identity-construction. It does so by substantiating the bifurcated society – hence, the citizen's privileged status – and by reinforcing relative proximity between the citizen and the different categories of foreigner.

Before elucidating in the following section how the "European," the non-GCC Arab and the unskilled Asian and African figure in the shaping of national identity in Gulf monarchies, I first examine a few particularly illuminating features of the set of arrangements that, for decades, has incorporated foreign labor. It is worth noting, though, that in recent years, some of the associated practices have been modified or eliminated in response to mounting international scrutiny and condemnation. Indeed, Qatar and its labor practices were much in the spotlight in advance of its hosting the FIFA World Cup games in 2022; the emirate was especially engaged in initiating reforms from roughly 2018.[23] Until then, there was, in fact, little variation among the Gulf monarchies in regard to the organization and management of foreign labor.

Labor Recruitment Practices

In the Gulf monarchies, the typical pattern of recruitment has been some variation of the following: local businesses, including public or private sector entities of varying size, wishing to hire expatriate labor apply for one or more permits through their Ministry of Labor (Willoughby 2006, 233–35; Gardner 2012, 50–6). The employer-sponsor then approaches a recruiter, a private licensed or unlicensed agency, sub-agent or individual broker, at home or abroad, whom they pay to find appropriate individuals and assist with their transfer. In the case of unskilled and semi-skilled labor,

---

[22] As Fuccaro (2008, 3–4) states: "The political, economic, and social segregation experienced by the 'guest' workers in contemporary Gulf cities forms one of the core tenets underpinning national consensus."

[23] For details, see International Labour Organization (ILO) 2020 and 2023.

the recruiter, in turn, "sells" the associated visa to aspiring migrants and may tack on additional fees to cover the physical transfer of the individual to their employer-sponsor. Thus, while in principle, the work visa and residence permit are provided by and through the employer-sponsor, in practice, the poorer strata of imported labor usually end up having to purchase them. As if to insist upon their inferior status, they must pay for the right to work for a Gulf citizen or entity – a practice that Andrew Gardner (2014, 6) refers to as the "commodification of the right to work."

The employer-sponsor may request more visas than they actually need and then sell the extras to recruiters. Alternatively, they can acquire visas from the government and sponsor migrants without intending to hire them; instead, they sell them what is known as a "free visa," and the migrants are left to find work (and lodging) on their own (Baldwin-Edwards 2011, 41). Thus, recruitment can be a lucrative business: For multiple parties in the importation of unskilled, predominantly Asian and African labor, there are profits to be made each step of the way (Bruslé 2012, 11; Gardner 2010b, 219; Jureidini 2014, 49). With the importation of skilled labor, recruiters are involved in the process, as well, but being relatively privileged, the skilled foreigner is not expected to pay for their visa, residence permit or related fees; these costs are borne by the employer-sponsor (Jureidini 2014, xii).

Although collecting fees for recruitment is illegal (Jureidini 2014, 35), there has been virtually no oversight and regulation of the process by government authorities. While some analysts have suggested that the state does not have the capacity to do otherwise (Crystal 2005, 168), it is certainly the case that the recruitment process is yet another way in which wealth gets distributed among citizens whose consumption, enrichment and relative power are thereby enhanced while foreigners vie for a better living, with some constrained in the host country more than others. Thus, citizens are not only conjoined and appeased, but vis-à-vis foreign labor and its various tiers, relative difference and distance (or the perceptions and aspirations thereof) – building blocks of identity-construction – are reinforced.

Contracts

As Longva (1999) and Lori (2012) point out, imported labor are always "temporary contract workers": They are expected to remain in the host country for the duration of their contract and required to leave upon its termination. Contracts are typically of limited duration: 2–3 years, renewable. As underscored by rigid citizenship laws, mentioned in Chapter 3, opportunities for permanent status are exceedingly rare. No doubt, permanence, in low-population states especially, could have a crowding-out effect; and it would allow for claim-making that, in turn, would threaten citizens' entitlements. This eventuality may seem especially foreboding for Qatar, in which a mere 12 percent of the total population of about 2.5 million in 2017 were citizens.

Nonetheless, many foreigners in these petro-monarchies have become "permanently temporary" (Fargues 2011, 280). Among the skilled and semi-skilled, few "Europeans," many Arabs as well as South Asians have lived in these countries for decades.[24] While their status allows them to be permanently temporary, as opposed to simply "temporary," as are the vast numbers of unskilled workers, the threat of deportation remains.[25] For example, in summer/fall 1990, some 800,000 Yemenis were deported by Saudi Arabia when their government, that had denounced Iraq's invasion of Kuwait, rejected the US-led military operation to "liberate" Kuwait. Not only were these Yemenis legal residents of the kingdom, but many had lived there for more than thirty years (Al-Saqqaf 1992). Then in March 1991, following the routing of the Iraqi occupation forces, the Kuwaiti government expelled the Palestinian population, then numbering about 200,000, since Yasser Arafat and the Palestine Liberation Organization had rejected the international military response to Iraq's invasion. And in March 2015, seventy Lebanese who had lived and worked in the UAE for decades were deported. Since the majority of those expelled were Shi'a, they may have been suspected of harboring sympathies for Hezbollah (hence, for Iran).[26] As for unskilled contract workers, they remain among the most vulnerable. In Saudi Arabia, for example, 1.2 million workers were forced out of their jobs and expelled from the country in the eighteen months following the beginning of the fall in oil prices in summer 2014 (Hanieh 2020, 119). Relative impermanence, corresponding to the "hierarchy of labor value," marks not only difference and distance, but also dispensability.

Lodging:

To reinforce difference and protect privilege, foreigners may be kept more-or-less physically separate from the national community.

---

[24] Citing a study conducted in Kuwait in 2013, Ulrichsen (2016) notes that "no fewer than 18 per cent of all non-nationals had been born in the country and lived in Kuwait for at least half their life" (183).
[25] For a fascinating study of the transformation of temporary residency in the UAE into permanent legal status through multiple ways – some more peculiar than others – see Lori (2019).
[26] www.dailymail.co.uk/wires/afp/article-2993016/Beirut-says-UAE-expel-70-Shiite-Lebanese.html.

104   Imported Labor: Building/Appeasing the Nation

As noted, lodging is one obvious means to apply separation. Depending on their status, that is, race/ethnicity and class, foreigners may live in particular parts of town. More often than not, upper- and middle-tier foreigners live in housing compounds akin to gated communities, or apartment blocs reserved for non-nationals who, unlike most citizens, rent their accommodations.[27] However, in Oman, the upper tier, and within it the European "expat" especially, but also the non-GCC Arab, enjoys somewhat greater residential integration with citizens.[28] As for semi-skilled and unskilled workers, they are lodged by their employer-sponsor either in company housing, as in an apartment building or a dormitory, or, for the poorest among them, in a "labor camp" on the periphery of the city and in squalid conditions. No doubt, such living arrangements limit the possibility of mingling with the citizen. Furthermore, by imposing what Gardner (2014b) has labeled an "enclave character" to the foreign presence, lodging practices not only regulate foreigners' infiltration of the national community but also facilitate surveillance, even of the "elite" among them (361–62). Still, the most vulnerable of foreigners are those who are truly invisible: domestic workers live in the homes and at the mercy of their employers, out of sight of any possible scrutiny, while "illegals" and those holding "free visas" must find ways to fend for themselves and elude arrest (Amnesty International 2014; Bajracharya 2012; Human Rights Watch 2010).

Although the right to own property was denied to foreigners beginning in the "oil bonanza" decade (1974–84), it has since been restored somewhat and to varying degrees (Ulrichsen 2016, 181–82). Essentially forbidden in Kuwait and Saudi Arabia until very recently, it is permitted in the UAE and in designated zones in Bahrain, Qatar and Oman. So stringent are property ownership regulations in Kuwait that since fall 2015, only Arab expatriates who are permanent residents could own a single property of a modest size in a residential area.[29] In Qatar until 2018 and in Oman until 2020, foreigners could own homes in a single, distinct location: "The Pearl" in Doha and "The Wave" in Muscat. In these fairly exclusive complexes, which combine lodging with commercial establishments, wealthy expats live side by side, sharing intimate space with citizens. Be that as it may, this kind of restriction on foreigners' property holding had several purposes: It prevented a possible

---

[27] Recall, however, the anomalous situation of home ownership in Saudi Arabia, referred to in Chapter 3.
[28] Interview with Omani journalist, Doha, 26 April 2015.
[29] "6 Expats Can Own Property," *Arab Times*, 19 Oct. 2015. www.arabtimesonline.com/news/6-expats-can-own-property.

"crowding out" effect by securing an almost complete monopoly over property ownership by local citizens, and it allowed citizens, the original owners of those properties, to make money off the foreigner. In short, such property ownership arrangements are about social control for the sake of protecting but also enriching the community of privilege while allowing a degree of scripted, "trans-national intimacy" between the citizen and the elite – predominantly "European" but also, select Arab – foreigner.

However, after several years of low oil prices (2014–21) and with the economic fallout from the coronavirus pandemic (2020–23), Gulf monarchies have been scrambling to attract investment at home. As part of this effort, they have relaxed property ownership laws somewhat. The Qatari government has increased the number of approved locations for foreign ownership to nine, while in Oman, foreigners can now own property throughout the Sultanate except in specified areas. In both countries, residency rights are extended to owners of higher-valued property.[30] As for Saudi Arabia and Kuwait, the former issued a directive in 2021 allowing non-Saudis who were legal residents to purchase a single property with restrictions. The latter proposed a similar reform in spring 2023 for non-Kuwaiti permanent residents.[31]

Financial Facilities

Foreigners employed in these Gulf states receive tax-free salaries. Moreover, until 2015 and the implementation of reforms in response to falling oil prices, described in Chapter 3, they enjoyed subsidized utilities in their lodgings, and most of the (officially) working foreigners had some health care provided by their employers. The highly skilled have benefited from other financial perks: Some, most notably the "European, " receive a premium, a so-called hardship allowance for the sacrifice they make working far from home in a supposedly less

---

[30] "Expats Can Now Own Properties Outside of ITCs," *Times of Oman*, 9 March 2022. https://timesofoman.com/article/114152-expats-can-now-own-properties-outside-itcs. "Qatar Allows Foreigners to Own Properties in More Areas," *Reuters*, 6 Oct. 2020. www.reuters.com/article/qatar-economy-property-int-idUSKBN26R1EB; Hazar Kilani, "Here's a List of Areas Where You Can Own Real Estate as a Foreigner," *Doha News*, 17 Jan. 2023. https://dohanews.co/heres-a-list-of-areas-in-qatar-where-you-can-own-real-estate-as-a-foreigner.

[31] "Saudi Arabia to Allow Foreigners to Purchase Property," *The Siasat Daily*, 30 March 2023. www.siasat.com/saudi-arabia-to-allow-foreigners-to-purchase-property-2557825; "Kuwait Announces Plan to Allow Expat Real Estate Investment: Report," *Arabian Business*, 16 May 2023. www.arabianbusiness.com/industries/real-estate/kuwait-announces-plan-to-allow-expat-real-estate-investment-report.

hospitable environment, while others, upon leaving their jobs, may receive a severance bonus.[32]

Especially illuminating is the matter of financial assistance to poor migrants. While Gulf Arabs are reputed to be generous philanthropists, as we will see in Chapter 6, foreign laborers have typically been unable to access assistance through ordinary channels. In Saudi Arabia in 2012, for example, I was told that the principal charities do not give to foreign workers except via *ifṭār* tables during Ramadan. They explained that workers' *kafīl* (sponsor), as well as their embassies, were supposed to take care of them.[33] Two prominent charities in Oman, one state-affiliated and the other private, as well as a foundation in Kuwait associated with a political-ideological movement, reported to me that they were not inclined to give, or at least not openly, precisely because the need was so great.[34] In other words, charitable organizations acknowledge the poverty of laborers in their countries, but many, if not most choose to turn the other cheek.[35] And while small, private initiatives to assist the poorest workers do exist, they are few.[36]

No doubt, imported labor should not be in need of charity in the host country; at a minimum, they should be paid a living wage. After all, in the mid-2010s, three of the six oil-rich monarchies were among the top ten countries, and a fourth was among the top twenty in the world in terms of per capita income. In 2017, for example, Qatar was ranked first, UAE seventh, Kuwait eighth and Saudi Arabia seventeenth.[37] Why, though, do Gulf Arabs tend not to give to migrant workers at home? While I address this more fully in Chapter 6, a possible explanation relates to the (circumscribed) notion of community. Indigent foreigners are not considered to be part of a community that matters: one to whom the host feels connected or for whom they feel some obligation, and this despite the host's acute dependence on their labor. Furthermore, the mass of restrictions imposed on the poor and unskilled, predominantly Asian and

---

[32] One of my interlocutors in Qatar, a Mashreqi Arab, told me that when he resigned from the company where he had worked for several years to take a different job, he received a bonus equivalent to about three-quarters of what his annually salary had been.
[33] Interview with spokesperson for Al-Wafā', a Saudi philanthropic society for women, Riyadh, 10 April 2012.
[34] Interviews: Muscat, 29 Oct. 2013; Kuwait City, 14 May 2012.
[35] In Qatar, however, one of the larger charities, Sheikh Eid bin Mohamad Al-Thani Foundation, has a program that targets the foreign worker specifically. See Chapter 6, pp. 131–32.
[36] See Chapter 6, fn. 63.
[37] Bahrain was ranked twenty-third and Oman twenty-ninth. It is also worth noting that in 2015, when the per capita income of Qatar (including both citizens and non-citizens) was equivalent to US$130,000, the lowest paid construction workers were earning about $160 per month (less than $2,000 per annum).

increasingly African laborers, are meant to underscore their absolute marginality and unambiguous difference *for the sake of the citizen.* Rendered invisible,[38] they cannot make claims on the "community of privilege" and take from what the ruler dispenses to his subjects.

In short, all foreigners brought to Gulf states to work are denied, in multiple ways and to varying degrees corresponding to their status (class) and origins (race and ethnicity), the possibility of making claims on, sharing space with, and even for some, being acknowledged by the national community. Relative difference and distance are thereby confirmed. As for the citizen-subject, who may in fact represent the real threat to the overwhelming power of the autocratic state, they are placated via their enrichment and the authority they enjoy in relation to the foreigner. Thus, the state secures their loyalty, while the collective identity of citizens as a community of privilege is reinforced.

Fashioning the Nation, Consolidating the State

Through the foreigner, through policies and practices effected to confront the presence of vast numbers of foreigners on whom the Gulf monarchies are dependent, citizens come together as a national community, and they do so, to varying degrees, despite inequalities among them. From stringent naturalization laws to the insistence on a bifurcated society and a distinct regime for the organization and management of imported labor, the purpose is to exclude the foreigner from access to resources while maintaining them as a resource from which the state and citizens profit. In this way, as John Chalcraft (2010, 23) has written, "rulers kept the population of patronage claimants low, increasing per capita the amount of patronage to be dispensed, and thus enhancing its political impact." The interests of rule are protected and the citizen, as dependent subject and recipient of patronage, is conciliated relative to the ruling elite's monopoly over power and wealth. Furthermore, not only can citizens identify themselves as constituting the community of privilege, but also their sense of belonging in the contemporary period is to a singularly "modern," national community that both enjoys special prerogatives and has found ways to gainfully manage its dependence on "others."

---

[38] "Behind the dust all you can see/is their broken souls and the shine/of new cars mirrored in their eyes. They are not as human as we are./They are nothing/but workers. We don't want/them in our malls, we choose/not to see them, to forget them./This army that builds our country/Remains invisible beneath the burning sun." (from the poem, "The Invisible Army" by Qatari writer, Maryam al-Subaiey, in Lodge et al. (2012, 171–72)).

How, though, do the different categories of foreigner – the whites of European descent, the non-GCC Arabs, the Asians and Africans – impact national identity in distinct ways? At the outset, recall that the varying degrees of deprivation imposed on the foreigner, depending on their status (class) and (racial/ethnic) origins, reflect the relative power in the international system of the particular category to which they belong. Hence, by adjusting the extent of exclusion on this basis, Gulf society reveals its perception, or aspiration, of the difference, distance and dissociation between itself and the European, the non-GCC Arab, the poor Asian and African.

To elaborate a more nuanced response to the question just posed, I return to the Islamic normative tradition and the notion of belonging (*intīma*) discussed in Chapter 2, and reference *musta'amin*: a non-Muslim present in Islamic civilization and acknowledged in Islamic jurisprudence (*fiqh*) as enjoying rights when in *dar al-Islam*, where Muslims live and rule. The beneficiary of *'amān*, a contract of security and safe conduct, the *musta'amin* who travels to *dar al-Islam* with the intention to stay for a short period, and usually for the purpose of engaging in economic activity, is both subject to Muslim rule and has the right to protection while there, for the duration of their stay (*Al-Mawsū'a al-Fiqhīa* 1997, 168–79; Hallaq 2009, 332–33).

Although no longer a legal category, the term *musta'amin* continues to have some resonance for it harks back to a historical period, an earlier moral order to which Muslims today claim to be connected. In fact, in spring 2003, Saudi authorities invoked this population of yore at a critical juncture. In response to an Al-Qaeda attack on a foreigners' housing compound in Riyadh where Europeans and Americans were living, the government publicly denounced the attack for "the victims were *musta'amān*."[39] But, when South Asian laborers died on construction sites in Doha, as was reported on several occasions in the years leading up to the 2022 World Cup Games,[40] did Qatari authorities remark that this was unacceptable for the victims were *musta'amān*? They did not. Recognition and the rhetoric of protection and inclusivity exist for one category of foreigner but not all categories. As such, they convey the GCC Arab's (imagined) proximity and (coveted) connection to the white European with their power, wealth and authority.

---

[39] Reported to me by a Saudi scholar, Doha, 16 March 2015. Note that Mednicoff (2011, 148–50) considers the appropriateness of the analogy between *musta'amān* and foreign labor in Gulf monarchies today.

[40] See, *inter alia*, Gibson and Pattisson (2014).

In fall 2003, a second foreigners' compound in Saudi Arabia, this time housing Arab and Asian workers, came under Al-Qaeda attack. Needless to say, the Arab residents, or at least the vast majority of them and many of the Asians, could not have been referred to as *musta'amān* for they were Muslims. Nonetheless, this variant may actually help us better understand how the non-GCC Arab complicates the matter of community and identity in Gulf petro-monarchies. For if the Islamic notion of belonging (*intīma'*), in which membership in the *umma* derives either from religious affiliation as a Muslim or from the special status extended to non-Muslims (that is, *dhimmī* and *musta'amān*), prevailed, the Muslim Arab migrant worker would enjoy all the rights and privileges of the Gulf Arab; there would be no difference between them.[41] Furthermore, recall that in the 1940s and 1950s, as Munif (1984) and Vitalis (2006) describe so compellingly, Arab workers from the Arabian Peninsula and beyond struggled together, resisting discriminatory treatment by the "European" and insisting on their rights. And in the 1950s through the 1970s, Arabs from within and beyond the Gulf engaged with each other and with Arab nationalism and other progressive ideologies of the time. It may be that this shared cultural baggage and historical experience have something to do with why, since the surge in oil-driven wealth, the non-GCC Arab has been considered a security threat. By virtue of who they are – the less affluent but arguably equally deserving (Arab-Muslim) cousin – their presence threatens the security of Gulf wealth and privilege. It is, indeed, a complicated relationship. The non-GCC Arab is denied at times so as to ward off the Gulf Arab's sense of (familial) obligation. They are relatively privileged at other times when, as with naturalization laws and the preference for Arab ethnicity, their "sameness" contributes to the safety and comfort of uniformity and the veneer of authenticity that Gulf elites so desperately seek.

What about the European, with their presumed authority and expertise, and the poor Asian and African with supposedly little apart from their labor power? Indeed, they are polar opposites in terms of their relative power and as a result, in the Gulf Arab's regard for them and the intimacy they seek with them. The European, who occupies the highest rung of the foreign labor hierarchy, experiences gentle marginalization; the poor Asian and African, whose difference is unequivocal even if they are Muslim, are shunned. How, though, do they intersect in identity-construction and the definition of community? As a preliminary answer,

---

[41] In principle, the same should be true for Muslim Asians. However, as with the Rohingya refugees discussed in Chapter 3, in the contemporary context, race and class trump religion.

I propose that the Gulf Arab's ambiguous relationship to the European – wanting what they have and anxious for their recognition – is soothed somewhat through the Asian and African. By underscoring hierarchy and privilege, the exclusion of the poor Asian and the poor African serves as an antidote to the uncomfortable ambiguity of being, in Homi Bhabha's (1984, 126) words, "almost the same, but not quite" vis-à-vis the European. In effect, by adopting the European organization of labor and re-ordering roles, the Gulf Arab has become "master."

Conclusion

The importation and organization of foreign labor in Gulf monarchies is a constitutive feature of the ruling project of community, nation and state. Through this practice, oil and gas revenues and returns on investments are mobilized and Islamic norms are manipulated to stimulate accumulation, appease particular social categories, enforce submission, encourage social cohesion and build the nation. Thus, ruling elites are assisted in their goal to maintain and secure their monopolization of power, wealth and authority.

The marginalization and differential incorporation of foreign labor function as means of social management and social control for the sake of protecting (relative) privilege. Indeed, the enrichment and empowerment of the citizen relative to the foreigner are nurtured. However, as with access to government distributions, some citizens benefit from this particular institutionalized practice more than others. Nonetheless, maintaining the citizen's relative entitlement is an implicit regime goal for it is a means to placate the citizen vis-à-vis the overwhelming power of the state and its ruling elites. As such, it secures their submission to, if not support for the state.

The importation and differential incorporation of foreigners contribute, as well, to consolidating the national community and constructing its identity. However, important tensions are revealed in the shaping of the boundaries of community and specifically, through exclusions. Despite the fact that these regimes broadcast their commitment to the faith and cite the *Shari'a* as a principal, if not the source of legislation, it is the case that not all Muslims are viewed as meriting inclusion, or even empathy. Wealthy, non-GCC Arab Muslims may be privileged in regard to naturalization and property ownership in Gulf monarchies, but that, along with the relatively gentle constraints on their autonomy and mobility, may be the extent of their prerogatives. Furthermore, in large numbers, non-GCC Arabs are considered a threat and this despite sharing both ethnicity and in most cases, religious affiliation with their

Conclusion

hosts. Other skilled and semi-skilled Muslims who have lived and worked in these countries for decades, such as tens of thousands of South Asians, tend to be denied these same privileges, among others. As for blue-collar foreigners, it matters little whether they are Muslims or not: poor Pakistanis and Bangladeshis are not unlike poor Nepalis and Filipinos in their denial of access to resources and protections. Within global capitalism's "hierarchy of labor value," poor Asians and sub-Saharan Africans occupy the lowest rung.[42] And it is this hierarchy, ultimately defined by race and class, that determines the extent of inclusion/incorporation.

Somewhat paradoxically, those who are excluded in fact contribute to defining the community of privilege, the nation. Exclusion is not only the other face of privilege, but when applied selectively, the exclusion of some may appease others and bring them together. At the same time, marginalization and differential incorporation assist in shaping the identity of the citizen in relation to both their entitlements and the different strata of the "expatriate" population.

Finally, the incorporation of foreign labor in Gulf monarchies reveals a reliance on the Islamic normative tradition and specifically, the notions of community and belonging, rather as an artefact or legacy, something to showcase and manipulate when it is expedient to do so. Both notions have been reconfigured to advance the agenda of dynastic autocracies and bolster their power, wealth and integration in global capitalism. I develop this latter idea more fully in the next chapters, which treat institutionalized practices – specifically, charitable giving and Islamic banking and finance – that are explicitly sanctioned by the faith and embody Islamic norms.

---

[42] For an important study of African labor migration to GCC states, see Atong et al. 2018. Included in the study are migrants from the states of North Africa, which include Arab populations. Note that by far, the largest numbers of African migrants to the Gulf are from Egypt and secondarily, from Sudan. Studies of sub-Saharan African migration to the Gulf are rare.

6 Charity as Politics "Writ Small"

Introduction

Another institutionalized practice, charitable giving in the petro-monarchies of the Gulf offers a window into the practice of politics and state–society relations. As these are Muslim societies, people are expected to share their wealth and give charity (zakat and *ṣadaqa*) regularly, to show their devotion to God by attending to the community's welfare and assisting those in need. Thus, examining this practice can illustrate how even secular objectives such as gaining recognition, building community and improving social welfare are advanced. It can also elucidate ways in which Islam is invoked and religious edicts are revised to facilitate meeting such objectives.

Gulf monarchies' giving is said to be substantial, although reliable data are lacking.[1] It is noted repeatedly, in fact, that governments do not publish all that they give bilaterally. And until recently, published figures on the size and sources of revenues, the extent of giving and the size and destination of donations by numerous charitable organizations were said to be incomplete, imprecise or unreliable. Insofar as individual giving is concerned, the challenge of conducting surveys effectively results in the absence of hard data.

Charitable giving is extended in a variety of ways and engages ruling families, governmental and non-governmental organizations, and private citizens. Moreover, it is actively promoted by ruling elites, anxious for both the symbolic capital it confers upon them as devotees of the faith and contributions of material support for social welfare from societal

---

[1] However, see Tok et al. (2014, 591) who write the following: "The Kingdom of Saudi Arabia (KSA), Kuwait and the United Arab Emirates (UAE) have been among the most active donors in the world, with official development assistance (ODA) averaging 1.5 percent of their combined gross national income (GNI) during the period 1973–2008, more than twice the United Nations target of 0.7 percent and five times the average of the OECD-DAC." For Qatar, Saudi Arabia and UAE's development assistance in sub-Saharan Africa, see Guijarro (2023).

Introduction

actors. As they encourage charitable giving among their subjects, these regimes at times employ a two-pronged rhetoric that identifies it, first, with Islamic doctrine, and second, with nation-building through social solidarity (*taḍāmun ijtimā'ī*) (LeRenard 2008, 148). Some go further by showcasing their own – that is, the ruler's or key family member's benevolence. For example, in 2013, the Emir of Kuwait made a very public, personal contribution of $300 million to Syrian refugees (Stafford 2017, 15) and in 2017, Saudi Crown Prince Mohamed bin Salman donated SR 23 million (US$6.16 million) from his "personal expense" to assist charity societies in Riyadh.[2] No doubt, that wealth is abundant, the possibilities for broad redistribution and the enhancement of social welfare, through charitable giving and otherwise, are vast. However, that poverty persists suggests that, as with government transfers (discussed in Chapter 3), charitable giving as a poverty alleviation strategy is insufficiently effective and its principal purposes lie elsewhere.

In this chapter I examine how charity is practiced in Kuwait, Qatar, Oman and Saudi Arabia and address the following questions: Who, or rather, what kinds of entities extend(s) charity? How do they give? To whom do they give, or not give? And why do they give as they do?[3] I consider giving both at home and abroad and by different donor types: public figures and private individuals, multinational agencies, governmental and non-governmental organizations – those that are explicitly charities and those that have a charity wing; those that are identity-based and those that have no obvious agenda apart from philanthropy. I highlight several key findings, some of which confirm what is considered to be universal in the world of charity and philanthropy or have been identified elsewhere in the Middle East or by other Gulf scholars.[4] First, benevolence may be motivated not only by charitable feelings or commitment to the faith but also by political ambitions. For most donor types, providing charity, whether at home or abroad, is an important source of political (or social) capital: a means to extend influence, establish networks and gain recognition. In fact, in three of the four countries, among the most prominent charitable foundations are ones created by members of the ruling family or by major political associations or interest groups.[5] Both instrumentalize

---

[2] "Charities Benefit from SR 23m Donated by Crown Prince," *Saudi Gazette*, 10 Aug. 2017. https://saudigazette.com.sa/article/514856.
[3] For an earlier version of this chapter, see Lowi (2019).
[4] See, for example, Atia (2013), Cammett (2014), Isik (2014), Jung and Petersen (2014), as well as Benthall (1999, 2003, 2018), Derbal (2011, 2014, 2022), Le Renard (2008), Petersen (2014).
[5] Given issues of transparency noted in fn.1, it is difficult to know which of the foundations are the best endowed financially and/or the most active in charitable initiatives.

charity and social welfare for political ends: to enhance legitimacy, deepen their penetration of society, shore up political power, gain adherents and advance a particular ideology. Second, when the state intervenes in the domain of charity by, for example, declaring how or to whom entities may (or may not) give, even at times by revising religious edicts, it is transforming charitable giving into a tool for social management and social control. It may aim thereby to appease a particular social category or demarcate the boundaries of community. Third, not unlike international giving that typically prioritizes Arab and Muslim countries and communities, private giving at home appears to favor family, tribe, ethnic and confessional community.[6] With few exceptions, labor migrants, for example, are, as noted in Chapter 5, excluded from access to charity. Hence, an "ethics of care" does not extend seamlessly to those at home who are perceived as distant, socially or otherwise.[7] These findings hint at features of statecraft, as well as the social or political interests of those who give.

I begin with a cursory examination of international giving undertaken by various multinational and governmental entities and explore its purposes, methods and target populations. I then turn to practices of giving at home and abroad by different types of semi- and non-governmental donor organizations in each of the four Gulf states and highlight their distinct features. Following that, I address the matter of access to charity and offer an explanation for the exclusion of certain social categories. Next, I turn to the private citizen. I describe their giving and then outline their views on why Gulf nationals and Gulf institutions extend charity as they do. I conclude by summarizing what my analysis of charitable giving elucidates about politics in Gulf monarchies and specifically, the intertwining and instrumentalization of oil revenues and Islamic doctrine in the ruler's project of community, nation and state.

International Giving: Multinational and Governmental Organizations

From the outset, international giving by Gulf monarchies has been a vehicle for advancing political interests. In the 1960s and early 1970s, several multilateral (aid) agencies were created with the Saudi monarchy

---

[6] Given the paucity of hard data, this finding is largely impressionistic, based exclusively on interviews with private citizens and specifically, on what they shared regarding their own habits and what they surmised about others'.

[7] By no means unique to Gulf states, see in this regard, Sethi 2017. Closer to home, consider the treatment of asylum seekers at the US southern border: for example, Michelle Hackman, "US Seeks Longer Detentions for Migrant Families," *Wall Street Journal*, 21 Aug. 2019. www.wsj.com/articles/trump-administration-unveils-plan-to-hold-migrant-children-in-long-term-detention-with-parents-11566394202.

as their driving force and with a distinctly political agenda: to combat the rising tide of secularism, leftism and republicanism in the Arab world, perceived as deeply threatening to the political authority of conservative royal families.[8] The basic strategy of these organizations was to promote Islamic identity – rather, a particular vision of Islam– and to do so by extending (oil-financed) aid and assistance in various forms, alongside religious instruction to Muslim populations. With Crown Prince and then King Feisal of Saudi Arabia at the helm as prime mover and the kingdom as chief financier, these organizations – among them, the Muslim World League (MWL) (1962), the Organization of the Islamic Conference (OIC) (1969)[9] and the World Assembly of Muslim Youth (WAMY) (1972) – contributed vastly to the spread of religious conservatism in general and Saudi-Wahhabi doctrine in particular, and to bankrolling Saudi influence across the Muslim world.[10] During the "oil bonanza" decade (1974–84), these politico-missionary, let's call them "*da'wist*" organizations, were joined by other religiously tinged entities created with a focus on charity, humanitarian aid or development assistance.

Da'wa, or "Missionary" Work

The Muslim World League (*rābiṭa al-islamiyya al-'ālimiyya*) was the first of those organizations to combine material assistance with indoctrination and political mobilization. Since its inception and with roughly 90 percent of its funding from the Saudi government, it has been funding schools and Islamic cultural centers, building mosques and clinics, distributing religious literature, training Imams and offering scholarships to study at Saudi religious universities.[11] It has also sent missionaries to Africa and elsewhere to spread Wahhabi doctrine, and has supported *salafi* groups in South Asia and beyond (Commins 2009, 152–53, 174–75). Similar in its mission to the MWL, WAMY was also created to combat various forms of secularism and promote Islamic identity by propagating Wahhabi views but with a focus on youth and, according to its secretary-general, through "development activities in the fields of education and institution-building." It builds schools, offers scholarships

---

[8] For Saudi Arabia's domestic response, see Bsheer (2017). For thoughtful treatments of the regional context within which (politico-)missionary entities were created, see Chalcraft (2016, 312–92), Farquhar (2017, 67–85).
[9] In 2011, the OIC's name was changed to Organization of Islamic Cooperation.
[10] For illuminating discussions of the "methods and operations of the transnational Wahhabi *da'wa*," led by Saudi Arabia and sponsored by Qatar and Kuwait, see, among others, Sells (2021, 292–96), Mandaville and Hamid (2018, 9–12).
[11] Interview with secretary-general of MWL, Jeddah, 17 April 2012.

and training courses and organizes summer camps.[12] Since 1988, it has also provided charity in the form of, for example, support for orphans (Bellion-Jourdan 2001, 177; Lacey 2014, 49).

The first of the international Muslim charities, the International Islamic Relief Organization, Saudi Arabia (IIRO or IIROSA) was founded in 1978 with royal approval as the humanitarian arm of the MWL, thereby explicitly integrating political interests, pursued via *da'wa*, with the Qur'anic injunction to be generous and compassionate by providing relief from hardship. It was through IIROSA, in fact, that the MWL became especially active in the 1980s and 1990s, first in Afghanistan, supporting *mujahidīn* materially in their struggle against the Soviet-backed government and Soviet forces while "spreading their messages in refugee camps," and then in post-Soviet Chechnya and Bosnia, combining material aid with "spiritual renewal" for the purpose of "re-Islamizing" society (Petersen 2012, 774; Bellion-Jourdan 2001).[13] In 1984, the International Islamic Charitable Organization (IICO) was created in Kuwait at the recommendation of Sheikh Yusuf al-Qaradawi, former member and spiritual leader of the Muslim Brotherhood. The IICO's expressed purpose was similar to that of Christian missionary-aid societies: to combine the provision of charity, relief and development assistance with the promotion of religious identity and practice (Petersen 2015, 65–9; www.iico.org).

Eventually, IIROSA and the IICO, along with the MWL and WAMY were brought under the umbrella of the International Islamic Council for Da'wa and Relief (IICDR) created at the behest of Saudi Arabia in 1988, the height of the war in Afghanistan. Its purpose was to coordinate activities, including charitable efforts of the organizations and their member states, while promoting a single vision of Islam (Benthall 2003, 75; Bellion-Jourdan 2001, 176–77). Indeed, from the inception of these related organizations until the early 2000s, and with burgeoning oil revenues after 1973, relief in the form of material support for Muslim communities and *da'wa* went hand in hand.[14] Political goals – to consolidate monarchical conservatism and absolutism while extending Saudi power and influence – couched in language about strengthening the *umma* in the face of external challenges, were at the forefront of their activities (Petersen 2015, 86).

Since the early 2000s, numerous Gulf-based entities that had been providing material assistance abroad have claimed to have modified their

---

[12] Interview: Riyadh, 4 April 2012.
[13] In 2014, its name was changed to the International Organization for Relief, Welfare and Development.
[14] Of course, Christian missionary work is often associated with humanitarian assistance/relief. See, for example, Rohde 2005.

activities significantly in response to post-9/11 suspicions of Western powers regarding the sources of *salafi-jihadi* financing.[15] In an interview in 2012, the MWL's leadership told me that the organization had cut by half its support for projects connected to religious instruction and practice. Instead, it focuses mostly on hosting conferences and promoting inter-faith and inter-cultural dialogue.[16] Nonetheless, according to Benthall (2018, 9), the MWL today remains "a vehicle for Saudi influence," while in the religious field it continues to promote a particular vision of Sunni Islam in an effort to confront both the rise of Shi'i Iran and the attraction of "jihadi ideology." The secretary-general of WAMY, at our meeting at its headquarters in Riyadh, insisted unprovoked that WAMY neither proselytizes nor engages with other (that is, non-Hanbali) *madhāhib*.[17] However, just a few years prior, other sources claimed that the organization remained explicitly engaged in *da'wa* by publishing and distributing religious literature, offering classes in *shari'a*, training young men to become Imams and then paying their salaries at mosques throughout the world (Commins 2009, 192–93).

As for IIROSA, considered until 2015 to have been the most prominent charity in Saudi Arabia that worked both inside and outside the kingdom, and said to have been the world's largest, or second largest Islamic charity in the mid-1990s (Benthall 2018, 2), its efforts, according to its spokespeople, no longer centered exclusively on Muslim communities and "faith-based causes" (al-Yahya 2014, 189). Nonetheless, a perusal of its Annual Report for 2011/12 suggests that the initial focus persisted: training in Islam continued and the universalization of aid pertained solely to emergency humanitarian relief. In fact, at least four of the seven programs described in that report were geared partially, if not exclusively to Muslims and included religious content.[18] Be that as it may, the King Salman Humanitarian Aid and Relief Center (KS Relief), that was created in 2015 by the king soon after he ascended the throne, is said to enjoy a monopoly over almost all Saudi foreign humanitarian aid. By royal decree, it has become the sole vehicle through which overseas aid can be extended. What's more, explicit religious content is absent from its programs and documentation (www.ksrelief.org; Benthall 2018, 1–2).

---

[15] For legislation in Saudi Arabia, for example, regarding philanthropic activity since 2001, see ICNL (2017, 8–12).
[16] Jeddah, 17 April 2012.   [17] 4 April 2012.
[18] Overall Performance Report of the International Islamic Relief Organization, Saudi Arabia (IIROSA) Projects and Programs for the Year 2011/2012 (1432/33 H). www.egatha.org/pdf/annualreport/iirosa_annualreport_3233_en.pdf. Besides, according to Benthall (2018, 16), it was only in 2011 that, for the first time, IIROSA appointed external auditors of its activities.

Despite some modifications in their operations, the five politico-*da'w-ist* agencies discussed have remained closely interconnected, as indicated by their leadership structures. For example, the secretary-general of WAMY, (Saudi national) Saleh al-Wohaibi (2002–present), is on the Board of Directors of the IICO, while (Saudi national) Abdullah Naseef, currently vice chairman of WAMY, had been secretary-general of the MWL (1983–94) and secretary-general of the IICDR some years later. Indeed, Saudi-dominated transnational collaboration, along with efforts at forging ideological unity by extending "material and spiritual sustenance" were fostered decades ago. While methods may have been revised, the efforts have persisted for the sake of achieving political ends: the consolidation of monarchical autocracy in the Gulf region, strengthening the position of the Saudi state vis-à-vis other states in the Gulf and the broader Arab region, and the related diffusion of a conservative Sunni Islam.

Development Assistance

As with charitable giving, Gulf-based development assistance through institutional channels took off in earnest after the 1973/74 "oil shock" and was brought under an umbrella organization, the Coordination Group of Arab National and Regional Development Institutions (CG-ANRDI, 1975) (Momani 2012, 616). Of the five multilateral aid agencies created by and with a heavy presence of the Gulf monarchies, the Islamic Development Bank (IDB) is the only one with an explicit religious orientation.[19] It was created as a "specialized institution" of the OIC to promote Islamic solidarity by addressing the "economic development and social progress" of its member states and assisting "Muslim communities within non-member states" by financing approved projects in accordance with principles of the Shari'a (Shushan 2011, 1970).[20] While its membership, composed in 2019 of fifty-seven countries with large Muslim populations, provides the IDB's capital through their contributions, Saudi Arabia, which houses the institution and has occupied

---

[19] The other four are: OPEC Fund for International Development (OFID), Arab Bank for Economic Development in Africa (BADEA), Arab Fund for Economic and Social Development (AFESD) and Gulf Arab Program for UN Development Organizations (AgFund). Three national aid organizations – Kuwait Fund for Arab Economic Development (KFAED), the Saudi Fund and the Abu Dhabi Development Fund – figure under the umbrella group, as well (Barakat 2010, 11–12; Momani 2012, 616–17).

[20] According to a senior researcher at the IDB (Interview: Jeddah, 16 April 2012), a percentage of its net income is earmarked for charitable activities, for example, the provision of scholarships and other forms of support to educational institutions.

the position of president since inception, is the largest shareholder by far – at 23.5–26.5 percent (depending on the source). The other GCC states combined had been contributing roughly 40 percent of the IDB's capital, according to one source (Lacey 2014, 23), although this proportion seems to have decreased considerably in recent years.[21] Despite the dominant position of Saudi Arabia, a senior researcher at the IDB said the following: "The IDB is independent of the Government of Saudi Arabia just as the World Bank is independent of the Government of the United States."[22] What he failed to add, however, is that, as with the World Bank, the political-ideological positions and policies of the IDB reflect those of its principal financiers.

Especially active in the domain of development assistance and part of the CG-ANRDI, bilateral organizations in several of the Gulf monarchies channel much of their governments' foreign aid disbursements. The largest donors, the Kuwait Fund for Arab Economic Development (KFAED, 1961) and the Saudi Fund for Development (SFD, 1975), are closely connected to, if not supervised by their Ministry of Foreign Affairs or of Finance. As such, it is neither surprising nor exceptional that their aid is politicized, in one form or another (Momani 2012, 617–18).[23] Indeed, most, if not all major donors have (had) powerful political agendas attached to their foreign assistance.[24]

Consider Kuwait, for example: Because of its perceived geopolitical vulnerability given its small size, peculiar demographic features and governance structure and the capriciousness of regional relations, regime security has been at the forefront of the ruling family's preoccupations since independence.[25] From the outset, therefore, as Mary Ann Tetreault (1991) has elucidated, oil revenues have been instrumentalized in its foreign relations for political capital – specifically, to legitimate and consolidate the rule of the Al-Sabah. In creating the KFAED, the very first national aid agency established in a developing country (1961) and the largest and most active Arab bilateral donor agency until 2006, the purpose was to "win friends" in the neighborhood (Leichtman 2017,

---

[21] In 2019, the IDB website (www.isdb.org) suggested that combined, they contributed only about 22 percent.
[22] Jeddah, 18 April 2012.
[23] Without providing details, Momani and Ennis (2012) report that the SFD extends two types of foreign aid: "one that is politically motivated and another that is oriented towards economic development." The first, according to them, is the larger of the two, and administered by the Minister of Finance, "by whom an unknown amount of aid is predominantly funneled to Arab countries largely based on political motivations" (619).
[24] For a searing critique of the development paradigm and its political ideology and motivations, see Escobar (1995).
[25] On its complicated relationship with Iraq, for example, see Crystal (2016, 129–60).

6–8). The regime aimed to do so, in this instance, by demonstrating a principled commitment to the normative model of Arabism despite the perceived threat that Arab nationalist currents had presented to the security of Gulf ruling families from the 1950s until, in the case of Kuwait, the early 1980s.[26]

Since the 1990s, a growing proportion of Gulf aid has gone to sub-Saharan Africa, Asia and even Latin America, but the preference remains to give to Arab and Muslim majority countries, followed by Muslim communities in non-Muslim majority countries (Momani and Ennis 2012, 613–14).[27] Nonetheless, as with charity, to whom and how development assistance is extended is determined in response to changes in political circumstances and interests, as Cammett (2014, 140–60) demonstrates with regard to welfare provision in Lebanon. Thus, post-9/11 suspicions and local concerns regarding negative publicity have caused numerous Gulf aid agencies to redirect their attention somewhat. As a former secretary-general of the MWL stated: "We need to show the world that we care about humanity, no matter who they are."[28]

Giving at Home and Abroad: Governmental, "Semi"- and Non-governmental

Across the Gulf, charitable foundations of various types abound. Often referred to as semi- or non-governmental, many of them are in fact closely connected to, if not created by members of the local ruling family, and many receive some portion of their funding and operating costs from the government.[29]

While some charitable foundations specialize in a specific region and/or sector – as with the Kuwaiti NGO, *'Awn Mubāshir* (Direct Aid) that works in Africa among Muslim communities, Qatar's Reach Out to Asia (R.O.T.A.) that supports education initiatives there, or the privately funded Qatif Charitable Society that provides services mainly to Shiʻa in Saudi Arabia's Eastern Province – most of the larger foundations conduct similar activities, with considerable overlap and negligible collaboration among them. They support the socially disadvantaged groups recognized in Islam: orphans, widows, the poor, the sick and disabled; they dig wells and fund educational endeavors and health services. Many

---

[26] On the Arab nationalist threat to the Al-Sabah, see Herb (1999, 163).
[27] For a rare but perhaps dated discussion of the main features of Arab development aid and a comparison with that of DAC member states, see Tok et al. (2014).
[28] Interview: Jeddah, 21 April 2012.
[29] For a rich study of the charity sector in Saudi Arabia, with a focus on four different types of organizations in the city of Jeddah, see Derbal (2022).

include an explicitly religious component, as in providing Islamic education, building mosques, preparing *ifṭār* tables during Ramadan or distributing sacrificial meat at *'Eid al-'Aḍḥa* (the Feast of Sacrifice). Some foundations respond to emergencies around the globe, while an increasing number, having adopted the language of empowerment, at times linking it discursively to the Islamic tradition, offer skill-building and job-training programs of various sorts.

In Saudi Arabia especially in Riyadh, among the largest and most visible foundations are those associated with members of the Al Sa'ud or their closest associates (Le Renard 2008, 144–45), while in Kuwait, they tend to be affiliated with religio-political organizations. Although variants of both features are found in Qatar, neither accurately characterizes the philanthropic landscape in Oman. Because of both the nature of absolutism in Oman, in which the sultan, and not the royal family, rules, and the country's religious diversity in which Ibaḍi, Sunni and Shi'a cohabit in a delicate balance, the late Sultan Qaboos was especially vigilant in preventing family members on the one hand and doctrinally defined religious movements on the other hand from gaining prominence. Since the assumption of leadership roles in institutionalized activities such as the provision of welfare can incur recognition and influence, those activities have had to remain apolitical.

In the Sultanate, the largest and best endowed charity is the Oman Charitable Organization (OCO), a public entity founded in 1996 by royal decree. Its board of directors is composed of several members of government, including, today, one Al BuSa'id, as well as prominent members of society. A spokesperson for the organization told me in 2013 that it received about half its funding from the government and roughly 10 percent from private donations; the remainder came from returns on its investments. Of the private donations, the bulk came from Omani companies that were expected to contribute 5 percent of their net income to social works. The OCO's activities comprise mostly relief work outside the country in coordination with international organizations, other Gulf states or local officials but also several social programs at home.[30]

Royal Connections

Many of the nominally "non-governmental" foundations in Saudi Arabia that operate internationally were established by royal decree for a member of the royal family, yet they are considered to be private; among

---

[30] Interview with representative: Muscat, 30 Oct. 2013.

them are the Sultan bin Abdelaziz Foundation (1995), Alwaleed bin Talal Foundation/Alwaleed Philanthropies (2003/2015) and King Abdallah International Foundation for Charity and Humanitarian Deeds (2010) (al-Yahya 2014, 180). One of the most visible of this type of philanthropic organization is the King Faisal Foundation (1976), established by the late king's children as waqf at the time of his death. While historically it built schools, libraries, hospitals and mosques, today it focuses primarily on supporting education, providing scholarships and funding research inside the country. Although created from the estate of a public figure whose wealth derived, in large measure, from the oil-infused public purse, the foundation claims to be fully private: It was created by "private" citizens, receives no funding from the government and cannot request donations from the public, although anyone can donate privately.[31]

In her early studies of different forms of institutionalized charity in Saudi Arabia, Nora Derbal (2011, 2014) explains that all not-for-profit philanthropic institutions, whether charity foundations (*mu'assasāt khairiyya*) or welfare associations (*jama'iyyāt khairiyya*), must be registered with the Ministry of Social Affairs (MoSA). However, organizations established by royal decree and financed from the assets of the founder, like the King Faisal Foundation, enjoy somewhat greater autonomy than the far more numerous welfare associations that do receive government funding and must follow MoSA's rules and regulations, including submitting all programs and procedures for its approval. Given its responsibility for supervising and evaluating such institutions engaged in welfare provision, MoSA enjoys considerable powers: among them, to veto programs, refuse particular board members, define eligible recipients of services, etc. (Derbal 2011, 48–50). However, Derbal (2022, 27–8) notes that since the issue by royal decree of Saudi Arabia's NGO law in December 2015, welfare associations are no longer referred to as such but rather as NGOs (*jama'iyyāt ahliyya*). Nonetheless, they remain under the authority of the responsible ministry and are required to submit to new regulations and more rigorous oversight (270–73).[32]

---

[31] Interview with a former employee, Riyadh, 26 March 2012. I was told that "the Foundation has no relationship to the government" and this despite the fact that prominent members of the ruling family both founded it and hold key positions in it. For the foundation's description of its aims and activities, consult its website (www.kff.com). For another description from twenty-five years ago, see Kozlowski (1998, 298–300).

[32] This information evokes Pollard's (2014) study of the charity field in Egypt pre-1945. Recognizing the potential influence of welfare provision, the Egyptian state, through the creation of the MoSA in 1939, assumed control over welfare associations. In so doing, it

As Caroline Montagu (2010) indicated in her study of the voluntary sector in Saudi Arabia, the royal family's efforts "reflect its concerns to control what could be a parallel power structure and threat" (77). No doubt, stripping these associations of their designation as welfare providers while expanding their monitoring by the state suggests that despite the rhetoric about liberalization under the kingdom's "Vision 2030," in fact the reins of power and authority have been tightened and avenues toward influence-gathering, constricted. The ruler alone is to be recognized as attending to the public good (*maṣlaḥa 'amma*) – in this case, through the provision of welfare.

Saudi royals are prominent in several of what had sometimes been referred to as "non-governmental" charitable associations, if not as founding members or patrons, then as board members. As LeRenard (2008, 150–52) notes, involvement in the charity sector is one of the principal roles of Saudi princesses. Moreover, their engagement is thought to be mutually beneficial. On the one hand, at least until the creation of the NGO law, it practically guaranteed the association's approval by the MoSA and may have lessened the ministry's oversight somewhat; it attracted important donations from private individuals, banks and companies; it improved networking possibilities and therefore, access to resources.[33] On the other hand, the participation of royals enhances the family's visibility and legitimacy. Royals appear intimately connected to civil society and responsive to its various needs; thus, they are associated with compassion and care. In these ways, they gain allegiance from the population while discreetly bolstering their monitoring of society.

The Al-Wafa' and the Al-Nahda Women's Philanthropic Societies, that focus exclusively on poor women, were created in the 1960s. They are headed by Princesses Latifa and Sara, respectively, both daughters of the late King Faisal but from different mothers. They receive funding from the government annually and donations from private enterprises, prominent individuals and other private citizens. The two foundations cooperate with each other insofar as they divide the poor neighborhoods

---

enhanced its ability to engage in surveillance and control of religious forces especially. More recently, according to Mittermaier (2020, 121–22), a "state-centralized alms-collection system," called *bayt al-zakat al-masri* (the Egyptian House of Zakat), was created in 2014 at the behest of President el-Sisi. A principal aim was to "undercut the hold Islamist organizations continue to have through what remains of their services."

[33] In April 2012, I attended a fundraiser in Jeddah for a charity that focused on the handicapped and was closely associated with Princess Adilah, a daughter of the late King Abdallah. Individual donations were as high as $45,000; the names of the donors were announced with great fanfare while attendees "rubbed shoulders" with the princess.

of Riyadh between them. In their designated areas, they provide a variety of similar services to women and their children (LeRenard 2008, 146–47).[34] Beyond that, Al-Wafa', for example, takes charge of individuals referred by the public hospital who travel to Riyadh for hospitalization and require lodging prior to and following their medical procedures. According to my interlocutors, the building in which these individuals are housed in Riyadh was provided *gratis* to the organization by a prominent donor – whose identity they did not share – who, at the end of each year, reimbursed Al-Wafa' for all that it had spent on this particular service.[35] Coincidentally, it was announced one year later (April 2013) that the Alwaleed bin Talal Foundation had made an important donation in kind to Al-Wafa''s patient lodging units in Riyadh.[36] To be sure, the family connection can make a big difference: royals support royals, especially when there is no competition between them.

Among its various activities at the time I visited, al-Wafa' ran a center for abused women and girls. However, it took in only those who had been referred by the Ministry of Interior. It would not provide sanctuary or assistance to an abused person from outside an official channel. Thus, its attachment to, endorsement of and collaboration with the Saudi government, as well as with other royals, was incontrovertible. In practice, therefore, Al-Wafa' is neither truly private, nor independent.[37] Emblematic of what Derbal (2014, 163) has referred to as the "intense entanglement not only of individual members of the royal family, but also that of the Saudi state with private charities," "loyalist" charities such as al-Wafa' actively uphold the national project of the state while providing another avenue for its infiltration of society.

In Jordan, an Arab monarchy outside the Gulf, a somewhat similar institution can be found, as described by Jung and Petersen (2014, 293). Originally called Queen Alia Social Welfare Fund, JOHUD (Jordanian Hashemite Fund for Human Development) was created in 1977 by royal decree but registered as private; it receives funding from several sources, including government ministries. It has been led, since its inception, by

---

[34] According to a representative at Al-Wafa' (Riyadh, 10 April 2012), in 2012 the organization was taking care of about 1,800 families, each with an average of seven members, in various ways including providing job training and helping them acquire official papers, pay monthly rent and food bills.

[35] Interview: Al-Wafa', Riyadh, 10 April 2012.

[36] www.alwaleed.com.sa/news-and-media/news/alwaleed-foundation-supports-al-wafa-philanthropic-association.

[37] It is important to note, however, that Al-Wafa' is not necessarily representative of women's organizations in Saudi Arabia, many of which would have found ways to circumvent certain state impositions, such as, until recently, the requirement that a woman produces consent from a *maḥram*, or male guardian.

Princess Basma bint Talal, sister of the late King Hussein and paternal aunt of King Abdallah II. Currently, one of her daughters is the executive director. According to its website, "JOHUD aims to ensure that its work is aligned with national strategies and contributes to poverty alleviation."[38]

In Qatar, most of the prominent charitable foundations were established as *awqāf* from the fortunes and in the names of members of the ruling al-Thani family – Sheikhs ʿEid bin Mohamed, Jassim bin Jabor, Thani bin Abdallah and Faisal bin Jassem – by their heirs. Some of these, like the *salafī*-leaning ʿEid bin Mohamed al-Thani Foundation, follow a particular religious orientation without being formally part of a politico-religious institution.[39] While these foundations are financially dependent upon their endowments, all but one rely increasingly upon private donations; at times, they solicit contributions through fundraising efforts for humanitarian crises.[40] Although their activities include assisting local needy families and funding projects abroad, it is said that more than 75 percent of Qatari charity goes outside the country since, in the words of a Qatari consultant to charities, "there are not many things to do here."[41] Despite their royal pedigree and branding, these establishments are considered to be private. No doubt, they enjoy close relations with the government (Mohamed 2014, 263).

In contrast, Qatar Charity, one of the oldest and largest charities in the country, was not created by royals. With an elected board and hired general-manager, it is regarded as independent even though its chairman, since 2002, has been an al-Thani. It is referred to as a "faith-driven organization" and said to "lean toward the Muslim Brotherhood."[42] However, like the ʿEid Foundation, among other charities in Qatar, its religious orientation is not "formalized through an institutional structure" (Freer 2018, 42). Neither the Brotherhood nor Salafi formations have an institutional presence in Qatar, as they do in Kuwait. While

---

[38] It goes even further, stating that "JOHUD participates in national level planning processes and also works closely in line with Jordanian government ministries." www.johud.org.jo.

[39] Interviews with: representative from ʿEid Foundation, Doha, 11 Nov. 2013; consultant to charities, Doha, 12 Nov. 2013.

[40] The Jassim and Hamad bin Jassim Charitable Foundation does not collect donations. As for the Sheikh ʿEid bin Mohammad Al Thani Charitable Foundation, its status was changed from waqf to that of a charity; as such, it receives an annual financial contribution from the government. Interviews with consultant to charities, Doha, 29 Feb. 2012 and 12 Nov. 2013.

[41] Interview: Doha, 22 Feb. 2012.

[42] Interview with consultant to charities, Doha, 12 Nov. 2013. Founded in 1992, Qatar Charity emerged from the "Qatar Committee for Orphans of Afghanistan," created in the 1980s (interview with representative from Qatar Charity, Doha, 13 Nov. 2013).

financially dependent upon donations, Qatar Charity, like all registered charities, as distinct from *awqāf*, receives an annual sum from the government. Moreover, it "absorbs some al-Thani initiatives"; that is to say, when the royal family wants to contribute to an effort abroad, it may choose to do so through Qatar Charity.[43]

One of a kind at home, Qatar Foundation (QF) comprises numerous sub-organizations, including charitable initiatives. Registered as a non-governmental organization, it was created as waqf in 1995 by the then-ruling emir, Shaykh Hamad bin Khalifa al-Thani, with the addition of public funds and land granted by the government.[44] His wife, Sheikha Moza, chairs the foundation; in addition to herself, three of their children are on the Board of Trustees and one on the Board of Directors (www.qf.org.qa). Reach Out to Asia (R.O.T.A.), a sub-organization and charitable initiative of the foundation, founded in 2005, is chaired by their daughter, Sheikha Myassa. Remarkably, Qatar Foundation is touted as "a private foundation for public purposes" even though it has been financed, both directly and indirectly, from the public purse. In its peculiarly public-private, "loyalist" nature, Qatar Foundation appears somewhat similar to the Syrian Trust for Development, an entity comprised of several government-created but supposedly non-governmental organizations, a number of which were initiated by Asma' al-Assad, the wife of President Bashar al-Assad (Ruiz de Alvira 2014, 334–40). With the resources to monopolize activities in the educational, cultural and philanthropic spheres, Qatar Foundation, like "The Trust," is a vehicle for "reproducing patterns of authoritarian rule" while enhancing the public image of regime figures (Ruiz de Alvira 2014, 335). To be sure, QF is the darling of the most powerful branch of the ruling family, providing it with tremendous visibility – indeed, a tentacular presence.

The involvement of royals, whether directly or indirectly, combined with the branding of foundations with their name, is noteworthy for the ubiquity and authority it signals, despite their being advertised as private (non-governmental) or even semi-private establishments. In the case of Qatar, consider that until the oil price downturn that began mid-2014, more than 75 percent of government revenues derived from oil and gas,[45] common property resources meant to be overseen by the leadership for the benefit of the community. In other words, the former emir

---

[43] Interview with Qatar Charity representative, Doha, 13 Nov. 2013.
[44] Interview with scholar and activist, Doha, 10 Nov. 2013.
[45] From 2006 to 2011, for example, 50–65 percent came from hydrocarbon exports and 25–30 percent came from investments made possible by resource rents (Ibrahim and Herrigan 2012). Since 2020, the contribution of exports alone has increased to 75–81 percent (US-EIA 2023).

established the Qatar Foundation from his "private" wealth, accrued in large measure from hydrocarbon exports (and related investments), and supplemented from the budget of the government, which he controlled at that time as monarch and head of state. What ensues, as Le Renard (2008) identified in Saudi Arabia, is a pernicious mixing of and calculated confusion between public and private. Royals take from what belongs to the people and invest those resources in the creation of entities that they oversee and that carry their name. By colonizing the charity field in this manner, they shore up a fabricated image of themselves as magnanimous benefactors and benevolent devotees of the faith, thereby bolstering their legitimation, both political and religious, and commanding allegiance. In fact, they have simply transformed public resources into private, or rather royal resources, and exploit them in ways that deepen their penetration of society, hence their power and domination.

Doctrinal Connections

Unlike in Qatar and Saudi Arabia, charities in Kuwait are not connected to the ruling family. Rather, the most prominent charities, excluding the Red Crescent Society, adhere to one or another religious tendency that may or may not be affiliated with a political movement.[46] In effect, the Al-Sabah have deliberately ceded this domain to the religious field and its promotion of social conservatism while still retaining authority over Islamist actors. They have done so for reasons having to do with the regime's vulnerabilities but also the peculiar political system that combines dynastic authoritarianism with parliamentarism, hence the need to make some concessions to popular forces. In this regard, it is important to recall that during the seven-month-long Iraqi invasion and occupation of the emirate (2 August 1990–25 February 1991), the Muslim Brotherhood became a "major political force." With the flight of the royal family, it organized resistance and assumed responsibility for social welfare (Freer 2018, 78–81) while a prominent member of the Salafi movement, Ahmed al-Baqir, led the popular government in Kuwait that negotiated with the government in exile (Azoulay 2013, 87). In fact, the Al-Sabah have both empowered and co-opted the Islamists. They have done so in an effort to protect themselves and secure their rule. In the 1970s and 1980s, for example, the royal family used the Brotherhood as a counterweight to the Arab nationalists, offering them ministries,

---

[46] Recall that political parties are banned in the four countries. In Kuwait, however, several political movements are tolerated and remain active in politics.

approving Islamic banking and extending different types of support (Freer 2018, 31). Then, by providing financial assistance for the creation in the 1980s of a ṣalafī charity, they encouraged the Kuwaiti Salafi movement to engage more fully domestically so that it would compete with the Brotherhood (Pall 2020, 16). Thus, the regime could control these movements more effectively, while allowing them some influence. Nonetheless, political power remains concentrated in the hands of the emir.

Jama'iyyāt al-Islaḥ al-Ijtimā'i (Society for Social Reform) and *Jama'iyyāt Ihya' al-Turāth al-Islāmī* (Society for the Revival of Islamic Heritage) belong to Kuwait's Muslim Brotherhood (*al-haraka al-dustūriyya al-islāmiyya* – Islamic Constitutional Movement [ICM or HADAS]) and *Salafī* movement (*al-Tajamm'u al-Salafī al-Islāmī* – Salafi Islamic Gathering), respectively. Both are active in Kuwaiti politics and typically hold seats in Parliament. Both associations are engaged in vast philanthropic activities at home but especially abroad – in the Middle East, Africa and Asia and in countries in crisis (e.g., Afghanistan and Bosnia in the 1990s, Syria since 2012). According to their representatives, their work is funded principally by donations from their adherents among Kuwaiti nationals and residents. Both are explicit that an important goal is to "preserve Islamic culture" wherever there is a Muslim community.[47]

Another charitable organization with a *ṣalafī* orientation, *'Awn Mubāshir* (Direct Aid) was created some thirty years ago by Abdelrahman al-Sumeit, a Kuwaiti physician and *'ālim*. Formerly called Africa Muslims Committee and reliant upon private donations and regular contributions from the government, the organization digs wells and builds schools, clinics and training centers in Africa. It also builds mosques, teaches Arabic and Islam and helps African Muslims make the pilgrimage. According to one of its representatives, "where there are Muslims, we work." Furthermore, "we are involved in helping Muslims be better Muslims" and so, "*da'wa* is part of our work."[48]

While *Jama'iyyāt al-Iṣlāḥ* insists that recipients of their aid do not have to be Muslims, *da'wa* is central to the mission of the three associations. According to a member of HADAS, "most charities in Kuwait have a *da'wa* component because in Islam you need to both encourage *da'wa* and help people live the best way as Muslims ... Much of the charity we

---

[47] Interviews with: representative of *al-Turāth*, Kuwait City, 13 May 2012; representative of *al-Iṣlāḥ*, Kuwait City, 14 May 2012.
[48] Interview, Kuwait City, 13 May 2012. See, www.directaid.org.

give is about supporting Muslims in their way of life."[49] In short, these three philanthropies combine the provision of assistance with efforts to strengthen the ranks of the Muslim community and especially, of their particular orientation within Islam.

To be sure, the *daʿwa* of the Brotherhood is distinct from that of the *Salafī* and certainly of the Shiʿa. In this regard, it is noteworthy that during my meeting at *Jamaʿiyyāt al-Iṣlāḥ* the representative mentioned Iran's charitable work, referring to the Islamic Republic as "a major competitor in Africa." He expressed concern about how Kuwaiti Shiʿa, who constitute roughly 35 percent of the citizen population, extend charity: "I'm convinced their money goes to initiatives supported by Iran and to strengthening Shiʿi networks (in West Africa)."[50] In short, charitable giving, as described, is intimately connected to politics and the struggle to gain adherents.

"Unaffiliated" Charity

Across the region, there are numerous charitable organizations that are linked neither to royal families, nor to religious tendencies or religio-political movements. To take but one example, in Oman, *Dar al-Iʿṭāʾ* is a well-known local charity. It was created in 2002 by a group of women married to Omani businessmen and became an official organization in 2006. Its revenues come exclusively from private sources, including companies, via a host of donation strategies and fundraising events. Its ambitions and capabilities are relatively modest, and its activities are confined to Muscat.[51]

Distinct in their status as "unaffiliated," prominent business families, like Bahwan in Oman and Al-Rajhi and Olayan in Saudi Arabia, who enjoy clientelistic relations with the regime, are engaged in broad-based philanthropic activities, while others, like the Sultan family in Kuwait, have created issue-specific entities.[52] Of the former, Azoulay (2013, 90–7) discusses the instrumentalization of charitable activities by relatively new Shiʿi merchant families in Kuwait. By donating to all segments

---

[49] More specifically, "of course daʿwa is very important: we can't just let anyone do the work of teaching Islam ... In Indonesia, for example, we have an Islamic training school where we train Imams and then send them elsewhere in Indonesia to work in a mosque we've built. We also write the Islamic curriculum for the schools we build" (interview with representative from *Majmaʿu Sanabīl al-Khīr, Jamaʿiyyāt al-Iṣlāḥ*, Kuwait City, 14 May 2012).
[50] Kuwait City, 7 May 2012. For Shiʿi charitable associations in Kuwait see, Azoulay (2013, 86).
[51] Interview with a founder, Muscat, 29 Oct. 2013.
[52] See Sultan Education Foundation. http://sultaneducationalfoundation.com.

of the diverse Shiʿi community, families like that of Jawaad Bukhamseen (of Bukhamseen Holding), who are close to the Al-Sabah, may use charity to "buy social prestige" among the Shiʿa. Their aim is to play the role of intermediary between the regime and the community. In effect, Azoulay argues, "they represent the interests of their patron" (93).

Who's In, Who's Out? The Politics of Exclusion

In the four countries, many charities extend assistance to long-term residents who do not carry the local citizenship. In fact, a representative of Al-Wafaʾ Women's Philanthropic Society claimed that 20–25 percent of those who request help from them are non-Saudi citizens with a residence permit.[53] However, except for very few cases, charities tend not to help poor labor migrants at home apart from offering *ifṭār* during Ramadan and Friday meals at some mosques.[54] Recall the claim of a Qatari national that "there are not many things to do here"[55] – and this despite the presence of vast numbers of indigent foreign laborers, often living in conditions of precarity.

One charity in Qatar and one in Oman told me that, in fact, they do give to laborers but not systematically and certainly without publicizing. The representative of the Omani charity elaborated thus: "Once you open that door, it will never close."[56] This rationalization, that obliquely acknowledges the need, was echoed, almost verbatim, by a representative of *al-Iṣlāḥ* (Kuwait): "If we open the door to helping the more than 1 million foreign laborers, our work would be insurmountable."[57] In contrast, "loyalist" Saudi charities, when asked about the exclusion, inclined toward a legalistic explanation: According to Ministry of Labor stipulations, the *kafīl* (sponsor) is supposed to take care of their workers. Apart from the *kafīl*, the worker's embassy is responsible for them.[58] Surely, the response of an *ʿālim* with the Omani Ministry of *Awqāf* and Islamic Affairs was remarkable: "We already do a lot for them: we allow them to come here and work."[59]

---

[53] Interview: Riyadh, 10 April 2012.
[54] On "food banks" and Ramadan food distributions in Saudi Arabia that also benefit non-Saudis and until recently, non-residents, as well, see Derbal (2022, 70–1,115–16, 212–214).
[55] *Supra* fn. 41.   [56] Doha, 13 Nov. 2013; Muscat, 29 Oct. 2013.
[57] Kuwait City, 14 May 2012.
[58] Interviews with representatives of: King Abdallah Foundation for Developmental Housing, Riyadh, 20 March 2012; Al-Wafaʾ, Riyadh, 10 April 2012.
[59] Muscat, 31 May 2013.

A more compelling explanation relates, as I suggested in Chapter 5, to the prevailing sense of community. In this regard, an Omani interlocutor noted that migrants' exclusion is "merely a matter of priorities": that, "charity begins at home."[60] He failed to add that for many, home is also where charity ends. As philanthropic organizations in these Gulf states routinely extend material support to causes and crises beyond their borders – for example, to Palestinian programs for decades, Syrians since 2012, victims of the 2004 tsunami in Southeast Asia and of other natural disasters since then – that they ignore needy foreigners in their midst, rendering them virtually invisible, suggests that *takāful* (solidarity) at home is a circumscribed notion that applies chiefly, if not solely to the community that matters. And compassion is not extended to those for whom one feels no obligation precisely because they are external to that privileged group.[61] No doubt, the tendency to prioritize one's own is universal, and the disadvantaged are more-or-less invisible everywhere. Nonetheless, the invisibility of the disadvantaged in Gulf monarchies is especially striking given the vast unearned wealth there from which they are excluded.[62]

While exceptions do exist, they are few. Nora Derbal (2022, 213–14) refers to two informal food distribution initiatives, "Half a Date" and "Feed the Need," which sprung up in Riyadh and Jeddah in 2013 and 2015, respectively, and disappeared just a few years later. They targeted South Asian laborers on the one hand, and workers and cleaners on the other. The founders and organizers remained anonymous and mobilized volunteers and donors via social media. By 2018, Derbal points out, the regime was openly opposed to the extension of even informal assistance to non-Saudis.

In my own work in the four Gulf countries, I encountered only three charitable initiatives, created by nationals, for the foreign community specifically.[63] Two of them, *Lajnat al-Ta'arīf b'il-Islam* (Islam Presentation Society) in Kuwait City and *ḍyūf Qatar* (Qatar's Guests)

---

[60] Interview with former minister, Muscat, 30 Oct. 2013.   [61] *Supra* fn. 7.
[62] *Supra.*, Chapter 5, fn. 37.
[63] There were, however, expatriate-founded initiatives that assisted migrants. In Oman, for example, the Charitable Wing of the Indian Social Club gave to needy Indians, and the Ecumenical Council for Charity, connected to the Reformed Church in America, gave to those in need, supposedly without discriminating. Another project that addressed migrants, albeit on a tiny scale, was "I Care." The inspiration of a young resident of Palestinian descent, it was active from May 2011 until 2017, bringing together volunteers to distribute bottled water at construction sites in Muscat and thank laborers for their work (interview with founder, Muscat, 29 Oct. 2013).

in Doha, targeted non-Muslims, offering Arabic language instruction, Islamic education and conversion. While they couched their activities in philanthropic sentiments, *da'wa* for the purpose of expanding the Muslim community was what motivated them.[64] The only program that, at least until summer 2015, explicitly addressed the material conditions of migrants was, like *ḍyūf Qatar*, part of the *salafī*-directed, Eid bin Mohammed al-Thani Charity Foundation. With the remarkable name, *ḥafiẓ al-niʿma* (Preserve Grace), its volunteers collect leftover food from hotels and private dinners in Doha and distribute in industrial zones where the poorest workers live.[65] They also distribute used clothing at construction sites. Moreover, a program officer mentioned to me, parenthetically, that preachers from *Ḍyūf Qatar* go to industrial zones following distributions to encourage conversion.[66] Alas, there is "no free lunch": Charity and proselytism often go hand in hand.[67]

Individual Giving

Recall that there are two types of individual giving in Islam: obligatory zakat – a tax of 2.5 percent levied on the equivalent of "capital gains," in one's possession for at least one year[68] – and elective *ṣadaqa*. In principle, zakat contributions are transferred to the public treasury (*beyt al-māl*) or its equivalent and then distributed among the poor, needy and other Qur'anically defined appropriate recipients. *Sadaqa* is given to whomever, however, and in whatever amounts the donor chooses. Among Muslim countries today, there is little uniformity in the role the state plays as collector and distributor of zakat. Furthermore, there is no consensus about whether zakat payment should be voluntary or obligatory, or even the forms of wealth that are "zakatable" (Kahf 1989; Kuran 2003, 277–83; May 2013).

---

[64] Such programs exist in Oman and Saudi Arabia, as well, through the Ministry of *Awqāf* and Islamic Affairs.
[65] This food collection and distribution program has been in place since 2008. See www.hifzalnaema.com. Interestingly, Al-Wafa' in Saudi Arabia also collects and distributes leftover food but among poor Saudis and non-Saudi residents only. Interview: Riyadh, April 10, 2012. For two quite distinct food distribution programs in Saudi Arabia – one, a CSR initiative of the Al Fozan Group and the other, the focus of *Jamaʿiyyat Ḥafẓ al-Niʿma*, a welfare association based in Jeddah, see Derbal (2022, 71).
[66] Interview, Doha, 11 Nov. 2013.
[67] Again, this is not uncommon (*Supra* fn. 14). In Egypt, for example, Atia (2013) notes that zakat committees at mosques make assistance conditional on submission to religious instruction (55–76).
[68] *Zakat* is meant to be levied on revenues that exceed *niṣāb*, a minimum, predetermined value, necessary for subsistence. Muslims whose assets fall below *niṣāb* are exempt.

Individual Giving 133

In Oman and Qatar, there is no formal, government-enforced collection of zakat; giving, in whatever form, is left to the individual. In Kuwait and Saudi Arabia, in contrast, governments impose and collect zakat from citizen-owned companies in the former and citizen- and GCC-owned companies in the latter.[69] In Saudi Arabia, funds are collected by the Ministry of Finance and transferred, in full or in part, to the MoSA/MoLSD for redistribution for the purpose of poverty alleviation. Zakat funds thus contribute to social security payments to those considered to be among the neediest Saudis, to allocations to charitable associations and to unemployment programs (LeRenard 2008, 142–43, 146; Derbal 2022, 80).

In Kuwait, it was only in 2006 that formal collection of zakat was imposed on companies, but interestingly, the mandatory 2.5 percent was reduced to 1 percent. Apparently, many had complained that the former was too onerous, while others suggested that since the country had a Shi'i population who were required to pay *khums*[70] to their religious leaders, it was preferable to reduce the obligatory contribution to the state and trust that each company would independently pay the remainder to an entity or initiative of its choosing.[71] Furthermore, of that 1 percent zakat payment, 0.5 percent goes into the government fund that subsidizes the salaries of private sector employees.[72] It is also worth noting that in Saudi Arabia until 2016 and the gradual imposition of the "White Land Tax Regulation, 2015,"[73] those extensive, undeveloped properties owned privately by wealthy Saudis (referred to in Chapter 3) were not subject to zakat. Remarkably, regime *'ulama* maintained that they constituted "hidden wealth" (*amwāl al-bāṭina*), which, according to several schools of Islamic jurisprudence, is exempt from zakat.[74] That the Kuwaiti and Saudi governments endorsed such respective claims, and in so doing essentially revised a religious edict, intimates that they aimed

---

[69] In cases of joint ventures in Saudi Arabia, the Saudi-owned portion has to pay zakat. For details, see, Oxford Business Group, "Updated Legislation Guides Zakat and Taxpayers Navigating Regulatory Framework." https://oxfordbusinessgroup.com/overview/path-forwards-updated-legislation-guides-zakat-and-taxpayers-navigating-regulatory-framework.

[70] A 20 percent tax on annual profits, half of which is meant for *marāji'* (the highest, Shi'i clerical authorities) and half for orphans, the poor and needy.

[71] Interviews with: MP for HADAS, Kuwait City, 7 May 2012; former MP for *tajama'a al-islāmī al-salafī*, Kuwait, 8 May 2012.

[72] *Supra* Chapter 3, fn. 56.

[73] Issued pursuant to Royal Decree no. (M/4), dated 12.2.1437H (Nov. 24, 2015), referred to in Chapter 3, p. 60.

[74] Interview with Saudi Shari'a scholar and specialist in Islamic finance, Riyadh, 25 April 2012. See al-Jassem 2013.

thereby to appease a particular social category. A tax, destined to assist the disadvantaged, was reformulated to benefit the rich.[75]

Alongside innovative forms of "zakat evasion,"[76] Kuwaiti companies, like their Saudi counterparts, may take advantage of the weak regulatory environment by failing to divulge their true net worth so as to contribute less than they would have otherwise.[77] In the words of a Saudi economist who sits on the shariʿa boards of several Islamic banks, "there is a lot of deception and trickery in the payment of zakat by the very rich. Many are not prepared to pay 2.5%, especially since 2.5% of a few billion [Saudi riyals] is a lot of money."[78] Thus, while zakat was meant to be a formula to counter hoarding, reduce inequality and combat material hardship, it, like taxation systems in Europe and North America, is routinely manipulated to facilitate private accumulation.

Although private giving is said to be substantial in Gulf states, statistics are lacking (Hartnell 2018, 42–3). Moreover, some who are employed in the philanthropic sector voice skepticism about the true extent of generosity. According to a representative of Oman Charity, "what is said and what is true are not always the same; there is a lot of exaggeration about the generosity of Gulf nationals."[79] A prominent Kuwaiti philanthropist went further: "We are still a tribal society, and being tribal means that in order to give, we need to first find out who is involved, who will get the credit, etcetera. We are not yet ready to give magnanimously."[80]

As elsewhere in the Muslim world, giving is greatest during the holy month of Ramadan and through mosques, especially following Friday prayers. People donate to different sorts of entities: individuals in need, government offices, charitable organizations or campaigns focused on particular causes or crises at home or abroad. There are hundreds of private charitable initiatives, as well as highly publicized, government-sponsored campaigns which, until recently, solicited contributions via telethons or television, or collection boxes in malls. However, due to transparency-related concerns, these latter collection methods are less common today.

No doubt, some private giving circumvents organizations, foundations and government agencies. In fact, several interlocutors explained that typically, individuals with means give to a select group of people

---

[75] For another example, see Chapter 7, p. **157** & fn. 38.
[76] Kuran (2003, 278–82) reminds us that opposition to and evasion of zakat payment were not uncommon even in early Islamic history.
[77] Interviews with: former MP for HADAS, Kuwait, 11 May 2012; member of Supreme Economic Council, Riyadh, 2 April 2012.
[78] Riyadh, 5 April 2012.   [79] Muscat, 30 Oct. 2013.
[80] Kuwait City, 15 May 2012. On characteristics of individual giving in the Gulf, according to one study, see Hartnell (2018, 30–5).

recurrently. In Qatar, for example, such individuals may have a roster, constituted over time, of needy individuals or families, inside and sometimes outside the country, as well, to whom they give on a regular basis. This roster, revised over time, may be handed down from one member to another within a family.[81] The billionaire Bahwan brothers in Oman, each with his own diversified business group, are said to "have envoys throughout the country who create a list of needy people who then receive monthly allowances." My interlocutor went on to say that "these men are loved and respected, but they have to be careful not to be seen as competing with the government and/or royals, and so, they tend to give quietly."[82] Nonetheless, in Kuwait and Oman, where an underdeveloped culture of giving outside the family was noted repeatedly by my interlocutors, the focus remains on one's tribe, ethnic or confessional community.[83] And across the region, building a mosque is another popular form of individual giving, as is establishing a waqf to address a particular concern.

What Do Citizens Say about Charitable Giving Today?

Many of my interlocutors pointed out that although giving is said to be extensive, poverty still exists in Gulf states – certainly in Bahrain, Oman and Saudi Arabia. They insisted that if zakat were paid and distributed appropriately, poverty would have been eliminated.[84] Some went further, suggesting that persistent poverty in these petro-monarchies is the result of greed, among Gulf elites especially.[85] Others suggested that in the current environment, characterized by material abundance and profligate consumption, "commitment to social welfare and recognition of the social value of money are wanting, while piety, to the extent it does exist, is de-linked from social responsibility."[86]

---

[81] Interviews with: lawyer and former minister, Doha, 21 Feb. 2012; director of a research institute, Doha, 22 Feb. 2012.
[82] Interview with: policy analyst, Capital Market Authority, Muscat, 4 Nov. 2013.
[83] Interviews with: member of one of most prominent business families, Muscat, 31 Jan. 2012; former minister, Muscat, 30 Oct. 2013; former member of *majlis al-dowla*, Muscat, 5 Nov. 2013; leading philanthropist and businessman, Kuwait, 15 May 2012.
[84] Interviews with: religious activist, Riyadh, 2 April 2012; economist with the Islamic Development Bank, Jeddah, 16 April 2012; religious scholar and former member of *majlis al-dowla*, Muscat, 4 Feb. 2012. Atia (2013, 111, 132) reports of similar comments by Egyptians, and Jung and Petersen (2014, 294–95) do likewise by Jordanians.
[85] Interviews with: professor, Shari'a College, Qatar University, 27 Feb. 2012; prominent economist and former member of *majlis al-shūra*, Riyadh, 1 April 2012; economist with the Islamic Development Bank, Jeddah, 16 April 2012.
[86] Interview with prominent philanthropist, Kuwait, 15 May 2012.

When asked about prevailing concerns for *maṣlaḥa 'amma* (the common good), several interlocutors responded sarcastically that *maṣlaḥa khaṣṣa* (private interest) was far more prevalent.[87] An oft-cited example was the penchant to construct a mosque and attach one's name to it. As a prominent Omani businessman remarked: "Mosque building ... is not about Islam; it's about status and posterity."[88] Indeed, the predilection for public posturing and ostentation, for cozying up to the powerful was underscored repeatedly:

> The preference is for big, well-advertised projects – promoted by the Emir, perhaps – that glorify the selves ... Some want to show off that they're giving. Look at charitable societies, like ...; money goes to the media first, to make a big splash about them, and the founder uses the foundation to enrich his other projects. He makes sure the Emir knows about his charitable acts and so, gives him more business.[89]

Of course, this is not unique to Gulf states. Similar behaviors have been identified in Syria among government-sponsored NGOs and "loyal philanthropists" (Ruiz de Elvira 2014, 337–40), as well as in Egypt (Atia 2013, 121), among other countries. According to some of my interlocutors, as noted in Chapter 4, "Islam is a big business ... it's an instrument for making more money and increasing popularity."[90]

There are, for sure, exceptions to these patterns, but they exist because "the philanthropist is exceptional."[91] *Bab Rizq Jameel* (Beautiful Gateway to Prosperity) is a community service initiative within the broader corporate social responsibility (CSR) program of the Saudi business organization, Abdellatif Jameel Group (AJG), named for its founder.[92] It was established in 2003, initially as a microfinance initiative modeled on the Grameen Bank of Bangladesh, to assist poor Saudis by supporting self-designed income-generating projects. Like Grameen, it

---

[87] Interviews with: professor, Shari'a College, Qatar University, 27 Feb. 2012; member of *majlis al-dowla*, Muscat, 5 Feb. 2012; renowned *'ālim*, Muscat, 13 Feb. 2012; philanthropist, Kuwait, 15 May 2012.
[88] Muscat, 31 Jan. 2012. Petersen (2015, 93) quotes from a manager at IIROSA who says that donors "want to see buildings ... They want somewhere they can place a sign."
[89] Interview with: professor, Shari'a College, Qatar University, Doha, 27 Feb. 2012. See, as well, LeRenard (2008, 151) and Derbal (2014, 153–54).
[90] Interview with: member of al-Thani family, Doha, 20 Feb. 2012.
[91] Interviews with: Lebanese scholar of religion, Muscat, 10 Feb. 2012; Saudi former deputy minister, Riyadh, 1 May 2012.
[92] Abdellatif Jameel began his career subcontracting with ARAMCO and operating gas stations, later becoming the sole distributor of Toyota vehicles in Saudi Arabia. Today, the AJG is the largest private independent distributor of Toyota in the world, with operations in the Middle East, Africa, Europe and Asia. It is involved in real estate and financial services, as well. In 2005, it endowed the Poverty Action Lab at the Massachusetts Institute of Technology.

lends to women who have a plan for a small business and have constituted a group of five borrowers – only one of whom may be a non-Saudi resident.[93] As in the Grameen Bank model, lending to the group is meant to encourage solidarity and shared responsibility. *Bab Rizq* also runs free job-training courses for poor, unemployed men and women, and assists successful graduates in finding employment. This multifaceted CSR operation, financed almost entirely from the family's fortune, is focused on helping the poor get themselves out of poverty.

Conclusion

Variations among the four states in the configuration of the charity domain, as noted, have much to do with the respective peculiarities of dynastic authoritarianism and the relationship with the religious sphere. In the case of Saudi Arabia, the Al-Saʿud, despite their historic alliance with Wahhabi religious forces, reign supreme. An absolutist monarchy, no non-state corporate group, religious tendency or individual may gain exclusive distinction for itself and certainly not for such consequential activities as welfare provision. In Qatar, the charity domain is one of the few spheres in which religious forces enjoy a role. Nonetheless, most of the charities that have a Salafi or Muslim Brotherhood orientation also have an Al-Thani in the leadership structure or as founder. Thus, not only has the ruling family co-opted the philanthropic sector, but also through their direct oversight they ensure that the influence of these religious orientations remains mostly informal and apolitical. Denying an institutional presence for religious forces in Qatar likely reflects the Al-Thani's concerns regarding their political autonomy and regime security in an environment in which they had originally sought political and tribal legitimacy in part by asserting their ideological affiliation to Wahhabism – then dominant in the Peninsula (Baskan and Wright 2011, 105–8). In Oman, where power is centralized in the sultan, preventing the emergence of other (potential) centers of power has been key. As noted, during the reign of the late Sultan Qaboos, even the royal family was kept mostly on the sidelines. Moreover, with multiple sects of Islam well-represented in the population, both the late Sultan Qaboos and the current Sultan Haitham have been careful to promote a "desectarian" Islam and impede the emergence of institutionalized religious forces in society. Hence, neither royals nor formalized religious tendencies are prominent in charitable institutions.

---

[93] Interviews with: CEO of AJG, Jeddah, 17 April 2012; representative at *Bab Rizq*, Jeddah, 21 April 2012.

What can be deduced about practices of giving and their implications for politics? First, a universal phenomenon, benevolence may be motivated by political ambitions in addition to charitable feelings. Giving at home and assistance abroad can be sources of political and/or social capital: means to extend influence, establish networks, gain recognition and secure allegiance. This is true for governing authorities and multilateral entities, as well as for clientelist business groups, "loyalist" and identity-based organizations. And as we have seen with ideology-driven entities, their generosity may be tied to adherence to their *da'wa*. Thus, conformism and obedience are enforced, the ranks of the believers grow and the particular ideology gains in influence.

Charitable giving may be a more-or-less deliberate conservatizing force. It is not a strategy to address poverty at its source or effectively mitigate inequality (Cammett 2014, 218–27; Isik 2014, 322; Mittermaier 2020, 123). Rather than promote real socioeconomic change, it is, as Derbal (2011, 63–4) observes in Saudi Arabia, a means to reinforce difference and consolidate the hierarchy in place. As an institutionalized practice, charity "diverts from the structural causes of need and poverty, thus disabling forms of resistance to such structural inequality and reproducing poverty and need" (Moumtaz 2021, 231). Furthermore, while named giving, in contrast to the Qur'anic preference for anonymity, may indeed provide a positive example for others to follow, it is, as well, an unequivocal expression of status and hence, a solicitation of recognition. Besides, named giving may offer the benefactor an array of public relations benefits of a social, political or economic nature and related to their ambitions (Cammett 2014, 203). Added to that, when not extended anonymously and/or when conjoined with ideology, benevolence presupposes indebtedness; and what more effective a way to repay a debt than through submission – to the benefactor's authority and/or their beliefs?

Second, when the ruler or members of the ruling family extend charity and/or are active in charitable associations, there is a blurring of the distinction between public and private, with important effects (LeRenard 2008, 145). The "royal," in the guise of an exclusively private citizen, is able to intervene more deeply in society. In so doing, they gain not only allegiance but also access to information that may be useful to the ruler (or ruling family) in his (or their) public function(s). Furthermore, when the state intervenes in the domain of charity by encouraging citizens to give, regulating the creation, organization and activities of charitable associations, decreasing requisite (zakat) contributions from some social categories or withholding access to charity from others, it is using charitable giving as a tool for social management and social control. By appeasing some and marginalizing others, it reinforces its domination of society while consolidating the contours of community.

Third, while international giving has prioritized Arab and Muslim countries and communities, giving at home tends to concentrate on family, tribe, ethnic and confessional community. Thus, those at home who are disadvantaged but not considered part of the community to which the Gulf state and citizen feel an obligation, are denied assistance. Recall, as well, that giving is also about getting in return: In the words of a prominent Kuwaiti philanthropist, "we give when we expect our generosity will bring us recognition."[94] In the case of migrant laborers, for example, not only are they perceived as distant and disassociated, but also, their allegiance is unnecessary and their submission, expected. Nothing of value is deemed to accrue to a donor by giving to them, even though citizens' quality of life is dependent upon them.[95]

Highlighting exclusions and other features of charitable giving in Gulf monarchies demonstrates that in these states, as in other environments, the normative inferences, supposedly at the source of charitable giving, are not always obvious or primary.[96] Furthermore, through this oil-financed institutionalized practice, ruling elites engage in not only manipulating but also regulating religion, however discretely, in their efforts to manage and control society. Indeed, secular goals related to the accumulation of capital (social, political, economic) are prominent, and regime priorities – its project of community, nation and state – are advanced.

---

[94] Kuwait City, 15 May 2012.
[95] Arguably, citizens' quality of life is dependent upon the migrant laborers' immiseration.
[96] Cammett (2014, 234) notes the same in her study of welfare provision by sectarian parties in Lebanon.

7 Islamic Banking and Finance
A Political Economy of Accumulation

Introduction

Recall that Islam is often described by its most loyal students as a total system (Chapra 1992; Naqvi 1994) that "deals with the whole field of human life" (Qutb 1953, 37, 113) or as an overarching moral-legal order to which the political and economic spheres are bound (Hallaq 2013). As such, all activities conducted by Muslims are meant to be suffused with the moral principles at the core of the religious tradition: the pursuit of justice and the actualization of goodness. While the central importance of charitable giving and the repudiation of *riba* ' are as old as the foundation of the Islamic community, a broad elaboration of something called "Islamic economics" is a modern development from the early twentieth century. Originally, the aim was to ensure the growth and development of Muslim societies in the face of the encroaching power of the capitalist West while preserving their Islamic identity. Economic transactions are to be carried out according to the Islamic ethical framework and for the sake of achieving justice and equity while improving the material condition of Muslims. Hence, productivity, efficiency and redistribution are integral to the Islamic "moral economy."

It is said that the Indo-Pakistani *'ālim*, Sayyid Abu al A'la Mawdudi (1903–1979) was the first to employ the term Islamic economics, describe its features and advocate for its adoption (Kuran 2004, 39). Mawdudi's goal, according to Timur Kuran, was for Muslims to recapture the sense of who they are and assert their singularity, and to do so by actually living their faith. In the later writings of Sa'id Qutb (1953) and especially, Baqir al-Sadr (1982), Islamic economics not only provided a means for Muslims to live their faith, but also it offered an indigenous – and in their view, a more humane – alternative to the economics practiced by the capitalist West: one that infuses meaningful economic engagement with Islamic values and understandings. Furthermore, if practiced appropriately, its advocates insist, Islamic economics would ensure sustainable growth and development, as well as equitable distribution. Thus, it would enhance both material well-being and social justice – indeed, *maṣlaḥa*.[1]

As interest in Islamic finance (IF) grew, from the 1970s especially, whatever "sacred intentions" may have inhered at the outset seemed to fall by the wayside, as Haniffa and Hudaib (2010, 86–8) point out, as did the pursuit of a more humane alternative to capitalist economics (Tripp 2006, 140–41). Rather, for Muslim rulers and elites, greater participation in advanced capitalism has remained at the forefront in the expansion of Islamic finance, alongside the assertion of a distinctive (Islamic) identity. In fact, some scholars suggest that Islamic Finance is primarily a means by which middle- and upper-class Muslims, deeply integrated into late capitalism, manage to preserve their religious identity in the face of tumultuous changes to their lives brought on by rapid modernization. Engaging with Islamic finance allows them to consume "in a Muslim way" (Pepinsky 2013, 157–58). Others suggest that it is, as well, a means by which regimes appease the more religiously motivated segments of their populations while at the same time enticing them to engage institutionally with advanced capitalism (Haniffa and Hudaib 2010, 88–90). Maxime Rodinson noted these conjoined objectives as early as in the mid-1960s; in *Islam and Capitalism*, he wrote the following of Islamic finance, then still in its infancy: "It has above all the virtue of enabling one to enjoy a good conscience as a Muslim and a human being ... without having to renounce the charms of a comfortable existence" (1978, 153). Indeed, the adoption of Islamic finance has provided yet another avenue to capital accumulation. This is especially noteworthy in the Gulf monarchies. There, it has also been instrumental in appeasing key segments of society and shaping the community of privilege.

Principles and Instruments of Islamic Banking and Finance

Foundational to Islamic finance is justice in economic transactions through the insistence upon several key principles. First among them is the prohibition of *riba'* – unlawful or undeserved gain, as in the charging of interest on a loan. The intention behind this principle is threefold: (i) to bar the lender of capital from profiting from the material need of the borrower; (ii) to inhibit extortion that could provoke or intensify impoverishment; (iii) to prevent accumulation in the absence of productive activity.[2] Hence, Islamic

---

[1] See, for example, Chapra (1994). For a rich discussion of intellectual production related to Islamic economics in its formative years see, Tripp (2006, 103–24).

[2] See Tripp (2006, 126–32) on different views regarding what actually constitutes *riba'*. Given that a loan must not be a "for profit" transaction, the only truly legitimate loan in Islam is the *qarḍ hassan*, in which the lender receives no monetary gain.

financial institutions neither charge nor pay their clients something they term "interest."

Loosely linked to *riba'* is the second principle: the prohibition of *gharār*, or (gain from) transactions that are based on uncertainty, as in betting and speculation. In short, where information is asymmetrical and outcomes are either unknown or unspecified in advance, unnecessary risk-taking is involved. Therefore, all financial transactions should be materialized: an actual object must change hands. This being the case, loans, for example, are transformed into trade arrangements insofar as a commodity that is (supposedly) bought from a merchant and then sold is introduced in the transaction between the financier and the client. Furthermore, participants in a transaction should share not only information but risk and returns, whether profits or losses, as well. For the proponents of Islamic banking and finance (IBF), therefore, equity financing of a business venture, in which an ownership interest is "sold" to financiers (investors) in the form of shares and the profits or losses that result from the venture are shared, is preferable to debt financing, in which funds are borrowed and then reimbursed with interest. This is because, if the venture for which the borrower required capital fails, they do not bear alone the full cost of the loss as they would with debt financing. And if the venture succeeds, the financier-investor who provided the capital shares in the profits, however great or small they may be. Given this preference, so-called participatory financial arrangements, those that include profit- and loss-sharing (PLS) between financiers and borrowers, are considered to be the most appropriate Islamically in that they protect and reward both parties. At the same time, they encourage owners of capital to make financial resources available to individuals and businesses while impeding their accumulation of "unearned" income in the form of interest (Khan 2010, 807–8). The final principle of Islamic banking and finance (IBF) is the prohibition of *harām*: goods and activities that are considered *harām* (unlawful and illegitimate) – for example, alcohol, pork and gambling – must not be financed.

Over time, a host of different instruments based on the aforementioned principles were devised by Shari'a scholars with expertise in *fiqh mu'āmalāt* – having to do with financial transactions and civil contracts – to allow for the possibility of engaging "Islamically" in banking and finance. Among the most common participatory contracts are *mudaraba*, *musharaka* and *sukūk*. *Mudaraba* is referred to as a "passive partnership" insofar as one person contributes capital and another, expertise and management. Profits are shared on a pre-arranged basis, while losses are borne by the financier alone. Deposits in Islamic banks, for example, tend to be placed in *mudaraba*-based accounts in which, rather than the depositor earning interest, they and the bank form a partnership to share in the profits that accrue from their joint

Introduction

investments. *Musharaka* is equivalent to "equity participation": The financier assumes a direct stake in the venture and all partners may participate in management. Profits are distributed in pre-arranged ratios, but losses are borne in proportion to respective capital contributions.[3] As for *sukūk*, they are similar to bonds except that they involve genuine ownership of a pool of assets, rather than simply the right to a return. Furthermore, they generate a return through income streams based on lease or rent payments, instead of fixed interest payments as in conventional bonds (Rethel 2011, 81).

Although considered weakly Islamic, non-participatory contracts exist, as well. The most common are *murabaha* and *ijāra* (or *mutājara*). *Murabaha* is equivalent to mark-up or cost-plus sale: A client asks the bank to purchase an item for them; having done so, the bank then sells it to the client for a predetermined, marked-up price, usually paid in installments. Those who defend the "shari'a compliance" of *murabaha* insist that: First, it avoids *riba* in that mark-up is simply payment to the bank for its services and second, the bank also incurs risk since it owns the item before selling it to its client (Tripp 2006, 143). *Ijāra* is a leasing arrangement in which the bank (lessor) leases an asset to a client (lessee) for agreed-upon payments and period of time, but in its most basic form, there is no option of ownership for the lessee.[4]

Brief History of IBF in the Gulf

The idea of Islamic banking gained in prominence in the Gulf states in the 1970s, initially as part of the Saudi-led effort that began in the 1950s to confront the political threat posed by leftism, Arab nationalism and republicanism in the region, and to do so by meting out repression and spending oil rents while hoisting the banner of Islam.[5] Recall that Faisal bin Sa'ud, first as crown prince (1953–64) and then king (1964–75), committed himself to both crushing leftist activism at home and spreading Saudi influence (and Saudi-Wahhabi ideology) within and beyond the Gulf region. In part to achieve the latter, and as noted in Chapter 6, he was instrumental in the creation of several pan-Islamic entities – among them, the Organization of the Islamic Conference (OIC) and the Islamic Development Bank (IDB) – in which the Al Sa'ud have played a dominant role.

---

[3] Definitions and descriptions of Islamic finance (IF) instruments rely on Khan (2010) and Warde (2010).
[4] For variants of *murabaha* financing – *musāwama, tawaroq, mutājara* – see Warde (2010) and Wilson (2012).
[5] *Supra.* Chapter 6, pp. 114–15, 120, 127–28.

Buoyed by the creation of the "shari'a-compliant" IDB, a son of King Faisal, Mohamed bin Faisal, established the Faisal Islamic Bank in 1977, as well as the International Association of Islamic Banks under the auspices of the OIC. Interestingly, the bank was set up first in the Sudan and then in Egypt but not in Saudi Arabia, since, as we will see, the Saudi monarchy had until recently spurned the creation of explicitly Islamic banks at home (Wilson 2009, 5–6). With other political but also religious figures, Mohamed bin Faisal established, as well, the *Dar al-Māl al-Islami* Trust in Switzerland in 1981; a multi-market banking conglomerate, its purpose was to "create(s), maintain(s), and promote(s) Islamic financial institutions" by providing "Islamic banking, Islamic investment, and Islamic insurance services to Islamic communities" (www.dmitrust.com). Mohamed bin Faisal's intentions were not far removed from those of his father: to enhance the kingdom's visibility and promote the royal family's reputation and its (political and material) interests abroad through the creation of institutions that had a religious imprimatur and could function in a "modern'" economy (Haniffa and Hudaib 2010, 87).

No doubt, the increased wealth and liquidity that accompanied the 1970s oil price boom meant that ruling families and their clients had far more money than ever before. Thanks largely to enhanced distributive mechanisms, described in Chapter 3, the standards of living of a growing proportion of Gulf nationals were improving, as well, although exclusions persisted. That, along with the expansion of the banking sector and the availability, for the first time, of non-conventional methods of banking that appeared to acknowledge religious sensibilities, augmented the demand for IBF in the Gulf.

From its slow beginnings, Islamic finance has become far more prominent and multifaceted since the 1990s especially, as both "identity politics" and the integration of Gulf states in global capitalism have gained ground.[6] In 2019, one-third of all active banks in the GCC were Islamic banks (Hanieh 2020, 531–32). And there are at least five different types of Islamic financial entities in the region: local banks, regional banking conglomerates, Islamic windows at conventional banks, specialized financial service entities (such as insurance companies) and highly capitalized local banks with tremendous support from power centers – either rulers or individuals/agencies closely linked to the national government – as founding sponsors and stakeholders (Rehman 2010, 114). By 2018, the six Gulf monarchies were acknowledged as the region with

---

[6] For a rich discussion of the latter see, Hanieh (2018, 29–62).

the largest share (42.3 percent) of the Islamic financial services industry, followed by Asia (28.2 percent). In terms of Islamic bank assets, they scored the highest – with US$704.8 bill. – of all regions, followed by the Middle East and North Africa (MENA) region (excluding the Gulf monarchies), with US$540.2 bill. (IFSB 2019, 10).

To uncover the actual goals and purposes of IBF in Gulf states, I first provide a brief overview of its development there, before turning to an investigation of the particularities of its form and substance. I address a set of issues related to, on the one hand, the adoption, governance and regulation of IBF and on the other hand, the conformity of its practice with its alleged purposes. I conclude by reiterating my argument: Over time, the institutionalized practice of Islamic banking and finance has become a means for Gulf regimes to both appease their restive populations and respond positively to the boundless (material) interests of a local and increasingly important "interest group" – that includes royals, as well as regime apparatchiks, ideologues and business associates – while cloaking their intentions in religiosity and ethical commitments. IBF represents the conjoined instrumentalization of (oil-derived) wealth and Islamic doctrine to build a community of (relative) privilege, facilitate the regime's management and control of society and beyond that, to bolster the royal family's political domination and material enrichment.

Development of IBF in GCC States

Whereas the Saudi regime resisted the creation of Islamic banks at home until the late 1980s and the Sultanate of Oman did likewise until sometime after the "Arab Spring" (2011) uprisings, the other Gulf monarchies have each had one or more Islamic banks from the mid-1970s/early 1980s. Most notable among them are the Dubai Islamic Bank, the first commercial Islamic bank, and the Kuwait Finance House, created in 1975 and 1977, respectively.[7] Bahrain introduced Islamic banking in 1979 and Qatar in 1982 (Wilson 2009, 6). Lacking the hydrocarbon wealth of its neighbors, Bahrain sought to build a reputation as an important service provider. To this end, it has cultivated a role, if not an image, as an Islamic financial hub, becoming known as the home of the Accounting and Auditing Organization for Islamic Financial Institutions (AAOIFI) since 1991, and of the International Islamic Financial Market (IIFM), created in 2002. Made up of a shari'a board of *fiqh* (jurisprudence) specialists, AAOIFI was created to address

---

[7] Interestingly, these remained the only Islamic banks in the UAE and Kuwait until the 2000s (Wilson 2009, 6).

matters related to Islamic financial products and their standardization, and to set guidelines for Islamic financial institutions to follow (Wilson 2009, 10).[8]

One of the first and largest Islamic banks in the Gulf region, the Kuwait Finance House (KFH) enjoyed tremendous support from the Al-Sabah family for many years. Its origins can be traced to local Islamist forces connected to the Muslim Brotherhood who were the object of considerable attention from the regime in the 1960s and 1970s, anxious as it was, as noted in Chapter 6, to counter the popularity of progressive, secular ideologies in the country and across the region. In fact, several members of Kuwait's merchant elite who dominated the Kuwait Chamber of Commerce and Industry (KCCI) and whose influence the emir sought to undercut, subscribed to Arab nationalism (Moore 2004, 90). Encouraged by this newfound attention in the oil-boom environment of the mid-1970s, Islamists who until then had limited their economic activities largely to charitable works, pushed their advantage and mobilized for the creation of a *riba*'-free financial institution (Smith 2004, 171–72). With support from the ruling family, including a government share of 49 percent of the bank's capital at the outset, plus freedom from Central Bank regulation until 2003, the KFH gained access to and came to dominate lucrative sectors of the economy, among them, construction and real estate (Hartley 2014). Like the UAE's DIB and eventually, Saudi Arabia's Al-Rajhi, it also developed global reach, with branches and/or subsidiaries elsewhere in the Middle East and Asia. Nonetheless, by the end of the first decade of the new millenium, it had lost its monopoly of the sector at home, as well as its outsized position in the economy. Newly created Islamic banking facilities such as Kuwait International and Boubian, having responded to legislation enacted in 2004 that opened up competition within the sector, emerged as dynamic players in an expanding field.[9] Moreover, in 2003, all Islamic banks were brought, for the first time, under the regulatory authority of the Central Bank of Kuwait.

By 2012, legislation had been introduced in each of the Gulf monarchies to both permit and regulate Islamic financing. However, the regulatory systems for banks are distinct in each state; even among the seven emirates that make up the UAE, a single regulatory framework is lacking (Wilson 2009, 7, 25). Furthermore, while Islamic financial institutions

---

[8] The OIC's Fiqh Academy (in Saudi Arabia) is another supranational body that issues guidelines for shari'a governance.

[9] In addition, KFH is said to have been plagued by internal power struggles and accusations of corruption. Interviews: Kuwait City, 10 May 2012.

now come under the authority of the Central Banks and are, for the most part, loosely regulated by them,[10] those located in financial free zones, as in the Qatar Financial Center (QFC) and the Dubai International Financial Center (DIFC), are considered to be part of a separate jurisdiction and therefore, have their own laws, regulatory guidelines and courts (Wilson 2009, 27–8). Hence, the regulation of Islamic banking and finance is fragmented not only within the Gulf region but also within individual states.

Particularities of Form: Adoption, Governance and Regulation

Adoption of or Resistance to IBF

As noted in the previous section, the first Saudi-created Islamic banks were based outside the kingdom, and it was not until 1987 that an Islamic bank (Al-Rajhi) received a license to operate inside. How can we explain the resistance of the Al-Saʿud to Islamic banking at home, while they paid lip service to the merits of Islamic finance and were keen to sponsor international Islamic financial institutions, like the Islamic Development Bank, headquartered in Jeddah?

Novel efforts to incorporate Islamic principles in the national economy, as in the creation of explicitly Islamic banks, seem to have been perceived as problematic for a royal family that has consistently insisted upon and laid claim to the Islamic identity of the Al Saʿud state. Explicitly Islamic banks would imply that domestic institutions were not already operating Islamically. Presumably, the regime favored the allusion that all banks in the kingdom adhered to the shariʿa without having to be labeled "Islamic." Furthermore, the creation of "Islamic" banks would call attention to the interest-bearing transactions of the banks that had been operating undisturbed until then. In this regard and as Charles Tripp (2006) has suggested, it is also likely that the regime initially feared that if imposed widely, the new Islamic financial instruments could threaten the vast financial interests of the ruling family and its closest associates, invested as they were, and remain, ever more deeply

---

[10] Aypadin vom Hau (2018) notes that Dubai Islamic Bank began without a shariʿa advisory board and had no "official regulatory framework" for its first six years. There was no Central Bank in Dubai until 1981 and the first official regulations of Islamic banking did not exist until 1985 (21). According to one of my interlocutors, a professor of Islamic economics, "it is because Islamic banks in the Gulf are under the authority of the (conventional) central bank of each state that they appear as conventional banks with a Muslim face" (Doha, 27 Feb. 2012).

in global financial markets (140). Hence, until 2005 when Saudi Arabia opened its market for financial services so as to gain membership in the World Trade Organization and thereby expand its integration in global capitalism, it was very difficult for Islamic banks to secure licenses in the kingdom (Henry 2006, 151–52). It is indeed noteworthy that until very recently, there was no mention of "Islamic banking" in Saudi banking legislation.[11] The Banking Control Law, introduced in 1966, had not been revised to include provisions for Islamic banks and this despite the fact that the sector has witnessed considerable growth, and one of the most prominent Islamic banks in the world, Al-Rajhi, is quintessentially Saudi (Wilson 2012, 139). However, in January 2023, a draft of a proposed new banking law and regulatory framework was finally issued.[12] Alas, in reviewing the emergence of IBF in Saudi Arabia, "Islamic authenticity" appears to be more of a veneer than a descriptor or even a clear objective, while the preference for unencumbered enrichment is indisputable.

In the case of Oman, it was not until after the uprisings in 2011 that the government finally approved the adoption of IBF. In 2013, Bank Nizwa, the first fully Islamic bank in the Sultanate, opened its doors. How can we explain the resistance to IBF until then, and its subsequent adoption? Insofar as asserting Islamic identity is concerned, recall that of the Gulf monarchies, Oman is quite distinct. As the Sultan, his family and the Grand Mufti are of the Ibaḍi tradition[13] – and Ibaḍi constitute, by most estimates, roughly 50 percent of the citizen population, the government treads lightly in its promotion of Islam. Because of both its unique status and its rule over a large Sunni population and several small Shiʿa (and Hindu) communities (5–10 percent),[14] the late Sultan Qaboos promoted a universalist – or, in Amal Sachedina's (2021, 11) terminology, "desectarian" – Islam that downplayed differences among the traditions while highlighting what is common to all Muslims. Introducing IBF in the Omani landscape would necessarily involve placing religious scholars from both Sunni and Ibaḍi traditions on shariʿa boards, and this may have been seen as potentially complicating the late sultan's public expressions of inclusivity and confessional harmony.

In my discussions with Omanis, two principal reasons were offered for the resistance to IBF. Some suggested that the appropriate authorities in

---

[11] However, see, Saudi Arabia Monetary Authority (Feb. 2020).
[12] As of July 2023, it does not appear to have gone into effect.
[13] In fact, Oman is the only independent state in the world where Ibaḍi are in power.
[14] The Omani government does not publish statistics on the size of the citizen population according to faith or sect. While Boghardt (2013) refers to Sunni as only 15–20 percent of the population, most other sources I have consulted suggest a range of 35–55 percent.

government, along with prominent financial regulators, did not find it to be significantly different from conventional banking and finance and so, not worth the investment. Furthermore, given the lack of standardization and other features that indicated relative underdevelopment of the sector, it appeared to them to be a potentially risky enterprise.[15] Other interlocutors explained that the Omani government tends to make decisions very slowly, and it was simply waiting to see how successful IBF would be elsewhere in the region before adopting it at home.[16]

The mobilizations in Oman in spring 2011 precipitated the introduction of IBF (Valeri 2015, 11). While the demonstrators did not invoke it specifically, demand for Islamic banks had been growing in the sultanate. In fact, a study conducted in Oman and published in 2011 indicated that about 60 percent of those Omanis who had been banking at conventional institutions expressed discomfort with engaging in transactions based on interest (Magd and McCoy 2014, 1625). And according to one of my interlocutors, many Omanis had been banking for years at Islamic banks in the UAE.[17] Hence, as another interlocutor pointed out, its introduction would "contribute to keeping Omani capital from going abroad to Islamic banks elsewhere; thus, it would result in increasing investment at home."[18] Furthermore, by finally allowing Islamic banks in the country, the late sultan sought greater stability at (what all autocratic rulers in the broader MENA region experienced as) an ominous historical moment. He did so by acknowledging societal demands and appeasing those forces who favored a greater role for Islam in daily life.[19] To be sure, tapping into popular preferences can secure political advantages for ruling elites. Thus, Islam was instrumentalized for the sake of social management and social control.

Governance and Regulation

If we compare Islamic banking and finance (IBF) in Gulf states with that in Malaysia and Indonesia, for example, the most significant differences between them lie in matters of governance and the role of the state. In the

---

[15] Interviews with: economist at Capital Market Authority, Muscat, 31 Jan. 2012; a rights activist, Muscat, 5 Feb. 2012.
[16] Interviews with: employee at Ministry of Awqāf, Muscat, 29 Jan. 2012; member of *majlis al-dowla* (State Council), Muscat, 2 Feb. 2012.
[17] Interview with a former banker and current advisor on IBF to governments and institutions, New Jersey, USA, 26 April 2018.
[18] Interview with a financial services regulator, Muscat, 31 Jan. 2012.
[19] Interviews with: employee at Ministry of Awqāf, Muscat, 29 Jan. 2012; member of *majlis al-dowla* (State Council), Muscat, 2 Feb. 2012; a former auditor general, Muscat, 5 Feb. 2012; a government minister, Muscat, 12 Feb. 2012.

Gulf, governments have been neither the initiators nor the principal advocates of IBF at home. Appearing more or less ambivalent, they have maintained, until now, a non-interventionist approach with the sector. In most cases, shariʿa governance is not centralized at the national level, as it has been in Malaysia and Indonesia since the 1990s, although some movement in this regard is currently underway.[20] And uniform rules, tools and oversight mechanisms remain weak, if not absent.

There are few elaborated laws governing Islamic banking and finance in Gulf monarchies. In Kuwait, the banking law of 1968 was amended in 2003 to address Islamic banking for the first time, essentially legislating that each bank could have its own shariʿa board (Wilson 2012, 127). Since then, a host of "instructions" for Islamic banks, many of a procedural nature, have been appended.[21] In Qatar, the central bank specifies in writing some regulations regarding IBF (Wilson 2012, 138–39), while plans for a centralized shariʿa supervisory body have been announced since 2019.[22] However, the Saudi Arabian Monetary Agency (SAMA), the kingdom's central bank, provided neither rules nor guidance until it issued the "Shariah Governance Framework" in 2020 (Alkhamees 2017, 173; SAMA 2020). In Oman in 2012, the banking law of 2000 was amended by royal decree to include six brief articles regarding Islamic banking; among them, article 126b stipulates that a "high Shariʿa supervision authority," a national shariʿa board, would be created and housed within and for the purpose of advising the Central Bank.[23] Shortly after the issuance of the amended law, the Central Bank of Oman released a fairly detailed "Islamic Banking Regulatory Framework" with which all Islamic Banks in the sultanate must comply. It includes specifications regarding, among other things, internal and external audits, the

---

[20] The UAE has begun to take steps in the direction of centralization (see fn. 23), and the central bank of Bahrain has issued guidelines for product systematization. See "Bahrain issues new guidelines for Islamic banks," *Saudi Gazette*, 19 Sept. 2017. http://saudigazette.com.sa/article/517599/BUSINESS/Bahrain. As for Saudi Arabia, see fn. 11.

[21] See, for example, Central Bank of Kuwait, "CBK Instructions for Islamic Banks," n.d. www.cbk.gov.kw/en/legislation-and-regulation/cbk-regulations-and-instructions/instructions-for-islamic-banks.

[22] See Qatar Financial Centre, Qatar Islamic Finance Hub Report 2019, www.qfc.qa/-/media/project/qfc/qfcwebsite/documentfiles/publications/research–insights-2019/qifr19.pdf.

[23] The interest in a national shariʿa board is not without precedent: In 1985, the UAE issued Federal Law no. 6 regarding Islamic banks and financial institutions and composed of ten articles, among them Article 5, which stipulates: "A Higher Shariah Authority shall be formed ... to undertake higher supervision over Islamic banks, financial institutions and investment companies ... The opinion of said Authority shall be binding." www.centralbank.ae/sites/default/files/2018-10/LawNo6-1985-IslaminBanks%281%29.pdf. However, it was not until the end of 2018 when the Higher Sharia Authority was finally created. See, Central Bank law (Decree-Law No. 14 of 2018).

composition, rights and responsibilities of shariʿa board members and the requirement to follow AAOIFI guidelines (CBO 2012).[24]

Although Oman is somewhat of an outlier in this regard, it is fair to say that as strict regulatory and supervisory mechanisms – including, for example, required audits at regular, specified intervals – have for the most part been absent in the Gulf monarchies, central banks do not exercise effective oversight of Islamic banks. Insofar as Qatari Islamic banks are concerned, shariʿa audits, external to the institution, have been carried out irregularly at best and almost exclusively at the behest of the bank management itself.[25] Moreover, except for those in Oman, Islamic banks have been under no obligation to follow shariʿa standards issued by any one of the supranational agencies, such as AAOIFI or the OIC-Fiqh Academy. Not only that, but according to Dar and Azmi (2015, fn. 7), they tend to rule either independent of or against those agencies' guidance. However, mounting criticism regarding compliance, oversight and accountability have prompted some governments to contemplate the initiation of reforms. For example, the governor of the Central Bank of Kuwait (CBK) announced in December 2016 that instructions on "shariʿa supervisory governance" for Kuwaiti Islamic Banks were being issued, and in fall 2020, the Higher Committee of Shariʿa Supervision was established at the CBK.[26]

Absent (effective) centralized governance of the sector, each and every Islamic bank has its own shariʿa board made up of at least three specialists in Islamic jurisprudence dealing with civil contracts and financial transactions; they are responsible for examining and evaluating products, contracts and operations, and providing their "stamp of approval." Appointees of the bank, their job is to assure that all transactions carried out by the particular bank and with its clients are, in their expert opinion, "shariʿa -compliant." However, as each shariʿa board is independent, it is not uncommon for there to be multiple interpretations and therefore, different sorts of products and methods of financing from one bank to the next within the same country. As a result, banks may compete with each other for "shariʿa -compliant" business.[27] And this may have the negative effect of incentivizing one financial institution to loosen its standards

---

[24] For a description and analysis of the articles related to shariʿa governance in the Framework, see Morrison (2015).

[25] Interview with shariʿa scholar, Doha, 5 March 2012.

[26] www.cbk.gov.kw/en/cbk-news/announcements-and-press-releases/press-releases/2020/10/202010051120-cbk-forms-the-higher-committee-of-shariah-supervision. For a description of its responsibilities, however vague, see www.cbk.gov.kw/en/about-cbk/committee-of-shariah/responsibilities.

[27] However, see the case of Qatar.

regarding "shariʿa authenticity" so as to retain or attract clients (Rehman 2010, 117–19).

Furthermore, shariʿa board members have few constraints placed upon them. For example, they are not vetted by a central authority and, except for in Oman, there is no limit to the number of boards on which they may sit.[28] In Qatar, for example, the same individual, Sheikh Waleed bin Hadi, chairs the shariʿa boards of four of the five Qatari Islamic banks (Barwa/Dukhan, Masraf al-Rayan, Qatar Islamic Bank, Qatar International Islamic Bank), and for several years until December 2020, the same three individuals were board members of those four institutions. In Kuwait, in contrast, shariʿa boards are composed of three to six members and there is far less overlap across boards than in Qatar. However, in Oman, scholars are not permitted to be on the shariʿa board of more than one competing institution, as in two or more Islamic banks, but they may be on the board of more than one non-competing institution, as in one Islamic bank and one takāful (Islamic insurance) company (CBO 2012).

According to a study published in 2011 (referred to in Hayat et al. 2013, 604–5), seven Gulf nationals – two Saudis, three Kuwaitis, one Qatari and one Bahraini – figured among the top ten shariʿa scholars in the world in terms of the number of shariʿa boards of Islamic financial institutions of which they were members; remarkably, that latter number ranged from a low of twenty-four to a high of eighty-five.[29] Moreover, the same ten individuals figured among the top twenty shariʿa scholars in terms of the number of boards of standard setting Islamic institutions of which they were members. In other words, at that time, "the monitors (are), in fact, monitoring themselves" (Hayat et al. 2013, 605). Thus, except for in Oman where they are restricted by law to a single board of a bank, there has been negligible concern on the part of either the state or the Islamic banks (or both) about conflicts of interest that may arise as a result of the same experts being employed by multiple entities and related institutions in a single industry and possibly across national borders. Finally, given the weakness of state oversight of the sector and the paucity of stringent, externally imposed regulatory mechanisms, the transparency of bank operations and reporting is indeed in question. Alas, there appears to have been scant concern about this, as well (al-Mutairi and al-Hunnayan 2016).

---

[28] Aypadin vom Hau (2018, 22) suggests that this freedom may constrain them somewhat in that, anxious to sit on multiple boards since they receive a salary from each bank, they may be inclined to be more conservative in their pronouncements so as to facilitate their hiring.

[29] For the actual data, see Funds@Work 2010.

How, then, should we make sense of the structuring of IBF in GCC states? In her work on Southeast Asia, Lena Rethel (2013, 122–23) indicates that IBF had been actively promoted in Malaysia for decades by former prime minister Mohamad Mahathir, who governed from July 1981 to October 2003 and from May 2018 to March 2020. He viewed IBF as a means to encourage the growth of a (largely indigenous) Muslim middle class in the multi-ethnic state and empower them relative to the economically dominant Chinese community. Systematic planning by the Malaysian financial bureaucracy followed suit. In a later study, Rethel (2017, 11–17) argues that the decision to centralize shariʿa governance through the creation of a single, national level shariʿa board and incorporate it within the "governance framework of the state apparatus" by housing it in the financial regulatory bureaucracy of the state was linked squarely to the regime's domestic development goals, as just noted, and to related concerns regarding organization and efficiency. Besides, structuring shariʿa governance thus allowed for greater transparency, as well as enhanced control by the state of the shariʿa board, its members and their pronouncements, as well as of the financial institutions, their operations and clients (Rethel 2017, 19–24).[30]

If we extrapolate from Rethel's research and analysis to better understand the structuring of IBF in the Gulf, we acknowledge that, in fact, and as noted by others, the introduction of IBF was not a "top-down" affair, as it was in Malaysia, Indonesia and Iran (Wilson 2012). For the most part, ruling elites of Gulf states did not perceive that such an alternative to conventional finance offered benefits to them and their projects of community, nation and state. While eventually each regime accepted its introduction and found ways to benefit from it, there were no obvious incentives at the outset for leaders to intervene, in either the direction or form of IBF, and assert control. The question remains, however, what particular interests of Gulf leaders did such a hands-off approach actually serve?

In her comparative study of governance of IBF in Malaysia and the UAE, Aypadin vom Hau (2018) argues that the variation in the configuration of regulatory frameworks depends upon the nature of political competition in authoritarian regimes. In Malaysia, characterized by institutionalized political competition, the leadership of the ruling party,

---

[30] In Indonesia, in contrast, the centralization of IBF governance was implemented so as to ensure "doctrinal purity." There, the national shariʿa board is closely linked to the religious bureaucracy and to the most important Islamic civil society organizations in the country (Rethel 2017, 17–18). Rethel refers to these different ways of institutionalizing centralized shariʿa governance as reflecting "specific settlements between state, market and religious actors" (18).

fearful of losing its incumbency to another party campaigning on a religious platform, chose to actively promote IBF as a means to win over religious segments of the population and gain their votes. To retain their support, the ruling party has sought to ensure the successful functioning of the sector and so, it both intervenes in the oversight and supervision of Islamic banks and insists upon the coordination of their activities. Thus, governance is centralized under the state's authority, regulatory institutions are a part of the state structure, carefully adjudicated shariʿa scholars are bound by explicit rules, and financial products and procedures are standardized throughout the country.

In contrast, in the UAE (and most other Gulf monarchies), autocratic rule persists and, except for in Kuwait, electoral political competition is absent. More or less complacent about their (absolute) hold on power, rulers demonstrate no "credible commitment to institution-building": there is little perceived need to create "complementary institutional layers," as in Islamic banking and finance, to entice popular support. Hence, the ruler and ruling elites have had no incentive to intervene in the regulation of the Islamic banking sector, nor in centralizing it under their authority (Aypadin vom Hau 2018). To be sure, it is less cumbersome and more cost-effective for them to delegate to the banks themselves and to shariʿa scholars chosen by the banks. Furthermore, shariʿa scholars thus situated are anxious to preserve their autonomy and maneuverability; they implicitly resist the centralization of governance and regulation of the sector for the constraints it would place upon them.

No doubt, the preferences of political leaders have everything to do with the structuring of Islamic banking and shariʿa governance. As long as the introduction of IBF would not undermine their interests, political leaders were prepared to respond positively to the demands of what tended to be the more conservative forces in society and accept the creation of an Islamically tinged alternative to, if not adaptation of, conventional banking. In so doing, ruling elites had little to lose: They would be stimulating the economic activity of a segment of the population that, until then, may have chosen to remain on the sidelines, while gently endorsing the incorporation (of another simulacrum) of Islamic piety into daily life. In some cases – Kuwait in the mid-1970s and Oman post-2011 – the introduction of Islamic banking actually served the political interests of rulers at those particular junctures.

In the early years, ruling elites felt little to no personal stake in the creation of the IBF sector or in its functioning. This may explain their non-interventionist role in what was, and has remained, a fragmented financial sector with a weak regulatory structure. More recently, however, the sector has grown rapidly across the region and the globe such

Table 7.1 *Islamic bank assets as percentage of domestic market, select GCC states, select years*

Country	2012	2014	2018	2021
Kuwait	60%	40%	40.6%	51.9%
Oman	NA	6	NA	15.3
Qatar	22	26	25	28.1
Saudi Arabia	35	50	51.5	77.2

Sources: IFSB 2022, 16; IFSB 2019, 10–11; IFSB 2015, 9; IFSB 2013, 8

that by the second quarter of 2018, for example, GCC states accounted for 42.3 percent of the global Islamic financial services industry;[31] in 2021, they accounted for 52.4 percent (IFSB 2022, 12). And within these states, Islamic bank assets as a proportion of the domestic market have also grown significantly. In Saudi Arabia, for example, they more than doubled in less than ten years: From 35 percent of total banking sector assets in 2012 (IFSB 2013), they grew to more than 75 percent in 2021 (IFSB 2022) (Table 7.1).[32]

With the expansion of the sector, combined with the demonstrated successes of an increasing number of Islamic financial institutions with significant asset bases, IBF was proving to be a means for both the accumulation of prodigious wealth and further integration of the Gulf states in global capitalism. Hence, ruling families, as well as individuals or agencies closely associated with the national government chose to actively participate as founding sponsors and stakeholders of what have become highly capitalized local Islamic banks, such as Alinma in Saudi Arabia and Masraf Al-Rayan in Qatar. Considered a private establishment, Alinma is in effect a joint stock company, established by royal decree in 2006 and with Saudi public enterprises – the Public Investment Fund, Public Pension Authority and General Organization for Social Insurance – as the founding shareholders, accounting for 30 percent of the bank's share capital (Rehman 2010). For several terms until 2019, the chairperson of the Board of Directors of Alinma, who was also the CEO (chief executive officer), was the late Abdelaziz al-Zamil. The first

---

[31] Of this, Saudi Arabia accounted for 20.2 percent, UAE 9.8 percent, Kuwait 6.3 percent, Qatar 6.2 percent, Oman 0.7 percent and Bahrain 0.7 percent (IFSB 2019, 12).

[32] In Qatar, the combined assets of the five fully Islamic banks increased from less than $1 bill. in 1990 to more than $30 bill. in 2008 (Tabash and Dhankar 2014, 54). According to another source, Islamic bank assets in Qatar grew 29 percent between 2009 and 2013, in the wake of the 2008 financial crisis (Ibrahim 2016, 64).

CEO of SABIC (Saudi Basic Industries Corporation) (1976–83) and a former Minister of Industry and Electricity (1983–95), he was from one of the most prominent, highly diversified business conglomerates, the Zamil Group Holding Company, in the kingdom.[33] Thus, ruling elites now enjoy more of a personal stake in the sector, as they and their (affluent) allies collaborate ever more closely and stand to reap far greater profits than before.

In this regard, it is worth noting that the chair of the Board of Directors in three of the four Qatari Islamic banks is an Al-Thani, and at least one-quarter of board members are Al-Thanis, as well; this has been the case from the opening of the banks until today (August 2023). In Oman, the Alizz Bank was chaired, from its opening in 2012 until 2016, by Taimur bin Asad bin Tariq bin Taimur. An Al BuSa'id, his father, Asad, was the late Sultan Qaboos' first cousin and personal representative; since 2000, he has also been the CEO of the highly capitalized, Asad Investment Company (Kamrava et al. 2016, 6). Bank Nizwa, the first Islamic bank in Oman, has an Al BuSa'id as a board member and until now (August 2023), it has been chaired by an al-Khalili, one of the renowned families of the sultanate.[34]

As for Kuwait, members of the Al Sabah hardly figure on the boards of directors; this may be an implicit concession to the business elite or a reflection of royals' more or less discrete involvement in business, as compared to other Gulf royal families. Indeed, it is only at the International Bank of Kuwait (IBK) that the board is chaired by an Al-Sabah. Nonetheless, the boards of Kuwaiti Islamic banks provide a who's who of the country's prominent business families: among them, al-Fulaij, al-Ghanim, al-Kharafi, al-Marzouq and al-Saqer. It is especially noteworthy that two members of the (Shi'a) Bukhamseen family, representing the new merchant elite, and one member of the (Shi'a) al-Wazzan family, representing the old merchant elite, are members of the Board of Directors of the IBK.[35] In Saudi Arabia, two of the four fully Islamic Saudi banks have been chaired by members of most prominent Saudi business families – al-Rajhi and until 2019, al-Zamil. As for the Middle

---

[33] See Hanieh (2018, 63–111) for rich detail on business conglomerates in GCC states and their interface with royal families.
[34] The bin Ali and bin Salim branches of the al-Khalili are prominent in finance and business, and hail from Bowsher in the Muscat Governorate. See the family conglomerates, Al-Taher Group and Al-Khalili Group. The Grand Mufti, the highest Islamic authority of Oman, Ahmad bin Hamad al-Khalili, is not a relative despite the patronym. He is from the Bani Rawahah tribe, from Bahla in the interior, the territory of the former Ibaḍi Imamate.
[35] See Chapter 6, pp. 129–30.

East's largest transnational Islamic bank, Al Baraka Banking Group (licensed in Bahrain), its founder and former chair was the late Salah Abdullah Kamel, Saudi billionaire businessman and founder of the massive holding company Dallah Al Baraka Group. Despite being from a prominent Meccan family with close ties to the Al Saʿud, he, like Mohamed bin Faisal, was unable to secure a banking license in the kingdom.[36]

Given the high stakes, it is not surprising that invested members of royal families, alongside well-heeled business families, function in this sector as a powerful, albeit informal financial lobby. As major shareholders, they have become, according to a former member of shariʿa boards in Saudi Islamic banks: "V.I.P.s whose interests and concerns have been given much consideration" in various aspects of the functioning of the sector.[37] To elaborate, this interviewee explained that in Saudi Arabia, Islamic banks collect zakat from their biggest shareholders and transfer the funds on their behalf to the authorities. However, to appease wealthy shareholders for whom 2.5 percent of their capital gains amounts to a lot of money, a decision was made that if the bank purchased government bonds, the cost of those bonds could be deducted from the requisite zakat to be paid. While this modification no doubt suited shareholders, buying a conventional government bond is considered *ḥarām* (unless it is of the *musharaka* sort).[38] Again, as noted in Chapter 6 with regard to the imposition of zakat on companies in Kuwait, a religious edict designed to promote equity and assist those in need was tweaked to benefit the rich and indulge their avarice.[39]

In their capacity as unconstituted lobbyists, the preference of what Adam Hanieh (2018, 63–111) aptly describes as a peculiarly interlocked, public-private elite is, no doubt, for an unencumbered financial sector. Hence, the IBF sector in Gulf monarchies has been given free rein more or less. AAOIFI guidelines are neither imposed, nor generally adopted because they are yet another level of regulation that constrains operations, behaviors and outcomes. Central banks do not favor the guidelines since imposing them would complicate their tasks and responsibilities, and clients do not demand them since they are either satisfied with or indifferent to the degree of authenticity (or, shariʿa-compliance) of banking operations and products (al-Ajmi et al. 2009; al-Mutairi and al-Hunnayan 2016; Tobin 2016, 161–72). Unbounded,

---

[36] In November 2017, Salah Kamel was arrested in Saudi Arabia in the alleged corruption crackdown conducted at the behest of Crown Prince Mohamad bin Salman.
[37] Riyadh, 5 April 2012. [38] Ibid. [39] Chapter 6, pp. **133–34**.

shari'a scholars sitting on multiple boards can issue their pronouncements and get paid handsomely.[40] What's more, the variety of pronouncements from one shari'a board to another and the diversity of products that result encourage business competition among Islamic banks in this environment described to me by one of the most prominent living scholars of Islam as *"le capitalisme sauvage."*[41]

While it is difficult to ascertain how much shari'a board members are paid for their services, Grassa and Matoussi (2014, 359–60) claim that the average per bank fee in GCC states from 2002 to 2011 was US $216,000 – ranging from a low of $19,600 to a high of $732,000. Hayat et al. (2013, 609) estimated the annual income during that same period for each of the top three shari'a scholars in the world – those who then occupied between seventy-one and eighty-five board positions (Nizam Yacoubi, Bahrain; Abd al-Sattar Abu Ghudda, Syria; and Mohamed Ali Elgari, Saudi Arabia) – at about US$4.5 million. To be sure, there are spectacular sums to be made in this industry.[42] Given both the opportunities they face in terms of their own personal enrichment and their (related) preferences regarding governance and regulation, shari'a board members themselves should be considered a part of the implicit, unconstituted financial lobby.[43] This is so even though their collaborations with the other segments of the lobby are rather virtual, and they veil their greed with religiosity. In sum, governance of the sector has been structured until now in such a way that all those who are invested in IBF – the bankers, their board members, shareholders and clients, as well as religious scholars – are appeased, and everyone is free to engage with the sector and accumulate.

---

[40] Consider the case of the late Abd al-Sattar Abu Ghudda: According to data collected in 2010 (Funds@Work 2010), Abu Ghudda was then the highest ranking shari'a scholar in the world in terms of the number of board positions he held in standard setting bodies (like AAOIFI). He was the second highest ranking in terms of the number of positions, amounting to a remarkable eighty-five, which he held on shari'a supervisory boards of banks and other financial institutions. In August 2019, according to the Islamic Markets website (www.islamicmarkets.com), he held positions on a total of fifty-six shari'a boards in the world, of which all but fourteen were in the Middle East and at least thirty were in GCC states.

[41] Jeddah, 19 April 2012.

[42] Furthermore, the market for financial *halal* certification is highly concentrated: According to Hayat et al. (2013, 604), at the end of 2011, the top twenty shari'a scholars (in terms of board positions) – equivalent to 5 percent of the total number – held 54 percent of the market, while the top three captured a remarkable 21 percent. Moreover, the average cost of *"halal* certifying" a financial product was estimated at $122,000 in 2011, while the requisite "monitoring" of that product cost an additional $34,000 each subsequent year (Hayat et al. 2013, 604–5).

[43] Monzer Kahf (2004) refers to a "power alliance" between the moneyed elite and shari'a scholars through IBF.

There are, of course, religious scholars in the region who object to how IBF is conducted, insisting that certain products like *murabaḥa* and *ijāra* are unacceptable according to Islam, that *ribaʾ* features in transactions but under another name and that weak assurance mechanisms allow for inappropriate behaviors that are considered *harām*. There are, as well, those who assert the need for a single, autonomous organization of shariʿa scholars, de-linked from power centers or financial institutions, to both advise and oversee Islamic banks.[44] However, since the sector has witnessed such important growth both globally and regionally and includes the engagement of Gulf royals as private actors (often in collaboration with private business associates), these religious scholars must be restrained in their criticism. As noted in Chapter 4, pushback from (non-establishment) religious forces has been significant at times; it has been met with repression even when combined with concessions.[45]

Substance, or the Conformity of the Practice with Its Alleged Purposes

Instrumentality: The Matter of Controversial Tools

It is interesting to note that despite the practically universal criticism by proponents of Islamic banking and finance (IBF) of debt-based/interest-based financing practiced by conventional banks and despite the availability in Islamic financial markets of several asset-based, profit and loss sharing (PLS) instruments – for example, *mudaraba* and *mushāraka* – debt-based, non-PLS instruments are far more common both globally and in the Gulf states (Asutay 2012, 103; Tripp 2006, 142–43). *Murabaḥa* and related types of "mark-up" financing or "cost-plus" sales have become increasingly popular over time, even though they are considered to be weakly Islamic. This is the case since mark-up can be understood as "interest," the financier's real ownership of the commodity is, at best, temporary, and there is no true risk-sharing in the

---

[44] Interviews with: senior researcher, Islamic Development Bank, Jeddah, 16 April 2012; prominent scholar of Islam, Jeddah, 19 April 2012; former dean of Shariʿa College, Qatar University, Doha, 22 Nov. 2013.
[45] Note the case of Hamza al-Salem, a Saudi religious scholar, economist and prominent critic of Islamic banking and finance. A heated debate on IBF between himself and Sheikh Ali Qara Daghi – which he referred to as "Juha Financing and the Lie of Sukūk" – could be viewed on YouTube from 2011 to 2021. Al-Salem was arrested in 2021 allegedly for his writings objecting to some of the economic dimensions of Saudi Vision 2030. "Saudi Academic Hamzah al-Salem's Fate Still Unknown after Forcible Disappearance Six Months Ago," *Saudi Leaks*, 25 April 2021. https://saudileaks.org/en/al-salem-2.

arrangement. In fact, these latter instruments dominate Islamic financial operations, not only for individuals and businesses but for projects initiated by governments and state-owned companies, as well (Wilson 2009, 20–1). For Al-Rajhi (Saudi Arabia) and the Kuwait Finance House, the largest and third largest Islamic banks in the region and globally in terms of their asset base (+US$125 bill. and +US$70 bill., respectively) in 2020,[46] *murabaha*-type instruments have been and remain their favored methods of financing.[47]

Defenders of *murabaha* arrangements explain their pervasiveness by stating that they are the simplest of IBF instruments and most similar to those utilized in conventional banking.[48] Moreover, for those intent upon unfettered personal gain, they avoid the disconcerting features of PLS contracts such as *musharaka* and *mudaraba*: among them, fluctuating returns, unpredictable losses and loan repayments via a share of profits rather than a fixed sum (Tripp 2006, 142–43).[49] Hence, concerns regarding the suitability of the instrument and confidence in the outcome of associated transactions appear to emanate from a basic preoccupation with "market share"; and these are at the source of the manifest popularity of what are, in principal, the more controversial contracts within the sector.

There is no doubt, then, that financial institutions and their clients are willing to forego a degree of "Islamic authenticity" for the sake of greater conformity, certainty and the expectation of superior returns. Likewise, the various justifications for otherwise dubious instruments confirm the claim that both unencumbered enrichment and "frictionless integration with the global financial system" are indeed the priorities of the Islamic finance sector and its adherents, rather than the institutionalization of an ethical alternative to advanced capitalism (Rethel 2011, 89) or even, simply, the conduct of business Islamically.

Institutional Transparency and the Matter of Compliance

As noted, transparency within the IBF sector has been deficient insofar as strict regulatory and supervisory mechanisms, external to and

---

[46] "Largest Islamic Banks 2021," *The Asian Banker*. www.theasianbanker.com/ab500/rankings/largest-islamic-banks.
[47] Khan (2010, 810–12) notes that the Islamic Development Bank that finances approved projects via interest-free loans, engages mostly in non-PLS activities, too.
[48] Interview with a former banker and current advisor on IBF to governments and institutions, New Jersey, 26 April 2018.
[49] It has also been said that the fees attached to these PLS contracts may in fact make them more expensive for the client than conventional ones (Khan 2010, 814).

independent of the institutions themselves, have for the most part been lacking.[50] This suggests that there could be no assurances regarding the shariʿa compliance of institutions in terms of their operations and the reporting of their true profits. Indeed, one of my interlocutors, a former shariʿa board member of two prominent Islamic banks in Saudi Arabia, pointed out that while the board is meant to review the bank's investment strategy as outlined by the executive committee, it tends to review only parts of the strategy, selected randomly. Board scholars are not inclined to examine meticulously every step in the operations undertaken by the financial institution or question the accuracy in reporting by banks that, after all, had hired them and pay their salaries. Given the spare oversight, cheating can occur.[51] This, no doubt, could have a negative impact on clients who, via one or another participatory arrangement – *mudaraba* or *mushāraka*, for example – have contracted to share in the profits of the financial institution. And while Islamic finance enthusiasts may insist that under-reporting does not occur because the profitability of the fund or business venture is known to both parties,[52] it is nevertheless the case that within the partnership, the agent – in this case, the financial institution – tends to have superior information (Iqbal and Llewellyn 2015, 12).

Be that as it may, studies indicate that such details appear to be of minor concern to those who patronize Islamic financial institutions. This is because patrons may be satisfied with the declared ethical orientation of the institution and its identification as "Islamic," while the minutia of its practices are irrelevant to them. Alternatively, they may have chosen to conduct their business there for reasons unrelated to shariʿa compliance (al-Ajmi et al. 2009; Pepinsky 2013; al-Mutairi and al-Hunnayan 2016). Still others, as Tobin (2016) found in Jordan, may be very critical of these institutions but continue to conduct their banking there "out of a sense of religious duty" (162). Furthermore, the state is not concerned about weak institutional transparency. Indeed, it has delegated governance of IBF to employees of the sector – (hired) experts in religion. For all intents and purposes, the state has prioritized consumption, material enrichment and social management.

---

[50] In Qatar, for example, and according to a shariʿa scholar based there, shariʿa audits were carried out irregularly at best and almost exclusively at the behest of the bank management itself. Interview: Doha, 5 March 2012.
[51] Interview with economist and shariʿa board member, Riyadh, 5 April 2012.
[52] Interview with a former banker and current advisor on IBF to governments and institutions, New Jersey, 7 June 2018.

Pursuing Maṣlaḥa: Consumption vs. Production, Accumulation vs. Redistribution

The growth in personal debt is said to be unremitting in Gulf monarchies. When not driven by need, this is certainly problematic from the Islamic perspective because it may reflect a lack of self-reliance, a desire for immediate gratification and little forethought. In fact, Islamic banks are routinely criticized for encouraging consumption and consumer indebtedness (Wilson 2009, 30; Rethel 2013, 129–30). Not only have they become especially active in the financing of real estate and consumer durables, but also, they aggressively market retail financial products and consumption loans via, for example, Islamic credit cards (Wilson 2012, 141).

When I asked an officer of an Islamic financial institution in the Gulf how he explains this propensity to encourage personal debt, he responded thus: "It's very simple: financial institutions profit more from putting people in debt than they do from urging them to save."[53] Needless to say, the practices of Islamic financial institutions both conform to and reproduce the environment within which they operate; and to quote an economist at the Islamic Development Bank (IDB), "the environment [in GCC states] does not encourage ethical behavior."[54] As Lena Rethel (2013) has argued with reference to Malaysia, Islamic banking does not represent "a genuine alternative or site of resistance" to capitalist development. Rather, it reproduces notions of capitalist development and "further entrench(es) the market state" (133).

Moreover, the vast wealth associated with IBF in the Gulf is not necessarily directed toward productive activities that foster development.[55] Rather, it has tended to circulate among the affluent at home who, as noted earlier, prefer short-term financing and investments in real estate (and other consumer durables) since they realize immediate returns in terms of monetary reward and/or personal gratification (Asutay 2012, 104–8). Furthermore, asset-backed transactions, which are meant to contribute to productivity by providing value-added, do not, in fact, achieve this purpose since the commodities introduced "have no value and do not promote development."[56] And more often than not, they remain in the possession of the financial institution only very briefly, if at all. Hence, Islamic banks' direct role in fostering growth, generating

---

[53] Ibid.   [54] Interview: Jeddah, 18 April 2012.
[55] Estimates of the Islamic banking assets of the six GCC states combined in 2021 were US $1.2 trillion, representing about 55 percent of the global total of $2.1 trillion. The Middle East and South Asia (combined) followed with US$477 bill. (IFSB 2022, 17).
[56] Interview with economist at the IDB, Jeddah, 18 April 2012.

jobs and stimulating local economies has been minimal, at best (Aksak and Asutay 2015, section 5.2; Rehman 2010, 121). However, as the economist I interviewed at the Islamic Development Bank noted, "if you criticize the Islamic banks for this, they respond: 'We are for profit; we cannot take care of the country!'"[57]

Given that Islamic banks encourage and profit from the predilection for consumption while their direct contributions to advancing growth and development are modest, does this negatively impact the efficacy of the Islamic finance sector? It does insofar as the conformity of the sector's practices with its alleged objectives is concerned. To be sure, many have criticized these institutions (and their governance structures) for having distanced themselves from the substance of Islam, the *maqāṣid* or purposes of the shariʿa, for an exclusive focus on its form – that is, *fiqh* (jurisprudence) and its *ḥukm* (*aḥkām*) or rules. In essence, as Zaman and Asutay (2009, 89) indicate, Islamic banks reveal "a mere technical process without a value system." In short, therefore, they may struggle to follow the letter of the shariʿa, but neither its matter nor its spirit. Reflecting the environment in which they operate, these banks are driven far more by pressures of the capitalist market and the acquisitive spirit than they are by precepts of the Islamic social and moral economy. Yet, like their rulers, they manipulate those precepts to advance their mundane interests. In the words of one of the most prominent living *ʿālim*: "It's not simply that Islamic banks are not interested in the poor, but they exploit people and exploit Islam for the sake of amassing wealth. They take advantage of Muslims' attachment to their religion so as to get them to put their money in their banks. The banks profit, but they do not distribute their gains justly."[58]

Indeed, the vast wealth associated with IBF in GCC states tends not to reach the needy in Muslim societies. Typically, it is not directed toward redistributive activities that alleviate hardship by, for example, extending micro-financing, creating employment opportunities or engaging in other socially responsible practices. As a Kuwaiti politician and former employee of an Islamic bank explained to me, "Islamic banks do not feel that it is their responsibility to encourage productivity or to offer channels to help people find work. As far as they are concerned, that is the

---

[57] Ibid. For confirmation, see fn. 59.
[58] Jeddah, 19 April 2012. See, as well, the following statement by a businessman and prominent economic analyst: "When Islamic banking started, many thought this was the way to heaven; there would be no guilt regarding the taking of *ribaʾ* ... But, with the built-in interest rate that tends to be even higher than in conventional banking, many people have come to realize that even Islamic banking is about power, money, and greed" (Kuwait City, 10 May 2012).

responsibility of the government."[59] Furthermore, Islamic financial institutions tend to be highly selective about the projects and partnerships they assume, at times incurring considerable upfront costs on feasibility studies to be assured in advance of the profitability of the proposed venture (Souaiaia 2014, 48). As for micro-finance, one could argue that it is unnecessary for the (relatively affluent) citizen population of Kuwait, Qatar and the UAE, but it would indeed be appropriate in Oman and Saudi Arabia and among the Bahraini Shiʻa, where poverty is not uncommon.[60] Alas, when I asked a prominent shariʻa scholar who chairs several shariʻa boards in Qatar about micro-financing, he laughed derisively and said, "this may be a good initiative for governments, but not for shareholders. We need to be pragmatic, and shareholders want to make money … We are, after all, commercial entities."[61]

Interestingly, shariʻa-compliant insurance, better known as *takāful*, has been growing steadily throughout the region in recent years. It has been booming in Saudi Arabia where in 2021 it was said to account for 100 percent of the insurance sector, in contrast to the rest of the GCC where its importance ranged from as little as 8 percent in Qatar to 40 percent in Kuwait (IFSB 2022, 46). Based on asset size, Saudi Arabia has remained the top market for *takāful* in the region (Alpen Capital 2022, 13). In fact, *takāful* and its variant, *micro-takāful*, serve as the core instruments of the so-called Kafala program – not to be confused with the sponsorship arrangements for foreign workers, discussed in Chapter 5. Implemented by the Saudi Industrial Development Fund in 2004, the program is meant to encourage financial institutions to extend small loans to small and medium enterprises and thereby encourage productivity and diversification while providing employment opportunities. The *takāful* provision in this program guarantees to the lending

---

[59] Kuwait City, 11 May 2012. Consider, as well, the words of a prominent senior researcher at the IDB in Jeddah (16 April 2012): "People's deposits in banks are public money and so, that money should be used to improve people's lives. Banks should invest those deposits in ways that promote greater justice. One way to do that is for the bank to enhance employment opportunities for need fulfillment. Since the bank takes resources from a large number of depositors, they should be redistributing to as many people as possible and doing things that would help as many people as possible. Hence, spending deposits on importing food or educational materials is a good thing, but spending them on importing a yacht for a rich person is not a good thing." He added that, "in the Gulf states, Islamic banks do not get involved in job creation; they have no vision."

[60] Recall *Bab Rizq Jameel* (Beautiful Gateway to Prosperity), the micro-credit program that is part of the CSR activity of the Abdelatif Jameel Group in Saudi Arabia, discussed in Chapter 6 (pp. 136–37). Although outside the "shariʻa-compliant" framework, this initiative is quite unique in the Gulf.

[61] Interview, Doha, 4 March 2012.

institutions that the government will cover part of the risk they incur in the event of loss, via default (Ahmed 2016, 5). Remarkably, this suggests that for Islamic financial institutions to contribute actively to social welfare, they require, at the very least, government backing so that their good works (ṣāliḥāt) remain cost-free to them.[62]

As for engagement in Corporate Social Responsibility (CSR), a model that appears to cohere with the notion of a "moral economy" and its underlying encouragement of both productive activity and social solidarity,[63] Islamic banks in the Gulf seem, for the most part, to have been weakly invested in such practices, as suggested by their reporting disclosures (Habbash 2016; Platonova et al. 2018). In addition, as pointed out by a Kuwaiti parliamentarian and former banker, not only is CSR fairly insignificant in the emirate, but also, "there is not a single entity here that tells us how it spends its money or how much of its earnings goes to the community."[64] No doubt there are exceptions. The Kuwait Finance House, for example, was singled out from among peer institutions in the Gulf in the early 2000s for its relatively important participation in social and philanthropic projects (Rashid and Hassan 2014) before it became engulfed in corruption scandals in later years. And all licensed banks in Oman, including the newly created Islamic banks, have been encouraged since 2013 to extend preferential assistance to small and medium enterprises (SMEs) in an effort to promote economic diversification; this is said to have had a positive effect on the sector (Almaimani and Johari 2015). Be that as it may, an examination of the practices, procedures and legal framework of the Islamic banking and finance sector attests to an ambivalent commitment to the foundations of an Islamic moral economy.

---

[62] In Saudi Arabia in 2008, I was told the following anecdote about a particular Islamic bank and the true intentions of "good works": "The ... Bank had announced on the eve of ʿeid al-adha (the Feast of Sacrifice) that instead of paying 650 SR for a sheep to slaughter, we (Saudis) could give the bank 350 SR and they would buy and slaughter a sheep in Bangladesh or Sudan, where sheep are cheaper and Muslims are poor, and distribute the meat there. Soon after, we learned that in those countries, a sheep costs much less than 350 SR - rather, closer to 200 SR. And so, the bank would have made a colossal profit. The initiative became a huge scandal, one that exposed how Islam has become a tool for making a lot of money" (emphasis my own). Interview with prominent Saudi businessperson, Al-Khobar, 13 April 2008.

[63] The principle behind CSR is that businesses have a responsibility to do what is best not only for their companies, but also for society at large. Indeed, they are expected to contribute to sustainable development and quality of life through initiatives that deliver economic, social and environmental benefits.

[64] Interview, Kuwait City, 11 May 2012.

Conclusion

The discussion of various elements of the form and substance of Islamic banking and finance (IBF) in Gulf monarchies confirms the findings of other scholars: The practice of IBF is detached from Islamic principles of promoting the common good and justice in distribution, and encouraging production over consumption. In effect, it shares goals of conventional finance related to profit maximization for the owners of capital and to deep integration in global capitalism and international finance.[65] However, it masks those mundane goals with the Islamization of language and structures, the fiction of an Islamic financial system. It is, indeed, a form of manipulation (Kuran 2004, El-Gamal 2006).[66]

Beyond that, Islamic finance has been incorporated into the ruler's project of community, nation and state. It has become a means for Gulf autocracies to appease their restive populations – among them, those who covet more, those who resent royal greed and those who favor a greater role for Islam in daily life – and gain their compliance. Furthermore, it has provided yet another way for these regimes to encourage consumption and enrichment while reinforcing, indeed refining the contours of the community of privilege and the particular hierarchy within it. Through IBF, regimes both endorse and stimulate the material interests of a local (and increasingly important) financial lobby: one that includes royals and their closest associates in the business and religious establishments. Thus, accumulation and social management go hand in hand; these are the true intentions. As with the other institutionalized practices discussed in this book, Islamic banking and finance represent both the coupling and instrumentalization of (oil) wealth and Islamic doctrine for the purpose of social control, and thus, the ongoing political domination and material enrichment of ruling elites.

---

[65] On a panel entitled, "How Ethical Is the Current Islamic Banking System?" (Center for Islamic Legislation and Ethics, Hamed bin Khalifa University, Doha, Qatar, 6 Dec. 2014), Mohamed Fadel points out that privately owned Islamic banks, like all privately owned businesses, are expected to make profits; that is part of their raison d'être. However, in an Islamic financial system, there must be banks that are not privately owned and therefore, are not-for-profit. www.youtube.com/watch?v=qkgJg7BEjQs&feature=youtube_gdata.

[66] El-Gamal (2006) insists that not only is IBF indistinguishable from conventional banking and finance but it is "Shari'a arbitrage" that makes it Islamic. IBF is all about finding a term in classical Arabic for "the Islamic analogy product" and using it so as to "justify and lend credibility to the Islamic brand name" (175–89).

8 Reflections on Islam and Politics in the Oil Era

> Through the many forms it came to assume, oil wealth fueled the state's sense of power over history while it undermined the moral trenches created to channel it to collective historical ends.
> Fernando Coronil, "Crude Matters: Seizing the Venezuelan Petrostate in Times of Chavez," 288

Just as redistribution is a fundamental norm within the Islamic tradition and a principal task of rentier states, Gulf monarchies assert their attachment to the faith and channel oil revenues to their citizens. That contemporary practices related to wealth circulation and resource allocation diverge from the teachings of a previously formed doctrine is neither surprising nor unusual. In these states as elsewhere, the structure of the domestic political economy outweighs all other factors in shaping policies and practices. Furthermore, as Maxime Rodinson (1978) explains,

the state power is, as a rule, in the hands of the property owners and the rich, and normally tends to favour them. Wealth makes possible a degree of luxury that, no less normally, prompts a lax attitude towards morality and the precepts of religion. The ruling authority usually tends to take steps, sometimes immoral and sometimes contrary to the religious law, with a view to strengthening itself and increasing the wealth of those who wield power.

This is "deplorably commonplace in human history. Islam offers no originality in this regard" (72). Over the course of Islamic history, as noted in Chapter 2, particular concepts, principles or practices were sidelined or watered down when doing so was deemed by power-holders to be politically expedient or otherwise appropriate. Hence, it follows that since the formation of national states in the Gulf, the religious tradition has been made to conform with the ruler's priorities. Typically, belief systems are subordinate to the pursuit of power. Nonetheless, they can be invoked "as a cloak for secular political ends" (Rodinson 1978, 207).

Distribution in the Gulf monarchies is a function of the relationship between the prevailing political structure, characterized by autocratic rule by a single, narrow group, and the economic structure of rentierism whereby vast revenues accrue to the state/ruling family from external sources. The combination of autocracy with behaviors and sentiments assumed to be fostered by rentierism and vast wealth – such things as rampant consumption, profligacy, complacency and entitlement – in an environment of advanced capitalism encourages "private interest" (*maṣlaḥa khaṣṣa*) and pushes to the sidelines an ethical code of conduct, be it religious or secular.[1] While in the Gulf monarchies, capitalist values and related notions of class, of hierarchy in the international system and inequality in domestic political economies have eclipsed whatever may have endured of the moral order defined by the teachings of Islam, the discourse of Islam nonetheless persists. It persists, in some measure, as insistence upon a distinctive primordial affiliation, but also as ritualized discourse. When touted by ruling elites, the discourse (and associated practices) may provide a veneer of authenticity or originality. However, it also functions as a form of manipulation for the purpose of securing objectives that have little if anything to do with religiosity or the normative tradition. To deter Saudi citizens from going into the streets in spring 2011, the Grand Mufti, Sheikh ʿAbd al-ʿAziz Al Sheikh, said the following, on behalf of King Abdullah: "Islam strictly prohibits protests in the kingdom because the ruler here rules by God's will."[2] Thus, the religious tradition is instrumentalized by ruling elites in their pursuit of regime goals. In this context, it should not be at all surprising that self-serving, politicized interpretations of the tradition may prevail. Be that as it may, that rulers invoke Islam (as belief system) in multiple ways, both discursively and practically, while their distributive practices appear impervious to restraints provided by religious doctrine or juridical interpretations, suggests peculiarities of the modern state in Gulf petro-monarchies.

In considering connections between oil revenues and Islamic norms, my purpose in conducting this study has been twofold: first, to uncover and examine some of the ways in which the two preeminent resources – one material, the other ideational – are instrumentalized by ruling elites to advance their interests; second, on the basis of my findings, to offer insights about distinctive features of politics in Gulf monarchies. Both oil rents and Islamic norms are, along with (the threat of) repression, important tools of governance. I refer to a ruling strategy, described as the intertwined instrumentalization of oil revenues – a shorthand for

---

[1] In a chapter entitled "Prayer and Shopping" in his memoir of the pilgrimage, Hammoudi (2005/2006, 74) writes: "Each time goods or services were distributed, each time a goal had to be reached, the religion of Me, Me first, Me before everyone else pushed Islam to the edge."

[2] Caryle Murphy, "Heavy Police Presence Deters Protesters in Saudi Arabia" reported by Agence France Presse, 11 March 2011. https://theworld.org/stories/2011-03-11/heavy-police-presence-deters-protesters-saudi-arabia.

revenues that accrue to states from both their hydrocarbon exports and from returns on their international investments (made possible, at the outset, from oil rents) – and Islamic doctrine (or its interpretations). Both are leveraged and repurposed, at times independently but often jointly, and intertwined in ways that allow ruling elites to redouble their management and control over society and advance their agenda. And I note that, in the process, Islamic norms may in fact be reconfigured, or their interpretation refined, so that through their instrumentalization, they could contribute more effectively to ruling priorities. Via a detailed examination of four government-sponsored institutionalized practices, associated with welfare and development, I have demonstrated some of those ways. The end goal of this ruling strategy, I argue, is to strengthen and protect these dynastic autocracies and specifically, their (more or less) absolute monopoly of power and wealth accumulation.

Of the four institutionalized practices, two have been made possible by – in fact they are distinct features of – the "extreme rent wealth" of Gulf regimes:[3] the governments' decades-long, massive distributions of goods and services, described in Chapter 3, and the employment of imported labor (Chapter 5), which has constituted well over half the labor force in each country since the mid-1980s and as much as 80–95 percent in Kuwait, Qatar and the UAE. The other two practices, charitable giving and Islamic banking and finance, are explicitly linked to Islam as belief system; they are meant to demonstrate, if not adherence to its teachings, however understood, then at least affiliation with the religious tradition.

While government distributions and the employment of foreign labor may have the most discernable effects on political and economic outcomes in Gulf monarchies, all four institutionalized practices fit neatly within the strategy to advance ruling priorities. The former have much to do with the project of community, nation and state: building the country, shaping and defining community, creating the nation and clarifying subjects' relationship to the state while reinforcing royal power and authority. With consumption as a veritable organizing principle, variable access to resources is a means to include some while excluding others, and exclude some even more than others, thereby creating hierarchies of relative privilege. In the process, community is delineated as those who, recognized (by the state) as belonging, are thus privileged relative to "outsiders" – that is, non-citizen residents and imported labor – and so, constitute the nation. In this context, social categories such as *umma* and *musta'mān* have little meaning. When invoked, they are a form of

---

[3] Herb (2017, 17) makes this observation with regard to the importation of foreign labor.

manipulation: to encourage national cohesion while fetishizing the normative tradition in the absence of adherence to its values. Furthermore, the government's development programs and lavish allocations of free or heavily subsidized goods and services ensure society's dependence on the state and that, along with the threat of coercion, enforces submission. The tiering of access to resources via government distributions (universal, selective, idiosyncratic), as well as the importation of labor and the associated *kafāla* system, are not only integral to the shaping of national community. They are also a means for the state to better manage and control society in that key social categories are appeased via the relative marginalization of others. Insofar as the organization of foreign labor is concerned, recall that maintaining the citizen's relative entitlement is an implicit regime goal for it is a means to placate the citizen vis-à-vis the overwhelming power of the state and its ruling elites. After all, the citizen is not merely a dependent subject but ultimately, the principal threat to state power.

The other two institutionalized practices, charitable giving and Islamic banking and finance, are also closely connected to shaping community and nation and consolidating state power by advancing the ruler's priorities. In both, oil rents and Islamic doctrine are deployed in ways that bolster the ruler's capacity to manage and control society so as to privilege the royal family's political and economic interests. In the discussion of charitable giving, I described ways in which ruling elites, in Qatar and Saudi Arabia especially, insert themselves in this domain, either in their capacity as royals or as if they were private agents.[4] In doing so, they gain political capital in the form of, for example, recognition for themselves and the ruler's agenda, or information about society. But I also proposed that when the state intervenes by stipulating how and/or to whom entities may (or may not) give, sometimes going so far as to modify a religious edict – as when the Kuwaiti state reduced the zakat obligation of businesses from 2.5 percent to 1 percent, or when the Saudi state enticed Islamic banks to purchase government bonds by allowing their shareholders' zakat obligation to be reduced by the price of the bond – it aims thereby to appease a particular, (no doubt, privileged) social category by affirming its material interests and facilitating its capacity to accumulate.

In the Islamic banking and finance (IBF) sector, the watering down of religious principles and practice for the sake of material gain is especially noteworthy. Not only are several of the associated financial tools and

---

[4] As noted in Chapter 6, Kuwaiti and Omani royals tend not to be active in charitable organizations for particular, context-driven reasons. See pp. 163–64 and pp. 155–56, respectively.

banking procedures weakly Islamic, but also, efforts at oversight and regulation of the sector are mitigated by the overriding concern, even on the part of shariʿa scholars on shariʿa boards, for accumulation without constraints. And while I noted, in the charity domain, the blurring of the distinction between public and private in the person of a royal as donor and/or their use of funds for charitable works, I described a different sort of but equally consequential public-private phenomenon in the IBF sector. There, ruling elites collaborate ever more closely with private sector business elites as founding sponsors, chief administrators and major shareholders of local Islamic financial institutions. Together with shariʿa board members, they accumulate, and they lobby for practices and procedures that promote their shared interests. Thus, there is a peculiar mixing, under the banner of Islam, of public and private, of governance (of the state and the Islamic banking sector) and accumulation. Through IBF, Gulf regimes exploit both oil revenues and the religious tradition not only as tools for consumption and enrichment but also to co-opt particular social forces and refine and reinforce the community of privilege while asserting their own religious credentials.

What, though, do these findings suggest about politics in the Gulf? Autocracy in Gulf monarchies is, in part, a product of the particular ways in which royal families exploit a religious narrative to promote their ambitions. Ruling interests relate to political stability, conceived as rulers' undisturbed power and control over society, which is in turn dependent upon uninterrupted revenue flows, coercion as a credible threat, foreign support and society's acquiescence to their rule. As the royal family's right to rule is, to varying degrees, intrinsically weak, it is fabricated, and in ways that both instrumentalize and interconnect Islam and oil: first, through uniforming (religious) rhetoric – a kind of ruling ideology[5] – and the flaunting of Islamic credentials; second, through a politics of oil-financed distribution and development that on the one hand, enforces society's dependence on the state and on the other hand, parades ruling elites as agents of modernity and the wellspring of progress.

It is not simply that the state uses hydrocarbon wealth to buy allegiance, as the rentier state literature has repeated *ad nauseum*. More pernicious is the smothering, numbing effect of hyper-materialism and rampant consumption, introduced by the Europeans/Americans and

---

[5] Although relatively weak in Kuwait, the ruling ideology combines a nationalist narrative with what could have been described (until recently) as hegemonic Wahhabism in Saudi Arabia, gentle Wahhabism (with a Muslim Brotherhood inflection) in Qatar and Oman's version of universal, or "desectarian" Islam.

encouraged by the example of the ruler alongside his development projects and distribution schemes. They offer appeasement, foster submission, and thereby facilitate social control. Furthermore, the model provided is one of greed but also selective indifference. Having assumed the vast national wealth for himself, to exploit as he chooses, the ruler is insouciant to inequities.[6] Following that model of behavior, the subject submits to commodity fetishism and to the ruler, purveyor of goods. They too disregard that which could disturb their comfort. (And the foreigner who has arrived to work – not so different, perhaps, from the *musta'amin* of yore – has instead become *mustaghal* (exploited).) Indeed, privilege depends upon hierarchy and exclusion. In this environment, therefore, community is not the *umma*, the de-territorialized community of believing Muslims and the protected non-Muslim residents. Rather, it is confined to those recognized by the state as linked to the ruler and his domain through parochial networks of privilege. As for the foreigner, they are, in fact, integral to the fashioning of the nation and, beyond that, a new moral order. They reflect the interests of rulers to contain, circumscribe and consolidate privilege; concentrate power and wealth; and intensify social control.

In the process of numbing and the associated submission, the meaning of *ḥaqq*, discussed in Chapter 2, has been reinterpreted. While it connotes in the normative tradition the right or entitlement of the needy to part of the wealth of those who have excess, it has become, in the contemporary period of oil-driven, externally supported dynastic authoritarianism and abundance, the *ḥaqq* of the ruler to overlook the moral dimension of his responsibilities as custodian of the common wealth, and instead assume the role of sole proprietor who distributes as he chooses, at least in part to enforce domination. It also signifies the *ḥaqq* of the privileged to have more, take more, expect more and overlook those who have less. This reinterpretation underpins the hierarchization of state and society in the Gulf monarchies, contributes to the demarcation of community and reinforces the interests of dynastic rule.

How, though, might inequalities and exclusions, described in preceding chapters, be rationalized by ruling elites in relation to the normative tradition that they espouse? Recall that since the ruler, as *walī al-'amr*, defines the common good (*maṣlaḥa*), he exploits resources as he deems appropriate. Moreover, while nepotism and hoarding contravene principles of the faith, Gulf monarchs peddle the Hanbali insistence that the ruler must not be contested; this is so even in (Ibaḍi) Oman and (Maliki)

---

[6] Arguably, to be otherwise would spell his undoing.

Kuwait, and elsewhere across the Middle East and North Africa. And as we have seen, the official 'ulama' go along with this: They "want to remain in the ruling alliance and so, they do not say anything that would compromise their position."[7] As for exclusion, rulers, with their compliant 'ulama', may explain it thus: *Maṣlaḥa* is served through political stability, and in this conjuncture of oil-financed development in low population states fixed on hyper-modernization and absolutely dependent upon foreign labor and expertise, stability requires that foreigners (and all who are defined as relative "outsiders") are denied privileges that citizens enjoy. In this way, citizens remain rich and therefore, appeased. (After all, it is the citizen-subject who represents the real threat to the overwhelming power of the autocratic state.) Non-citizens retain low expectations; they refrain from making demands upon the state and depleting its resources. Thus, the new norm of exclusion, elaborated to address potential threats to privilege, promotes *maṣlaḥa* – a refined common good, as understood by *walī al-'amr* (the governor).[8]

As for charity and IBF, they are metaphors for politics. Charity functions as another numbing agent that promotes complacency in that it offers evidence to the giver of their goodness and adherence to the faith. At the same time, it supports the ruler's priorities by providing ruling elites with sought-after recognition, legitimation and a probing presence while enforcing submission and consolidating the contours of community. In turn, Islamic banking and finance extend the fiction of a religious moral order while encouraging consumption and enrichment. Accumulation by another means, IBF is supported by ruling elites in an effort to appease their populations and thus enhance their management of society while they and their closest associates in the business and even the religious field profit handsomely from engagement with the sector and with each other.

Thus, religious doctrine is both reinterpreted and, like oil rents, instrumentalized. In the embrace of Gulf rulers, it too becomes a mechanism for social control. Even as a rhetorical device, its purposes may be coercive: to assert rulers' right to rule and identify them with justice; to insist upon surface uniformity and enforce conformism and obedience. Manipulating Islamic doctrine and its interpretations thus facilitates social management – hence, the state's domination of society – and the

---

[7] Interview with high-ranking technocrat, Al-Khobar, 14 April 2012, who added that, "they are not the ones who will insist upon the true values of Islam." A renowned *'ālim* added: "The 'ulama' get their salaries from the Government and so, their tongues are tied" (Jeddah, 16 April 2012).

[8] However, as Zaman (2012, 116–18) remarks, when something considered as *maṣlaḥa* contradicts the shari'a, it is not *maṣlaḥa* at all.

fashioning of a new (moral) order. In the contemporary period, the particular ways in which Gulf rulers exploit and entwine oil revenues and Islamic doctrine are intrinsic to their dynastic ambitions, both political and material.

Ruling elites in Gulf monarchies are deeply engaged in the regulation of religion and of society. However, in Oman, Qatar, Saudi Arabia and to a lesser extent in Kuwait, they refuse the regulation of politics – that is, their own power (and the participation of their publics). Thus, they refuse a negotiated understanding of the common good. That being the case, when ruling elites' instrumentalization of oil and Islam proves insufficient for preserving their interests and advancing their agenda, as noted in Saudi Arabia in 1979 and 2017, in Oman in 2011 and more discretely in Kuwait in 1992 and since then, the use of force – indeed, the intensification of authoritarianism – is what remains in their tool kit.

Appendix

Villagio is an opulent mall located in what's called the "Aspire" zone of Doha. Next to the renowned "Aspire Tower" (also referred to as "The Torch") – a 300-meter-tall skyscraper, housing a luxury hotel, a revolving restaurant and a cantilevered swimming pool at 80 meters above ground – Villagio is designed to look like Venice. Canals, with floating wood gondolas, crossed by neat Italian footbridges, extend down the middle of each of the three wings of high-end shops, while representations of Italian loggias bedeck the second level, above exclusive designer boutiques. The dome-shaped ceiling is a baby-blue Italian sky with buoyant clouds, bright stars and the hint of a rainbow. Where the three wings meet at the far end, there is a fabulous Olympic size (water- and energy-intensive) skating rink, home of the Qatar Ice Hockey League.[1] Surrounding the rink is every fast-food joint imaginable: the proverbial McDonald's and Burger King but also stalls selling Asian, Indian, Middle Eastern and Mexican cuisine. "Life is good," as the saying goes.

Tucked away in a far corner adjacent to an exit, we happen upon a sight that is willed "unseen": a modest booth with an even more modest sign offering "International Money Transfers," and a long queue of poor South and Southeast Asian workers who wait patiently to send back home some of their meager but hard-earned cash in this wonderland of Aspire, Villagio and what some refer to as "modern-day slavery."

On May 28, 2012, a fire broke out in the Villagio Mall. While it appears to have started in a sporting goods shop when a light bulb with

---

[1] Qataris are among the highest consumers of water per capita per day – around 400 litres. Moreover, with very high rates of energy use, Qatar, for the past twenty years, has had the highest per capita carbon dioxide emissions in the world, more than double the emissions of people in the US and about 60 percent higher than Kuwait, the next highest per capita emitting country. While activities such as natural gas processing, water desalination, electricity production and air conditioning require vast amounts of energy, absolutely free and unregulated access to water and electricity for Qataris contributes to their high rate of energy use.

flammable components burst, it spread quickly to a daycare center below. By the time the fire was brought under control, nineteen people had died, of whom thirteen were children. Although a complete report of the investigation into the tragedy remained unavailable ten months later, some information regarding deficiencies in safety conditions and fire standards had come to light. According to several on-site sources and news outlets, on that day a number of fire alarms were not working, and some emergency exits, including one at the daycare, were locked. Rescue teams arrived to the scene quickly, but the blueprints they had of the building were incorrect; besides, they were not informed of the existence of a nursery in the mall until thirty minutes after they had arrived. There had been rumors, as well, of the existence of highly flammable paint and illegal flammable moldings that would have caused the fire to spread very quickly and pick up in intensity.

In the words of one of my Qatari interviewees, in reference to the condition of foreign labor in the emirate – but which seem apropos to the Villagio Mall tragedy: "The main problem is with our mentality: the soul of society has been snatched away for the appearance of modernity. I insist that it is only the 'appearance' of modernity, because this (Qatar) is not modernity" (Doha, 22 Feb. 2012).[2]

---

[2] For representations of "modernity on steroids" in the UAE and Saudi Arabia, see, Lowi (2016).

Bibliography

Abou El Fadl, Khaled. *The Great Theft: Wresting Islam from the Extremists*. Harper Collins, 2005.
——. "Conflict Resolution as a Normative Value in Islamic Law: Handling Disputes with Non-Muslims." In *Faith-Based Diplomacy: Trumping Realpolitik*, edited by Douglas Johnston, 178–209. Oxford University Press, 2003.
Abu-Sahlieh, Sami Aldeeb. "The Islamic Conception of Migration." *International Migration Review* 30, no.1 (1996): 37–57.
AbuKhalil, As'ad. "A New Arab Ideology? The Rejuvenation of Arab Nationalism." *Middle East Journal* 46, no.1 (1992): 22–36.
Ahmed, Attiyah. "Migrant Domestic Workers in Kuwait: the Role of Institutions." In *Viewpoints: Migration and the Gulf*, 27–9. Middle East Institute, 2010.
Ahmed, Mamdouh Hamza. "Micro Takaful Insurance as a Tool to Guaranteeing Financing and Protecting Micro Enterprises." *Journal of Business and Financial Affairs* 5, no.4 (2016): 1–11.
Al-Ajmi, Jasim, Hameeda Abo Hussain and Nadhem Al-Saleh. "Clients of Conventional and Islamic Banks in Bahrain: How They Choose Which Banks to Patronize." *International Journal of Social Economics* 36, no.11 (2009): 1086–1112.
Ajwad, Mohamed Ihsan, Johannes Koettl-Brodmann, Ismail Radwan, Thomas Farole, Javier Sanchez-Reaza, Carole Chartouni, Jumana Jamal Subhi Alaref, Nayib Rivera Guivas, Venkatesh Sundararaman, Zeina Afif and Gharam Alkastalani Dexter. *Towards a National Jobs Strategy in Kuwait: Overview*. World Bank Group, 2022. http://documents.worldbank.org/curated/en/099155109292260319/P16615507094f70ac09ff10e025ddcfd40b
Aksak, Ercument and Mehmet Asutay. "The Maqasid and the Empirics: Has Islamic Finance Fulfilled Its Promise?" In *Islamic Finance: Political Economy, Values and Innovation*, edited by Mehmet Asutay and Abdullah Turkistani, 187–220. Gerlach Press, 2015.
Al-'Alayli, 'Abd-allah. "Ayn al-Khiṭā'?: Taṣḥīḥ mafāhīm wa-naẓra tajdīd" (Where Is the Error? Rectifying Concepts and a Perspective of Renewal). Beirut: dar al-'ilm l'il-malāyyin, 1978; second printing, Dar al-Jadid, 1992.
Albertus, Michael, Sofia Fenner and Dan Slater. *Coercive Distribution*. Cambridge University Press, 2018.

Bibliography

AlKhamees, Ahmad. *A Critique of Creative Shari'ah Compliance in the Islamic Finance Industry*. Brill, 2017.

Allarakia, Luai and Hamad H. Albloshi. "The Politics of Permanent Deadlock in Kuwait." The Arab Gulf States Institute in Washington. 11 March 2021. https://agsiw.org/the-politics-of-permanent-deadlock-in-kuwait

Alpen Capital. GCC Insurance Industry. 8 February 2022.

AlShehabi, Omar. *Contested Modernity: Sectarianism, Nationalism and Colonialism in Bahrain*. Oneworld Academic, 2019.

"Show Us the Money: Oil Revenues, Undisclosed Allocations and Accountability in Budgets of the GCC States." *LSE Kuwait Programme Paper Series* no.44 (2017).

"Histories of Migration to the Gulf." In *Transit States: Labour, Migration and Citizenship in the Gulf*, edited by Abdelhadi Khalaf, Omar AlShehabi and Adam Hanieh, 3-38. Pluto Press, 2014.

Alvaredo, Facundo, Lydia Assouad and Thomas Piketty. "Inequality in the Middle East." VOX CEPR Policy Portal. 13 August 2018. https://voxeu.org/article/inequality-middle-east

Alzahrani, Majed M. "The System of Kafala and the Rights of Migrant Workers in GCC Countries – with Specific Reference to Saudi Arabia." *European Journal of Law Reform* 16, no.2 (2014): 377–400.

Amnesty International. "'My Sleep Is My Break': Exploitation of Migrant Domestic Workers in Qatar." 23 April 2014. www.amnesty.org/en/documents/mde22/004/2014/en

Amnesty International. "Saudi Arabia: Imminent Execution of Seven Young Men Would Violate Kingdom's Promise to Abolish Death Sentence for Youth." 15 June 2023. www.amnesty.org/en/latest/news/2023/06/saudi-arabia-imminent-execution-of-youths-would-violate-kingdoms-promise-to-abolish-death-penalty-for-juveniles

Arab Times. "6 Expats Can Own Property." Arab Times, 19 October 2015. www.arabtimesonline.com/news/6-expats-can-own-property

Arabian Business. "Kuwait Announces Plan to Allow Expat Real Estate Investment: Report." *Arabian Business*, 16 May 2023. www.arabianbusiness.com/industries/real-estate/kuwait-announces-plan-to-allow-expat-real-estate-investment-report

"Saudi Arabia to Become First GCC Country to Impose Sin Tax." *Arabian Business*, 28 May 2017. www.arabianbusiness.com/saudi-arabia-become-first-gcc-country-impose-sin-tax-675875.html

Al-Arabiya. Saudi Crown Prince Mohammed bin Salman Interview on Vision 2030, Part 3/3, Liwan al-Mudaifer program, 28 April 2021. www.youtube.com/watch?v=xqXl0L3lL8w

ArabLit and ArabLit Quarterly. "Qatari Poet Muhammad Al-Ajami, Serving 15-Year Sentence, Pardoned by Emir." *ArabLit and ArabLit Quarterly*, 16 March 2016. https://arablit.org/2016/03/16/qatari-poet-muhammad-al-ajami-in-jail-on-15-year-sentence-pardoned-by-emir

The Asian Banker. "Largest Islamic Banks 2021." www.theasianbanker.com/ab500/rankings/largest-islamic-banks

Askari, Hossein and Noora Arfaa. "Social Safety Net in Islam: The Case of Persian Gulf Exporters." *British Journal of Middle Eastern Studies* 34, no.2 (2007): 192–201.

Bibliography

Asl, Nima Khorrami. "Oman's Economic Ambitions." Sada: Carnegie Endowment for International Peace, 14 December 2018. https://carnegieendowment.org/sada/77972

Asutay, Mehmet. "Conceptualising and Locating the Social Failure of Islamic Finance: Aspirations of Islamic Moral Economy vs the Realities of Islamic Finance." *Asian and African Area Studies* 11, no.2 (2012): 93–113.

Asutay, Mehmet and Abdullah Turkistani, eds. *Islamic Finance: Political Economy, Values and Innovation*. Gerlach Press, 2015.

Asutay, Mehmet, Ahmet Faruk Aysan and Cenk C. Karahan. "Reflecting on the Trajectory of Islamic Finance: from Mit Ghamr to the Globalisation of Islamic Finance." *Afro Eurasian Studies* 2, nos.1 & 2 (2013): 5–14.

Atia, Mona. *Building a House in Heaven: Pious Neoliberalism and Islamic Charity in Egypt*. University of Minnesota Press, 2013.

Atong, Kennedy, Emmanuel Mayah and Akhator Odigie. "African Labour Migration to the GCC States: The Case of Ghana, Kenya, Nigeria and Uganda." African Regional Organization of the International Trade Union Confederation (ITUC-Africa), 75. 2018. www.ituc-africa.org/IMG/pdf/ituc-africa_study-africa_labour_migration_to_the_gcc_states.pdf

Attareiry, Abd al-Wahhab. Prophetic Anecdotes: The Prophetic Biography from New Angles. unpublished ms., n.d.

Aziz, Saba. "'We're Broken': Rohingya on Hunger Strike in Saudi Detention." Al-Jazeera, 17 April 2019. www.aljazeera.com/news/2019/4/17/were-broken-rohingya-on-hunger-strike-in-saudi-detention

Azoulay, Rivka. "The Politics of Shi'i Merchants in Kuwait." In *Business Politics in the Middle East*, edited by Steffen Hertog, Giacomo Luciani and Marc Valeri, 67–100. Hurst & Co., 2013.

Babar, Zahra R. "The Cost of Belonging: Citizenship Construction in the State of Qatar." *Middle East Journal* 68, no.3 (2014): 403–20.

Bajracharya, Rooja and Bandita Sijapati. "The Kafala System and Its Implications for Nepali Domestic Workers." *Centre for the Study of Labour and Mobility* (Nepal). Policy Brief no.1 (2012).

Baldwin-Edwards, Martin. "Labour Immigration and Labour Markets in the GCC Countries: National Patterns and Trends." *Kuwait Programme on Development, Governance and Globalisation in the Gulf States*, no.15. London School of Economics and Political Science, London, 2011.

Barakat, Sultan and Steven A. Zyck. "Gulf State Assistance to Conflict-Affected Environments." *Kuwait Programme on Development, Governance and Globalisation in the Gulf States*, no.10. London School of Economics and Political Science, London, 2010.

Baskan, Birol and Steven Wright. "Seeds of Change: Comparing State-Religion Relations in Qatar and Saudi Arabia." *Arab Studies Quarterly* 33, no.2 (2011): 96–111.

Bassens, David, Ben Derudder and Frank Witlox. "Setting Shari'a Standards: On the Role, Power and Spatialities of Interlocking Shari'a Boards in Islamic Financial Services." *Geoforum* 42 (2011): 94–103.

Bazoobandi, Sara. *Political Economy of the Gulf Sovereign Wealth Funds: A Case Study of Iran, Kuwait, Saudi Arabia and the United Arab Emirates*. Routledge, 2012.

BBC. "Saudi Arabia Triples VAT to Support Coronavirus Hit Economy." *BBC*, 11 May 2020. www.bbc.com/news/business-52612785

"Saudi Arabia's King Salman Reverses Public Sector Pay Cuts." *BBC*, 23 April 2017. www.bbc.com/news/world-middle-east-39683592

Beaugrand, Claire. *Stateless in the Gulf: Migration, Nationality and Society in Kuwait.* I. B. Tauris, 2018.

"Framing Nationality in the Migratory Context: The Elusive Category of Biduns in Kuwait." *Middle East Law and Governance* 6, no.3 (December 2014): 173–203.

Bellin, Eva. "Faith in Politics: New Trends in the Study of Religion and Politics." *World Politics* 60, no.2 (2008): 315–48.

Bellion-Jourdan, Jérôme. "Les organisations de secours islamique et l'action humanitaire." *Esprit* (2001): 173–85.

Benthall, Jonathan. "The Rise and Decline of Saudi Humanitarian Charities." *Center for International and Regional Studies Occasional Paper*, no.20. Georgetown University Qatar, 2018. https://repository.library.georgetown.edu/bitstream/handle/10822/1051628/CIRSOccasionalPaper20Jonathan Benthall2018.pdf?sequence=1&isAllowed=y

"Financial Worship: The Quranic Injunction to Almsgiving." *Journal of the Royal Anthropological Institute* 5, no.1 (March 1999): 27–42.

Benthall, Jonathan and Jérôme Bellion-Jourdan. *Charitable Crescent: Politics of Aid in the Muslim World.* I. B. Tauris, 2003.

Bhabha, Homi. "Of Mimicry and Man: The Ambivalence of Colonial Discourse." *October 28*, Discipleship: A Special Issue on Psychoanalysis (1984): 125–33.

Bin Bayyah, Abdullah. Maqāṣid al-Muʿāmalāt wa-Marāṣid al-Wāqaʿāt (Purposes of Transactions and Observations of Safeguards). 2nd edition, markaz dirāsāt maqāṣid al-shariʿah al-islamiyya, 2010.

Birks, J. S. and C. A. Sinclair. *Arab Manpower: The Crisis of Development.* London: Croom Helm, 1980.

Bishara, Azmi. "Mudākhila b'shaʿan al-ʿadāla: suʾal fi al-siyāq al-arabī al-muʿāṣir" (Intervention on the Matter of Justice in the Current Arab Context). *Tabayyun* 5 (2013): 7–26.

Boghardt, Lori Plotkin. "The Muslim Brotherhood in the Gulf: Prospects for Agitation." *Washington Institute for Near East Policy* Policy Analysis/Policy Watch 2087, 10 June 2013. www.washingtoninstitute.org/policy-analysis/muslim-brotherhood-gulf-prospects-agitation

Bonner, Michael. "Poverty and Economics in the Qurʾan." *Journal of Interdisciplinary History* 35, no.3 (2005): 391–406.

"Poverty and Charity in the Rise of Islam." In *Poverty and Charity in Middle Eastern Contexts*, edited by Michael Bonner, Mine Ener and Amy Singer, 13–30. State University of New York Press, 2003.

"The Kitab al-Kasb attributed to Al-Shaybani: Poverty, Surplus, and the Circulation of Wealth." *Journal of the American Oriental Society* 121, no.3 (2001): 410–27.

Boodrookas, Alex and Arang Keshavarzian. "The Forever Frontier of Urbanism: Historicizing Persian Gulf Cities." *International Journal of Urban and Regional Research* 43, no.1 (2019): 14–29. DOI:10.1111/1468-2427.12664

Brown, Nathan. "Citizenship, Religious Rights and State Identity in Arab Constitutions: Who Is Free and What Are They Free to Do?" In *Freedom of Religion, Secularism and Human Rights*, edited by Nehal Bhuta, 53–68. Oxford University Press, 2019.

Arguing Islam after the Revival of Arab Politics. Oxford University Press, 2016.

"Rethinking Religion and Politics: Where the Fault Lines Lie in the Arab World." *POMEPS Studies* 15: Islam and International Order. (22 July 2015): 42–4. http://pomeps.org/wp-content/uploads/2015/07/POMEPS_Studies_15_Islam_Web.pdf

Bruslé, Tristan. "What Kind of Place Is This? Daily Life, Privacy and the Inmate Metaphor in a Nepalese Workers' Labour Camp (Qatar)." *South Asia Multidisciplinary Academic Journal* 6 (2012): 1–25.

Bsheer, Rosie. *Archive Wars: the Politics of History in Saudi Arabia*. Stanford University Press, 2020.

"A Counter-Revolutionary State: Popular Movements and the Making of Saudi Arabia." *Past and Present* 238, no.1 (2018): 233–77.

"The Property Regime: Mecca and the Politics of Redevelopment in Saudi Arabia." *Jadaliyya* (8 September 2015). www.jadaliyya.com/Details/32436

"Poverty in the Oil Kingdom: An Introduction." *Jadaliyya* (30 September 2010). www.jadaliyya.com/Details/23527/Poverty-in-the-Oil-Kingdom-An-Introduction

Bu Haliqah, Iḥsaan. "kayfa tabada'a al-ru'iya fi mukāfaḥa al-faqr? ("How Does the 'Vision' Begin to Fight Poverty?"), Al-Arabiya, 30 October 2016. www.alarabiya.net/saudi-today/2016/10/30/كيف-تبدأ-الرؤية-في-مكافحة-الفقر؟.

Cammett, Melani. *Compassionate Communalism: Welfare and Sectarianism in Lebanon*. Cornell University Press, 2014.

Cammett, Melani, Ishaq Diwan, Alan Richards and John Waterbury. *A Political Economy of the Middle East*. 4th edition, Routledge, 2015.

Carapico, Sheila. "Arabia Incognita: An Invitation to Arabian Peninsula Studies." In *Counter-Narratives: History, Contemporary Society and Politics in Saudi Arabia and Yemen*, edited by Madawi Al-Rasheed and Robert Vitalis, 11–34. Palgrave MacMillan, 2004.

Carré, Olivier. *Mysticism and Politics: A Critical Reading of Fi Ẓilal al-Qur'an by Sayyid Qutb (1906–66)*. Leiden: Brill, 2003.

"Religion et Développement dans les pays musulmans: éléments d'économie islamique." *Social Compass* 39, no.1 (1992): 55–65.

Central Bank of Kuwait. "CBK Instructions for Islamic Banks." n.d. www.cbk.gov.kw/en/legislation-and-regulation/cbk-regulations-and-instructions/instructions-for-islamic-banks

Press Statement. "CBK Forms the Higher Committee of Shari'ah Supervision." 5 October 2020. www.cbk.gov.kw/en/cbk-news/announcements-and-press-releases/press-releases/2020/10/202010051120-cbk-forms-the-higher-committee-of-shariah-supervision

Press Statement. "The Higher Committee of Shari'ah Supervision Responsibilities." www.cbk.gov.kw/en/about-cbk/committee-of-shariah/responsibilities

Central Bank of Oman (CBO). "Islamic Banking Regulatory Framework," 18 December 2012. https://cbo.gov.om/Pages/IslamicBankingRegulatoryFramework.aspx

Chalcraft, John. *Popular Politics in the Making of the Modern Middle East.* Cambridge University Press, 2016.

"Migration and Popular Protest in the Arabian Peninsula and the Gulf in the 1950s and 1960s." *International Labor and Working-Class History* 79, no.1 (2011): 28-47.

"Monarchy, Migration and Hegemony in the Arabian Peninsula." *Kuwait Programme on Development, Governance and Globalisation in the Gulf States* no. *12*, London School of Economics & Political Science, 2010.

Chapra, M. Umer. *Islam and Economic Development: A Strategy for Development with Stability in the Light of Justice and Islamic Teachings.* Washington, DC: International Institute of Islamic Thought, 1994.

Islam and the Economic Challenge. Leicester: Islamic Foundation, 1992.

Césari, Jocelyne. *The Awakening of Muslim Democracy: Religion, Modernity and the State.* Cambridge University Press, 2014.

Chaudhry, Kiren Aziz. *The Price of Wealth: Economies and Institutions in the Middle East.* Cornell University Press, 1997.

Commins, David. *The Gulf States: A Modern History.* I. B. Tauris, 2012.

The Wahhabi Mission and Saudi Arabia. I. B. Tauris, 2009.

Cook, Michael. *Commanding Right and Forbidding Wrong in Islamic Thought.* Cambridge University Press, 2001.

Cooke, Miriam. *Tribal Modern: Branding New Nations in the Arab Gulf.* University of California Press, 2014.

Coronil, Fernando. "Crude Matters: Seizing the Venezuelan Petrostate in Times of Chavez." In *The Fernando Coronil Reader*, 266–306. Duke University Press, 2019.

The Magical State: Nature, Money and Modernity in Venezuela. University of Chicago Press, 1997.

Crystal, Jill. *Kuwait: The Transformation of an Oil State.* 2nd edition, Routledge, 2016.

"Public Order and Authority: Policing Kuwait." In *Monarchies and Nations: Globalisation and Identity in the Arab States of the Gulf*, edited by Paul Dresch and James Piscatori, 158–81. London: I. B. Tauris, 2005.

Oil and Politics in the Gulf: Rulers and Merchants in Kuwait and Qatar. Cambridge University Press, 1990.

Daily Mail. "Beirut Says UAE to Expel 70 Mostly Shiite Lebanese." *Daily Mail*, 13 March 2015. www.dailymail.co.uk/wires/afp/article-2993016/Beirut-says-UAE-expel-70-Shiite-Lebanese.html

Dar, Humayon A. and Wan Nursofiza Wan Azmi. "Shariah Governance Regimes in the Gulf Cooperation Council Countries: A Comparative Study." In *Islamic Finance: Political Economy, Values and Innovation*, edited by Mehmet Asutay and Abdullah Turkistani, 63–78. Gerlach Press, 2015.

De Bel-Air, Françoise. "Demography, Migration, and the Labour Market in Oman." Explanatory Note no. 7/2018. Gulf Labour Markets, Migration and Population (GLMM) programme of the Migration Policy Center (MPC) and the Gulf Research Center (GRC), 2018. http://gulfmigration.org

Bibliography

Deloitte. "International Tax: Qatar Highlights 2019." June 2019. www2.deloitte.com/content/dam/Deloitte/global/Documents/Tax/dttl-tax-qatarhighlights-2019.pdf

Derbal, Nora. *Charity in Saudi Arabia: Civil Society under Authoritarianism.* Cambridge University Press, 2022

"Domestic, Religious, Civic? Perspectives on the Institutionalized Charitable Field in Jeddah, Saudi Arabia." In *Gulf Charities and Islamic Philanthropy in the "Age of Terror" and Beyond,* edited by Robert Lacey and Jonathan Benthall, 145–67. Gerlach Press, 2014.

"Lifestyle and Liberty in the Name of Piety: Philanthropy in Jeddah, Saudi Arabia." In *Takaful 2011 – The First Annual Conference on Arab Philanthropy and Civic Engagement,* edited by John D. Gerhart Center for Philanthropy and Civic Engagement, 46–75. Cairo University Press, 2011.

Dito, Mohammed. "Kafala: Foundations of Migrant Exclusion in GCC Labor Markets." In *Transit States: Labour, Migration and Citizenship in the Gulf,* edited by Abdelhadi Khalaf, Omar Al-Shehabi and Adam Hanieh, 79–100. Pluto Press, 2014.

Doumato, Eleanor. "Gender, Monarchy, and National Identity in Saudi Arabia." *British Journal of Middle Eastern Studies* 19, no.1 (1992): 31–47.

Dresch, Paul. "Foreign Matter: The Place of Strangers in Gulf Society." In *Globalization and the Gulf,* edited by J. W. Fox, N. Mourtada-Sabbah and M. Al-Mutawa, 200–22. Routledge, 2006.

"Debates on Marriage and Nationality in the United Arab Emirates." In *Monarchies and Nations: Globalisation and Identity in the Arab States of the Gulf,* edited by Paul Dresch and James Piscatori, 136–57. I. B. Tauris, 2005.

Dunning, Thad. *Crude Democracy: Natural Resource Wealth and Political Regimes.* Cambridge University Press, 2008.

Escobar, Arturo. *Encountering Development: The Making and Unmaking of the Third World.* Princeton University Press, 1995.

Al-Fahad, Abdelaziz. "The 'Imama vs. the 'Iqal: Hadari - Bedouin Conflict and the Formation of the Saudi State." In *Counter-Narratives: History, Contemporary Society, and Politics in Saudi Arabia and Yemen,* edited by Madawi Al-Rasheed and Robert Vitalis, 35–75. Palgrave Macmillan, 2004.

Fargues, Philippe. "International Migration and the Nation-State in Arab Countries." *Middle East Law and Governance* 5, nos. 1–2 (2013): 5–35.

"Immigration without Inclusion: Non-nationals in Nation-Building in the Gulf States." *Asian and Pacific Migration Journal* 20, nos.3–4 (2011): 273–92.

Farouk-El-Adé, Farouk. "L'Exploitation Petrolière à la Lumière du Droit Islamique." parts 1 and 2. *Arab Law Quarterly* 14, nos.i & ii (1999): 3–15,148–58.

Farquhar, Michael. *Circuits of Faith: Migration, Education and the Wahhabi Mission.* Stanford University Press, 2016.

Foley, Sean. *The Arab Gulf States: Beyond Oil and Islam.* Lynne Rienner Publishers, 2010.

Foltz, Richard C., Frederick M. Denny and Azizan Baharuddin, eds. *Islam and Ecology: A Bestowed Trust.* Harvard University Press 2003.

France 24. "Saudis Arrested for Criticising King Abdullah on YouTube." The Observers. France 24, 1 April 2014. https://observers.france24.com/en/20140401-saudis-chastise-king-abdullah-youtube-get-arrested

Freer, Courtney. "The Symbiosis of Sectarianism, Authoritarianism, and Rentierism in the Saudi State." *Studies in Ethnicity and Nationalism* 19, no.1 (2019a): 88–108.

"Mapping Religious Authority in Wahhabi States: An Examination of Qatar and Saudi Arabia." *Baker Institute for Public Policy*, 20. Center for Middle East, Rice University (2019b).

Rentier Islamism: The Influence of the Muslim Brotherhood in Gulf Monarchies. Oxford University Press, 2018.

Fromherz, Allen J. *Qatar: A Modern History.* New York: I. B. Tauris, 2012.

Fuccaro, Nelida. "Arab Oil Towns as Petro-Histories." In *Oil Spaces: Exploring the Global Petroleum-Scape*, edited by Carola Hein, 129–44. Routledge, 2022.

"Rethinking the History of Port Cities in the Gulf." In *The Persian Gulf in Modern Times: People, Ports and Cities*, edited by Lawrence G. Potter, 23–46. Palgrave/MacMillan, 2014.

"Between Imara, Empire and Oil: Saudis in the Frontier Society of the Persian Gulf." In *Kingdom without Borders: Saudi Political, Religious and Media Frontiers*, edited by Madawi al-Rasheed, 39–64. Columbia University Press, 2008.

Funds@Work. "The Small World of Islamic Finance: Shariah Scholars and Governance – A Network Analytic Perspective." 5 October 2010. https://funds-at.work/wp-content/uploads/2018/02/Sharia-Network-by-Funds-at-Work-AG.pdf

El-Gamal, Mahmoud A. "'Islamic Finance' after State-Sponsored Capitalist-Islamism," working paper, Baker Institute, Rice University (December 2017).

Islamic Finance: Law, Economics and Practice. Cambridge University Press, 2006.

Gardner, Andrew. "Ethnography, Anthropology and Migration to the Arabian Peninsula: Themes from an Ethnographic Research Trajectory." Gulf Research Centre: Gulf Labour Markets and Migration, GLMM-EN-no. October 2014.

"How the City Grows: Urban Growth and Challenges to Sustainable Development in Doha, Qatar." In *Sustainable Development: An Appraisal from the Gulf Region*, edited by Paul Sillitoe, 343–66. Berghahn Press, 2014b.

"Why Do They Keep Coming? Labor Migrants in the Gulf States." In *Migrant Labour in the Persian Gulf*, edited by Mehran Kamrava and Zahra Babar, 41–58. New York: Columbia University Press, 2012.

"Labor Camps in the Gulf States." In *Viewpoints: Migration and the Gulf*, 55–7. Middle East Institute, 2010a.

"Engulfed: Indian Guest Workers, Bahraini Citizens and the Structural Violence of the Kafala System." In *The Deportation Regime: Sovereignty, Space, and the Freedom of Movement*, edited by Nicholas De Benova and Nathalie Mae Peutz, 196–223. Duke University Press, 2010b.

Gardner, Andrew, Silvia Pessoa, Abdoulaye Diop, Kalthama Al-Ghanim, Kien Le Trung and Laura Harkness. "A Portrait of Low-Income Migrants in Contemporary Qatar." *Journal of Arabian Studies* 3, no.1 (2013): 1–17.

Gause III, F. Gregory. *The International Relations of the Persian Gulf.* Cambridge University Press, 2010.

Geertz, Clifford. "After the Revolution: The Fate of Nationalism in the New States" In *The Interpretation of Cultures*. 234–54. Basic Books, 1973.

General Secretariat for Development Planning (GSDP). *Qatar National Development Strategy, 2011–2016: Toward Qatar National Vision 2030*. Doha: GSDP, 2011.

Gengler, Justin. "Collective Frustration, but No Collective Action, in Qatar." MERIP Online (MERO), Middle East Research and Information Project (MERIP), 7 December 2013. www.merip.org/mero/mero120713

al-Ghazali, Abdelhamid. *The Mysteries of Almsgiving*. Translated by Nabih Amin Faris. American University of Beirut, 1966.

Al-Ghazali, Muhammad. *Al-Islam w'al-Manāhij al-ishtirakiyya* (Islam and Socialist Methodology). Egypt: Ennahda Publishing, 2005.

Gibson, Owen and Pete Pattisson. "Death Toll among Qatar's 2022 World Cup Workers Revealed." *The Guardian*, 23 December 2014. www.theguardian.com/world/2014/dec/23/qatar-nepal-workers-world-cup-2022-death-toll-doha

Gill, Anthony. "Religion and Comparative Politics." *Annual Review of Political Science* 4 (2001): 117–38.

Gill, Anthony and Arang Keshavarzian. "State Building and Religious Resources: An Institutional Theory of Church-State Relations in Iran and Mexico." *Politics and Society* 27, no.3 (1999): 431–65.

Grassa, Rihab and Hamadi Matoussi. "Corporate Governance of Islamic Banks: A Comparative Study Between GCC and Southeast Asia Countries." *International Journal of Islamic and Middle Eastern Finance and Management* 7, no.3 (2014): 346–62.

Grzymala-Busse, Anna. "Why Comparative Politics Should Take Religion (More) Seriously." *Annual Review of Political Science* 15 (2012): 421–42.

Guermat, C., A. T. Al-Utaibi and J. P. Tucker. "The Practice of Zakat: An Empirical Examination of Four Gulf Countries." Economics Department Discussion Papers Series, paper no. 03/02, University of Exeter, November 2003. http://business-school.exeter.ac.uk/economics/papers

Guijarro, Oscar Garrido. "Emiratis, Saudis and Qataris Cross the Red Sea: What Are the Gulf Monarchies Doing in Africa?" Instituto Español de Estudios Estrátegicos (IEEE). Analysis paper 45, 6 July 2023. www.ieee.es/Galerias/fichero/docs_analisis/2023/DIEEEA45_2023_OSCGAR_Emiratos_ENG.pdf

Gulf News. "Oman's Sultan Introduces Changes to Laws Regulating Marriage of Omanis to Foreigners." *Gulf News*, 16 April 2023. https://gulfnews.com/world/gulf/oman/omans-sultan-introduces-changes-to-laws-regulating-marriage-of-omani-citizens-to-foreigners-1.1681675027709

Habbash, Murya. "Corporate Governance and Corporate Social Responsibility Disclosure Evidence from Saudi Arabia." *Journal of Economic and Social Development* 3, no.1 (2016): 87–103.

Hackman, Michelle. "US Seeks Longer Detentions for Migrant Families." *Wall Street Journal*, 21 August 2019. www.wsj.com/articles/trump-administration-unveils-plan-to-hold-migrant-children-in-long-term-detention-with-parents-11566394202.

Hallaq, Wael. *The Impossible State: Islam, Politics, and Modernity's Moral Predicament.* Columbia University Press, 2013.
Shari'a: Theory, Practice, Transformations. Cambridge University Press, 2009.
Hamade, Riad, Zaid Sabah and Vivian Nereim. "KSA Triples VAT, Cuts State Allowances Amid Crisis." *Bloomberg*, 10 May 2020. www.bloomberg.com/news/articles/2020-05-11/saudi-arabia-plans-26-6-billion-austerity-cuts-triples-vat-ka1uss4c
Hammoudi, Abdellah. *A Season in Mecca: Narrative of a Pilgrimage.* Farrar, Straus and Giroux, 2006.
Hanieh, Adam. "Rethinking Class and State in the Gulf Cooperation Council." In *Critical Political Economy of the Middle East*, edited by Joel Beinen, Bassam Haddad and Sherene Seikaly, 105–22. Stanford University Press, 2021.
"Variegated Finance Capital and the Political Economy of Islamic Banking in the Gulf." *New Political Economy* 25, no.4 (2020): 572–89.
Money, Markets and Monarchies. Cambridge University Press, 2018.
Haniffa, Roszaini and Mohammad Hudaib. "Islamic Finance: From Sacred Intentions to Secular Goals?" *Journal of Islamic Accounting and Business Research* 1, no.2 (2010): 85–91.
Hartley, Robert. "Kuwait Progresses toward Islamic Banking Vision." *The Banker*, 1 April 2014. www.thebanker.com/Kuwait-progresses-towards-Islamic-banking-vision-1396339489
Hartnell, Caroline. "Philanthropy in the Arab Region: A Working Paper,"Philanthropy for Social Justice and Peace in association with Alliance, Arab Foundations Forum, John D. Gerhart Center for Philanthropy, King Khalid Foundation, Philanthropy Age, SAANED and WINGS. March 2018. www.alliancemagazine.org/wp-content/uploads/2018/03/Philanthropy-in-the-Arab-region-March-2018.pdf
Hasenclever, Andreas and Volker Rittberger. "Does Religion Make a Difference? Theoretical Approaches to the Impact of Faith on Political Conflict." *Millenium: Journal of International Studies* 29, no.3 (2000): 641–74.
Hayat, Raphie, Frank Den Butter and Udo Kock. "Halal Certification for Financial Products: A Transaction Cost Perspective." *Journal of Business Ethics* 117 (2013): 601–13.
Haykel, Bernard. "Oil in Saudi Arabian Culture and Politics: From Tribal Poets to Al-Qaeda's Ideologues." In *Saudi Arabia in Transition: Insights on Social, Political, Economic and Religious Change*, edited by B. Haykel, T. Hegghammer and S. Lacroix, 125–47. Cambridge University Press, 2015.
Heard-Bey, Frauke. "From Tribe to State: The Transformation of Political Structure in Five States of the GCC," vol. 2, *CRiSSMA Working Paper* no.15. Catholic University Milan, 2008.
Hegghammer, Thomas and Stephane Lacroix. "Rejectionist Islamism in Saudi Arabia: The Story of Juhayman al-Utaibi Revisited." International Journal of Middle East Studies 39, no.1 (2007): 103–22.
Held, David and Kristian Ulrichsen, eds. *The Transformation of the Gulf: Politics, Economics and the Global Order.* Routledge, 2011.
Henry, Clement M. "Islamic Finance in the Dialectics of Globalisation: Potential Variations on the 'Washington Consensus'" (originally published in *Journal*

of Arabic, Islamic and Middle Eastern Studies 5, no.2 (1999): 25–37, reprint in Akbarzadeh, Shahram, ed. Islam and Globalization, vol. IV. Routledge, 2006: 143–58.

Henry, Clement M. and Robert Springborg. *Globalization and the Politics of Development in the Middle East*. Cambridge University Press, 2001.

Henry, Clement M. and Rodney Wilson, eds. *The Politics of Islamic Finance*. Edinburgh University Press, 2004.

Herb, Michael. *The Wages of Oil: Parliaments and Economic Development in Kuwait and the UAE*. Cornell University Press, 2018.

"Ontology and Methodology in the Study of the Resource Curse." *LSE Programme Paper Series* no.43 (2017).

Hertog, Steffen. *Princes, Brokers, and Bureaucrats: Oil and the State in Saudi Arabia*. Cornell University Press, 2010.

"The Sociology of the Gulf Rentier Systems: Societies of Intermediaries." *Comparative Studies in Society and History* 52, no.2 (2010b): 282–318.

"Defying the Resource Curse: Explaining Successful State-Owned Enterprises in Rentier States." *World Politics* 62, no.2 (2010b): 261–301.

"National Cohesion and the Political Economy of Regions in Post-World War II Saudi Arabia." In *Saudi Arabia in Transition: Insights on Social, Political, Economic, and Religious Change*, edited by Bernard Haykel, Thomas Hegghammer and Stephane Lacroix, 97–124. Cambridge University Press, 2015.

Hodgson, Marshall G. S. *The Venture of Islam*, Volume 2: The Expansion of Islam in the Middle Periods. University of Chicago Press, 1975.

The Venture of Islam, Volume 1: The Classical Age of Islam. University of Chicago Press, 1974.

Hoffman, Jon. "The Evolving Relationship between Religion and Politics in Saudi Arabia." Arab Center Washington, DC, 20 April 2022. https://arabcenterdc.org/resource/the-evolving-relationship-between-religion-and-politics-in-saudi-arabia

Hoffman, Valerie. *The Essentials of Ibadi Islam*. Syracuse University Press, 2012.

Hopper, Matthew. *Slaves of One Master: Globalization and Slavery in Arabia in the Age of Empire*. Yale University Press, 2015.

Human Rights Watch. "Saudi Arabia: Cleric Held 4 Months without Charge." Human Rights Watch, 7 January 2018.

"Rights on the Line: Human Rights Watch Work on Abuses against Migrants in 2010." Human Rights Watch, December 2010: 48–83.

Hvidt, Martin. "The Development Trajectory of the GCC States: An Analysis of Aims and Visions in Current Development Plans." In *Gulf Politics and Economics in a Changing World*, edited by Michael Hudson and Mimi Kirk, 11–28. World Scientific, 2014.

Ibrahim, Abdul-Jalil. "Empirical Findings on the Profitability of Banks in Qatar: Islamic versus Conventional." *International Journal of Business and Commerce* 5, no.4 (2016): 63–78.

Ibrahim, Ibrahim and Frank Herrigan. "Qatar's Economy: Past, Present and Future." *QScience Connect*, September 2012. http://dx.doi.org/10.5339/connect.2012.9

Bibliography

IIROSA. "Overall Performance Report of the International Islamic Relief Organization." Saudi Arabia (IIROSA) Projects and Programs for the Year 2011/2012 (1432/33 H). www.egatha.org/pdf/annualreport/iirosa_annualreport_3233_en.pdf

International Center for Not-for-Profit Law (ICNL). "Saudi Arabia Philanthropy Law Report." ICNL March 2017. www.icnl.org/news/Saudi%20Arabia%20Philanthropy%20Law%20Report.pdf

International Energy Agency (IEA). World Energy Outlook 2010. Online database available at www.iea.org/subsidy/index.html

International Labour Organization (ILO). "Overview of Qatar's Labour Reforms." ILO 2023. www.ilo.org/beirut/countries/qatar/WCMS_760466/lang–en/index.htm#banner

"Dismantling the Kafala System and Introducing a Minimum Wage Mark New Era for Qatar Labour Market." ILO 30 August 2020. www.ilo.org/global/about-the-ilo/newsroom/news/WCMS_754391/lang–en/index.htm

International Monetary Fund (IMF). Kuwait: IMF Country Report no. 18/22, January 2018.

Iqbal, Munawar and David T Llewellyn, eds. *Islamic Banking and Finance: New Perspectives on Profit-Sharing and Risk*. Edward Elgar Press, 2015.

Isik, Damla. "Vakif as Intent and Practice: Charity and Poor Relief in Turkey." *International Journal of Middle East Studies* 46, no.2 (2014): 307–27.

Islamic Financial Services Board (IFSB). *Islamic Financial Services Industry Stability Report 2022*. Kuala Lumpur, 2022.

Islamic Financial Services Industry Stability Report 2019. Kuala Lumpur, 2019.

Islamic Financial Services Stability Report 2013. Kuala Lumpur, 2013.

Al-Jassem, Diana. "Zakat on Owned Land as Solution to Housing Problem." *Arab News*, 19 March 2013. www.arabnews.com/news/445343

Al Jazeera. "Oman Shuffles Cabinet amid Protests." *Al Jazeera*, 26 February 2011.

Johnston, David L. "Intra-Muslim Debates on Ecology: Is Shariʻa Still Relevant?" *Worldviews* 16 (2012): 218–38.

Jones, Toby. *Desert Kingdom: How Oil and Water Forged Modern Saudi Arabia*. Harvard University Press, 2010.

"Saudi Arabia's Not So New Anti-Shiʻism." *Middle East Report* 242 (2007): 29–32.

Jung, Dietrich and Marie Juul Petersen. "'We Think That This Job Pleases Allah': Islamic Charity, Social Order, and the Construction of Modern Muslim Selfhoods in Jordan." *International Journal of Middle East Studies* 46, no.2 (2014): 285–306.

Jureidini, Ray. *Migrant Labour Recruitment to Qatar*. Report for Qatar Foundation. Migrant Worker Welfare Initiative: Bloomsbury Qatar Foundation Journals, 2014.

Kahf, Monzer. "The Rise of a New Power Alliance of Wealth and Shariʻa Scholarship." In *The Politics of Islamic Finance*, edited by Clement M. Henry and Rodney Wilson, 17–36. Edinburgh University Press, 2004.

"Zakat: Unresolved Issues in the Contemporary Fiqh." *Journal of Islamic Economics* 2, no.1 (1989): 1–22.
Al-Kahlut, Abd al-Aziz. Al-Islam w'al-Tharwa (Islam and Wealth). ṣaḥīfa al-daʿwa al-islamiyya, 1982.
Kamali, Mohammad Hashim. "Citizenship: An Islamic Perspective." *Journal of Islamic Law and Culture* 11, no.2 (2009): 121–53.
"Have We Neglected the Shariah Law Doctrine of Maslahah?" *Islamic Studies* 27, no.4 (1988): 287–303.
Kamrava, Mehran. *Qatar: Small State Big Politics*. Cornell University Press, 2013.
ed. *The Political Economy of the Persian Gulf*. Columbia University Press, 2012.
"Royal Factionalism and Political Liberalization in Qatar." *Middle East Journal* 63, no.3 (2009): 401–20.
Kamrava, Mehran and Zahra Babar, eds. *Migrant Labor in the Persian Gulf*. Columbia University Press, 2012.
Kamrava, Mehran, Gerd Nonneman, Anastasia Nosova and Marc Valeri. "Ruling Families and Business Elites in the Gulf Monarchies: Ever Closer?" *Research Paper, Middle East and North Africa Programme*, Chatham House: The Royal Institute of International Affairs, 2016.
Kanna, Ahmed. *Dubai: The City as Corporation*. University of Minnesota Press, 2011.
"The 'State Philosophical' in the 'Land without Philosophy': Shopping Malls, Interior Cities and the Image of Utopian Dubai." *Traditional Dwellings and Settlements Review* 16, no.2 (2005): 59–73.
Kapiszewski, Andrzej. "Arab versus Asian Migrant Workers in the GCC Countries." Paper delivered to *United Nations Expert Group Meeting on International Migration and Development in the Arab Region* (UN/POP/EGM/2006/02). Beirut, 22 May 2006.
Kareem, Mona. "An Invisible Nation: The Gulf's Stateless Communities." Jadaliyya, 21 August 2012.
Karl, Terry Lynn. "Ensuring Fairness: The Case for a Transparent Fiscal Social Contract." In *Escaping the Resource Curse*, edited by Macartan Humphreys, Jeffrey Sachs and Joseph Stiglitz, 256–85. Columbia University Press, 2007.
Karpat, Kemal. "Commentary: Muslim Migration: A Response to Aldeeb Abu Sahlieh." *International Migration Review* 30, no.1 (1996): 79–89.
El-Katiri, Laura, Bassam Fattouh and Paul Segal. "Anatomy of an Oil-Based Welfare State: Rent Distribution in Kuwait." *Kuwait Programme in Development, Governance and Globalization in the Gulf States*, no.13. London School of Economics (2011).
Khadduri, Majid. "Maṣlaḥa." *Encyclopedia of Islam*, 2nd edition, 2013.
Khalaf, Abdelhadi. "The Politics of Migration." In *Transit States: Labour, Migration and Citizenship in the Gulf*, edited by Abdelhadi Khalaf, Omar Al-Shehabi and Adam Hanieh, 39–56. Pluto Press, 2014.
Khalaf, Sulayman. "Gulf Society and the Image of the Unlimited Good." *Dialectical Anthropology* 17, no.1 (1992): 53–84.
Khalaf, Sulayman and Saad Alkobaisi. "Migrants' Strategies of Coping and Patterns of Accommodation in the Oil-Rich Gulf Societies: Evidence from the UAE." *British Journal of Middle Eastern Studies* 26, no.2 (1999): 271–99.

Khalid, Fazlun and Joanne O'Brien, eds. *Islam and Ecology*. Cassell, 1992.

Khalili, Laleh. *Sinews of War and Trade: Shipping and Capitalism in the Arabian Peninsula*. Verso, 2020.

Khan, Feisal. "How 'Islamic' Is Islamic Banking?" *Journal of Economic Behavior and Organization* 76 (2010): 805–20.

al-Khatib, Muʿtaz. "Al-ʿAdl fī al-tafkīr al-islāmī: al-mafāhīm w'al-siyāqāt" (Justice in Islamic Thought: The Concepts and the Context). *Al-Tafahom* 47 (2015): 11–34.

Al-Khouri, Ali M. "The Challenge of Identity in a Changing World: The Case of GCC Countries." *Conference Proceedings: The 21st Century Gulf: The Challenge of Identity*, 30 June–3 July 2010, University of Exeter.

Al-Khūlī, Al-Bahī. *Al-Tharwa fī Ẓil al-Islām* (Wealth in the Shadow of Islam). Kuwait: Dar al-Qalam, 1981.

Kilani, Hazar. "Here's a List of Areas Where You Can Own Real Estate as a Foreigner." *Doha News*, 17 January 2023. https://dohanews.co/heres-a-list-of-areas-in-qatar-where-you-can-own-real-estate-as-a-foreigner

Kinninmont, Jane. "Citizenship in the Gulf." In *The Gulf States and the Arab Uprisings*, edited by Ana Echague, 47–57. FRIDE and the Gulf Research Center, 2013. http://fride.org/download/The_Gulf_States_and_the_Arab_Uprisings.pdf

Kirschgaessner, Stephanie. "Saudi Woman Given 34-year Prison Sentence for Using Twitter." *The Guardian*, 16 August 2022. www.theguardian.com/world/2022/aug/16/saudi-woman-given-34-year-prison-sentence-for-using-twitter

Kozlowski, Gregory C. "Religious Authority, Reform, and Philanthropy in the Contemporary Muslim World." In *Philanthropy in the World's Traditions*, edited by Warren F. Ilchman, Stanley N. Katz and Edward L. Queen II, 279–308. Indiana University Press, 1998.

Krane, Jim. *Energy Kingdoms: Oil and Political Survival in the Persian Gulf*. Columbia University Press, 2019.

"Subsidy Reform and Tax Increases in the Rentier Middle East." *POMEPS Studies* no.33 (2019): 18–24.

Krane, Jim and Shih Yu Hung. "Energy Subsidy Reform in the Persian Gulf: The End of the Big Oil Giveaway." *Issue Brief*, Baker Institute for Public Policy, 28 April 2016, Rice University.

Kuran, Timur. *Islam and Mammon: The Economic Predicaments of Islamism*. Princeton University Press, 2005.

"Islamic Redistribution through Zakat: Historical Record and Modern Realities." In *Poverty and Charity in Middle Eastern Contexts*, edited by Michael Bonner, Mine Ener and Amy Singer, 275–93. State University of New York Press, 2003.

"The Provision of Public Goods under Islamic Law: Origins, Impact and Limitations of the Waqf System." *Law and Society Review* 35, no.4 (2001): 841–98.

Kuwait Ministry of Foreign Affairs. "Kuwait Vision 2035 'New Kuwait.'" State of Kuwait: MOFA, 2021. www.mofa.gov.kw/en/kuwait-state/kuwait-vision-2035.

Kuwait Times. "Kuwaitis' Private Sector Allowance Will Not Stop," Kuwait Times, 4 August 2022. www.kuwaittimes.com/kuwaitis-private-sector-allowance-will-not-stop

al-Kuwari, Ali Khalifa. *al-ṭafra al-nafṭiya al-thālitha w'anʿakāsāt al-māliyya al-ʿālimiyya* (The Third Oil Boom and the Repercussions of the Global Financial Crisis). Beirut: Center for Arab Unity Studies, 2009.

al-Kuwari, Soad. "Modernity in the Desert." In *Gathering the Tide: An Anthology of Contemporary Arabian Gulf Poetry*, edited by Jeff Lodge, Patty Paine and Samia Touati, 167. Ithaca Press, 2012.

Lacey, Robert and Jonathan Benthall, eds. *Gulf Charities and Islamic Philanthropy in the "Age of Terror" and Beyond.* Gerlach Press, 2014.

Lacroix, Stéphane. *Les Islamistes Saoudiens: Une Insurrection Manquée* (The Saudi Islamists: A Failed Insurrection). Presse Universitaire de France, 2010.

Laoust, Henri. *La Politique de Ghazali*. Paris: éditions Geunther, 1970.

Lapidus, Ira. "State and Religion in Islamic Societies." *Past and Present* no.151 (1996): 3–27.

Le Renard, Amélie. "Poverty and Charity in Saudi Arabia: The Royal Family, the Private Sector, and the Welfare State." *Critique Internationale* no.41 (2008).

Leichtman, Mara A. "Kuwaiti Humanitarianism: The History and Expansion of Kuwait's Foreign Assistance Policies." *Changing Landscape of Assistance to Conflict-Affected States*, Policy Brief #11, George Mason University/Stimson Center, August 2017.

Limbert, Mandana E. *In the Time of Oil: Piety, Memory and Social Life in an Omani Town*. Stanford University Press, 2010.

"Marriage, Status and the Politics of Nationality in Oman." In *The Gulf Family: Kinship Policies and Modernity*, edited by Alanoud Alsharekh, 167–79. Middle East Institute at School of Oriental and African Studies, University of London, 2007.

Longva, Anh Nga. "Nationalism in Pre-modern Guise: The Discourse on Hadhar and Badu in Kuwait." *International Journal of Middle Eastern Studies* 38, no.2 (2006): 171–87.

"Neither Autocracy nor Democracy but Ethnocracy: Citizens, Expatriates, and the Socio-Political System in Kuwait." In *Monarchies and Nations - Globalisation and Identity in the Arab States of the Gulf*, edited by Paul Dresch and James Piscatori, 114–35. London: I. B.Tauris, 2005.

"Citizenship in the Gulf States: Conceptualization and Practice." In *Citizenship and the State in the Middle East*, edited by N.A. Butenschon, U. Davis and M. Hassassian, 179–200. Syracuse University Press, 2000.

"Keeping Migrant Workers in Check: The Kafala System in the Gulf." *Middle East Report* 211 (1999): 20–2.

Lori, Noora. *Offshore Citizens Permanent Temporary Status in the Gulf*. Cambridge University Press, 2019.

"Temporary Workers or Permanent Migrants? The Kafala System and Contestations over Residency in the Arab Gulf States." *Note de l'IFRI*. French Institute for International Relations: Center for Migrations and Citizenship (2012): 1–35.

Louër, Laurence. "The State and Sectarian Identities in the Persian Gulf Monarchies: Bahrain, Saudi Arabia and Kuwait in Comparative Perspective." In *Sectarian Politics in the Persian Gulf*, edited by Lawrence Potter, 117–42. Oxford University Press, 2014.
Lowi, Miriam R. "Charity as Politics 'Writ Small' in Gulf Petro-Monarchies." *Journal of Muslim Philanthropy & Civil Society* 3, no.2 (2019): 26–53.
"Identity, Community, and Belonging in GCC States: Reflections on the Foreigner." *Sociology of Islam* 6, no.4 (2018): 401–28.
"Justice, Charity and the Common Good: In Search of Islam in Gulf Petro-Monarchies." *Middle East Journal* 71, no.4 (2017): 563–85.
"Modernity on Steroids: The Promise and Perils of Climate Protection in the Arabian Peninsula." In *Re-imagining Climate Change*, edited by Paul Wapner and Hilal Elver, 69–87. Routledge, 2016.
Oil Wealth and the Poverty of Politics: Algeria Compared. Cambridge University Press, 2009.
Lyall, Angus. "A Moral Economy of Oil: Corruption Narratives and Oil Elites in Ecuador." *Culture, Theory and Critique*, 16 August 2018: 1–20. https://doi.org/10.1080/14735784.2018.1507752
Lysa, Charlotte. "Governing Refugees in Saudi Arabia (1948–2022)." *Refugee Survey Quarterly* no.42 (2023): 1–28.
Lysa, Charlotte and Andrew Leber. "Onwards and Upwards with Women in the Gulf." Middle East Report Online (MERO), 11 January 2018. https://merip.org/2018/01/onwards-and-upwards-with-women-in-the-gulf
Magd, Hesham and Mark McCoy. "Islamic Finance Development in the Sultanate of Oman: Barriers and Recommendations." *Procedia Economics and Finance* 31 (2015): 677–88.
Mahdavy, Hossein. "The Patterns and Problems of Economic Development in Rentier States: The Case of Iran." In *Studies in the Economic History of the Middle East: From the Rise of Islam to the Present Day*, edited by Michael Cook, 37–61. Oxford University Press, 1970.
Al-Maimani, Jamal and Fuadah Binti Johari. "Enhancing Active Participation of SMEs and Islamic Banks towards Economic Diversification in Oman." *Procedia Economics and Finance* 31 (2015): 677–88.
Maktabi, Rania. "Female Citizenship and Family Law in Kuwait and Qatar: Globalization and Pressures for Reform in Two Rentier States." *Nidaba: an Interdisciplinary Journal of Middle East Studies* 1, no.1 (2016): 20–34.
Mandaville, Peter. *Transnational Muslim Politics: Reimagining the Umma*. Routledge, 2001.
Mandaville, Peter and Shadi Hamid. "Islam as Statecraft: How Governments Use Religion in Foreign Policy." Foreign Policy at Brookings, November 2018.
Marlow, Lousie. *Hierarchy and Egalitarianism in Islamic Thought*. Cambridge University Press, 1997.
Marx, Anthony. *Making Race and Nation: A Comparison of South Africa, the United States and Brazil*. Cambridge University Press, 1998.
Marzooq, Adel. "Qatar's Legislative Elections: A Debate for Citizenship Rights against Tribal Dominance." Sada: Carnegie Endowment for International Peace, 23 September 2021.

Matthiesen, Toby. *The Other Saudis: Shi'ism, Dissent and Sectarianism*. Cambridge University Press, 2015.

May, Samantha. "Political Piety: The Politicization of Zakat." *Middle East Critique* 22, no.2 (2013): 149–64.

Mazaheri, Nima. "The Saudi Monarchy and Economic Familism in an Era of Business Environment Reforms." *Business and Politics* 15, no.3 (2013): 295–321.

al-Mawsū'a al-Fiqhiyya (Encyclopedia of Islamic Jurisprudence). "Musta'min," part 37, 168–91. Kuwait: Ministry of Endowments and Islamic Affairs, 1997.

McMillen, Michael J. T. "Islamic Banking Law Decree in the Sultanate of Oman." 2013 Oman Law Blog of Curtis, Mallet-Prevost, Colt & Mosle LLP, 9 June 2013. https://papers.ssrn.com/sol3/papers.cfm?abstract_id=2276282

Mednicoff, David. "The Legal Regulation of Migrant Workers, Politics and Identity in Qatar and the United Arab Emirates." In *Migrant Labor in the Persian Gulf*, edited by Mehran Kamrava and Zahra Babar, 187–215. Hurst & Co., 2012.

"National Security and the Legal Status of Migrant Workers: Dispatches from the Arabian Gulf." *Western New England Law Review* 33, no.1 (2011): 121–62.

Menoret, Pascal. *Graveyard of Clerics: Everyday Activism in Saudi Arabia*. Stanford University Press, 2020.

Joyriding in Riyadh: Oil, Urbanism, and Road Revolt. New York: Cambridge University Press, 2014.

Menoret, Pascal and Nadav Samin. "The Bleak Romance of Tahliyah Street." *Middle East Journal of Culture and Communication* 6 (2013): 213–28.

Metcalf, Thomas. *Imperial Connections: India in the Indian Ocean Arena, 1860–1920*. University of California Press, 2007.

Mitchell, Jocelyn Sage and Justin Gengler. "What Money Can't Buy: Wealth, Inequality, and Economic Satisfaction in the Rentier State." *Political Research Quarterly* 72, no.1 (2018): 75–89.

Mitchell, Timothy. "Ten Propositions on Oil." In *A Critical Political Economy of the Middle East*, edited by Joel Beinin, Bassam Haddad and Sherene Seikaly, 68–84. Stanford University Press, 2021.

Carbon Democracy: Political Power in the Age of Oil. Verso, 2011.

"McJihad: Islam in the U.S. Global Order." *Social Text* 20, no.4 (2002): 1–18.

Mohamed, Abdul Fatah. "The Qatar Authority for Charitable Activities (QACA) from Commencement to Dissolution (2005-2009)." In *Gulf Charities and Islamic Philanthropy in the "Age of Terror" and Beyond*, edited by Robert Lacey and Jonathan Benthall, 259–71. Gerlach Press, 2014.

Momani, Bessma and Crystal A. Ennis. "Between Caution and Controversy: Lessons from the Gulf Arab States as (Re-)emerging Donors." *Cambridge Review of International Affairs* 25, no.4 (2012): 605–27.

Montagu, Caroline. "Civil Society and the Voluntary Sector in Saudi Arabia." *Middle East Journal* 64, no.1 (2010): 67–83.

Moumtaz, Nada. *God's Property: Islam, Charity and the Modern State*. University of California Press, 2021.

Morrison, Scott. "Oman's Islamic Banking Regulatory Framework: the Corporate Governance of Shariah Compliance in a New Jurisdiction." *Arab Law Quarterly* 29 (2015): 101–37.

Munif, Abdelrahman. *Cities of Salt*. Translated by Peter Theroux. Vintage, 1989.

Murphy, Caryle. "Heavy Police Presence Deters Protesters in Saudi Arabia." *GlobalPost*, 11 March 2011. https://theworld.org/stories/2011-03-11/heavy-police-presence-deters-protesters-saudi-arabia

Al-Mutairi, Abdullah and Al-Hunnayan, Sayed. "Attitudes of Customers towards Islamic Banks in Kuwait." *International Journal of Business and Management* 11, no.11 (2016): 59–69.

Naffee, Ibrahim. "Saudi Arabia-Born Expats Face an Identity Crisis." *Albawaba*, 18 April 2011. www.albawaba.com/saudi-arabia-born-expats-face-identity-crisis

Nagy, Sharon. "Making Room for Migrants, Making Sense of Difference: Spatial and Ideological Expressions of Social Diversity in Urban Qatar." *Urban Studies* 43, no.1 (2006): 119–37.

Naithani, Pranav. "Challenges Faced by Expatriate Workers in Gulf Cooperation Council Countries." *International Journal of Business and Management* 5, no.1 (2010): 98–103.

Al-Najjar, Baqer. "Al-ʿAmāla al-ʾAjnabiyya w'qaḍāya al-hawiyya fi'l-khalīj al-ʿarabī" (Foreign Labor and the Question of Identity in the Arabian Peninsula). *Omran* no.3 (2013): 1–24.

Nakhoul, Samia, Angus McDowall and Stephen Kalin. "A House Divided: How Saudi Crown Prince Purged Royal Family Rivals." *Reuters*, 10 November 2017. www.reuters.com/article/us-saudi-arrests-crownprince-insight/a-house-divided-how-saudi-crown-prince-purged-royal-family-rivals-idUSKBN1DA23M

Nakhleh, Emile. *Political Development in a Modernizing Society*. Lexington Books, 2011.

al-Nakib, Farah. "Modernity and the Arab Gulf States: The Politics of Heritage, Memory, and Forgetting." In *Routledge Handbook of Persian Gulf Politics*, edited by Mehran Kamrava, 57–82. Routledge, 2020.

Kuwait Transformed: A History of Oil and Urban Life. Stanford University Press, 2016.

"Revisiting 'Hadar' and 'Badu' in Kuwait: Citizenship, Housing and the Construction of a Dichotomy." *International Journal of Middle East Studies* 46, no.1 (2014): 5–30.

Naqvi, Syed Nawab Haider. *Morality and Human Well-Being: A Contribution to Islamic Economics*. The Islamic Foundation, 2003.

Islam, Economics, and Society. Kegan Paul International, 1994.

Nasr, Seyyed Vali Reza. "Mawdudi and the Jamaʿat-i-Islami: The Origins, Theory, and Practice of Islamic Revivalism." In *Pioneers of Islamic Revival*, edited by Ali Rahnema, 98–124. Zed Press, 2006.

The National News. "Oman Introduces 5% VAT on Goods and Services." *The National News*, 17 April 2021. www.thenationalnews.com/business/economy/oman-introduces-5-vat-on-goods-and-services-1.1204907

"All in the Details for Value Added Tax in the GCC." *The National News*, 4 February 2017. www.thenationalnews.com/business/all-in-the-details-for-value-added-tax-in-the-gcc-1.29091

Nereim, Vivian. "Saudi Arabia Begins Payouts to Buffer Belt-Tightening Blow." Bloomberg, 21 December 2017. www.bloomberg.com/news/articles/2017-12-21/saudi-arabia-begins-payouts-to-buffer-belt-tightening-blow

Noreng, Oystein. *Oil and Islam: Social and Economic Issues*. Wiley & Sons, 1997.

Ochsenwald, William. *Religion, Society, and the State in Arabia: The Hijaz under Ottoman Control 1840–1908*. Columbus: Ohio State University Press, 1984.

Okruhlik, Gwenn. "Dependence, Disdain, and Distance: State, Labor, and Citizenship in the Arab Gulf States." In *Industrialization in the Gulf: A Socioeconomic Revolution*, edited by Jean-François Seznec and Mimi Kirk, 125–42. Routledge, 2011.

Ollero, Antonio M., Sahar Sajjad Hussain, Sona Varma, Grzegorz Peszko, Helena Al-Naber and Munir Freih. "Economic Diversification for a Sustainable and Resilient GCC." *Gulf Economic Update* no.5. World Bank Group, December 2019. http://documents.worldbank.org/curated/en/886531574883246643/Economic-Diversification-for-a-Sustainable-and-Resilient-GCC

Onley, James. *The Arabian Frontier of the British Raj: Merchants, Rulers, and the British in the Nineteenth Century Gulf*. Oxford: Oxford University Press, 2007.

Onley, James and Sulayman Khalaf. "Sheikhly Authority in the Pre-oil Gulf: An Historical-Anthropological Study." *History and Anthropology* 17, no.3 (2006): 189–208.

Oxford Business Group. "Kuwait's Sharia-Compliant Financial Sector on the Rise." *Country Reports*, 2015. https://oxfordbusinessgroup.com/overview/growing-impact-despite-some-remaining-challenges-sharia-compliant-financial-sector-rise

"Updated Legislation Guides Zakat and Taxpayers Navigating Regulatory Framework," n.d. https://oxfordbusinessgroup.com/overview/path-forwards-updated-legislation-guides-zakat-and-taxpayers-navigating-regulatory-framework

Ozaral, Basak. "Islam and Moral Economy." In *The Sociology of Islam: Secularism, Economy, and Politics*, edited by Tugrul Keskin, 21–44. Ithaca Press, 2011.

Pall, Zoltan. "The Development and Fragmentation of Kuwait's al-Jama'a al-Salafiyya: Purity over Pragmatism." *Middle East Journal* 74, no.1 (2020): 9–29.

Parolin, Gianluca P. *Citizenship in the Arab World: Kin, Religion and Nation-State*. Amsterdam University Press, 2009.

Peck, Jennifer R. "Can Hiring Quotas Work? The Effect of the Nitaqat Program on the Saudi Private Sector." *American Economic Journal: Economic Policy* 9, no.2 (2017): 316–47.

Pepinsky, Thomas. "Development, Social Change, and Islamic Finance in Contemporary Indonesia." *World Development* 41 (2013): 157–67.

Perrault, Thomas. "Extracting Justice: Natural Gas, Indigenous Mobilization and the Bolivian State." In *The Politics of Resource Extraction: Indigenous*

Peoples, Multinational Corporations and the State, edited by Suzana Sawyer and Edmund Terence Gomez, 75–102. Palgrave MacMillan, 2012.

Petersen, Marie Juul. *For Humanity or for the Umma? Aid and Islam in Transnational Muslim NGOs*. Oxford University Press, 2015.

——— "Sacralized or Secularized Aid? Positioning Gulf-based Muslim Charities." In *Gulf Charities and Islamic Philanthropy in the "Age of Terror" and Beyond*, edited by Robert Lacey and Jonathan Benthall, 25–52. Gerlach Press, 2014.

——— "Trajectories of Transnational Muslim NGOs," *Development in Practice* 22, nos.5–6 (2012): 763–78.

Peterson, J. E. "Tribe and State in the Arabian Peninsula." *Middle East Journal* 74, no.4 (2020/21): 501–20.

——— "The Solitary Sultan and the Construction of the New Oman." In *Governance in the Middle East and North Africa: A Handbook*, edited by Abbas Kadhim, 319–29. London: Routledge, 2013.

——— "Oman's Diverse Society: Northern Oman." *Middle East Journal* 58, no.1 (2004): 31–51.

Platonova, Elena, Mehmet Asutay, Rob Dixon and Sabri Mohammad. "The Impact of Corporate Social Responsibility Disclosure on Financial Performance: Evidence from the GCC Islamic Banking Sector." *Journal of Business Ethics* no.151 (2018): 451–71.

Platteau, Jean-Phillipe. *Islam Instrumentalized: Religion and Politics in Historical Perspective*. Cambridge University Press, 2017.

——— "Political Instrumentalization of Islam and the Risk of Obscurantist Deadlock." *World Development* 39, no.2 (2011): 243–60.

Pollard, Lisa. "Egyptian by Association: Charitable States and Service Societies, circa 1850–1945." *International Journal of Middle East Studies* 46, no.2 (2014): 239–57.

Potter, Lawrence G. "Society in the Persian Gulf Before and After Oil." *Occasional Paper #18*. Center for Regional and International Studies, Georgetown University in Qatar, 2017.

——— ed. *Sectarian Politics in the Persian Gulf*. Oxford University Press, 2014.

Powers, David. "The Islamic Family Endowment [waqf]." *Vanderbilt Journal of Transnational Law* no.32 (1999): 1167–90.

PWC. "Doing Business in Kuwait: A Tax and Legal Guide" PricewaterhouseCoopers International, Ltd, 2015. www.pwc.com/m1/en/tax/documents/doing-business-guides/doing-business-guide-kuwait.pdf; updated January 2022: https://taxsummaries.pwc.com/kuwait/corporate/taxes-on-corporate-income

Al-Qaradawi, Yusuf. *Kayfa nataʿamal maʿa al-turath waʾl-tamadhhub waʾl-ikhtilāf* (How Do We Deal with Tradition, Doctrines and Difference?) Cairo: Maktabat waḥba, 2001.

——— *Fiqh al-Zakat* (Islamic Jurisprudence of Zakat), vols. 1 and 2. Dar al-Irshad, 1969.

Al-Qassemi, Sultan. "Tribalism in the Arabian Peninsula: It Is a Family Affair." *Jadaliyya e-zine*, 1 February 2012. www.jadaliyya.com/pages/index/4198/tribalism

Qiblawi, Tamara. "MBS Once Sought Advice from This Cleric. Now Saudi Prosecutors Want Him Executed." *CNN*, 25 July 2019. www.cnn.com/2019/07/25/middleeast/saudi-cleric-sheikh-salman-al-awda-intl/index.html

Qutb, Sayyid. *Social Justice in Islam*. Islamic Publications International, 1953.

Rahman, Anisur. "Migration and Human Rights in the Gulf," 16–18. In Middle East Institute, (Viewpoints Series) *Migration and the Gulf*. Middle East Institute, 2010.

al-Rasheed, Madawi. *Muted Modernists: The Struggle over Divine Politics in Saudi Arabia*. C. Hurst & Co., 2015.

"The Minaret and the Palace: Obedience at Home and Rebellion Abroad." In *The Political Economy of Arab Gulf States*, edited by Kristian Coates Ulrichsen, 720–38. Edward Elgar Publisher, 2013.

Contesting the Saudi State: Islamic Voices from a New Generation. Cambridge University Press, 2007.

"Transnational Connections and National Identity: Zanzibari Omanis in Muscat." In *Monarchies and Nations: Globalisation and Identity in the Arab States of the Gulf*, edited by Paul Dresch and James Piscatori, 96–113. I. B. Tauris, 2005.

A History of Saudi Arabia. Cambridge University Press, 2002.

Rashid, Mamunur and M. K. Hassan. "The Market Values of Islamic Banks and Ethical Identity." *American Journal of Islamic Social Sciences* 31, no.2 (2014): 43–74.

Rashid, Ahmed. *Taliban: Militant Islam, Oil and Fundamentalism in Central Asia*. Yale University Press, 2010.

Rehman, Aamir. *Gulf Capital and Islamic Finance: The Rise of the New Global Players*. McGraw Hill, 2010.

Rethel, Lena. "Economic Governance beyond State and Market: Islamic Capital Markets in Southeast Asia." *Journal of Contemporary Asia* 48, no.2 (2017): 301–21. https://doi.org/10.1080/00472336.2017.1404119

"Islamic Finance in Malaysia: Global Ambitions, Local Realities." In *The Everyday Political Economy of Southeast Asia*, edited by Juanita Elias and Lena Rethel, 116–36. Cambridge University Press, 2013.

"Whose Legitimacy? Islamic Finance and the Global Financial Order." *Review of IPE* 18, no.1 (2011): 75–98.

Reuters. "Oman Income Tax Expected in 2022 in Fiscal Shake-Up." Reuters, 2 November 2020. www.reuters.com/article/oman-economy-int/oman-income-tax-expected-in-2022-in-fiscal-shake-up-idUSKBN27I0XZ

"Qatar Allows Foreigners to Own Properties in More Areas." *Reuters*, 6 October 2020. www.reuters.com/article/qatar-economy-property-int-idUSKBN26R1EB

Rodinson, Maxime. *Islam and Capitalism*. University of Texas Press, 1978 (original edition 1966).

Rohde, David. "Mix of Quake Aid and Preaching Stirs Concern." *New York Times*, 22 January 2005. www.nytimes.com/2005/01/22/world/worldspecial4/mix-of-quake-aid-and-preaching-stirs-concern.html

Roper, Steven D. and Lilian A. Barria. "Understanding Variations in Gulf Migration and Labor Practices." *Middle East Law and Governance* 6, no.1 (2014): 32–52.

Rouhana, Nadim N. and Nadera Shalhoub-Kevorkian, eds. *When Politics are Sacralized: Comparative Perspectives on Religious Claims and Nationalism*. Cambridge University Press, 2021.

Ross, Michael L. *The Oil Curse: How Petroleum Wealth Shapes the Development of Nations*. Princeton University Press, 2012.

"Does Oil Hinder Democracy?" *World Politics* 53, no.3 (2001): 325–61.

"The Political Economy of the Resource Curse." *World Politics* 51, no.2 (1999): 297–322.

Ruiz De Elvira, Laura and Tina Zintl. "The End of the Baʿthist Social Contract in Bashar Al-Asad's Syria: Reading Sociopolitical Transformations through Charities and Broader Benevolent Activism." *International Journal of Middle East Studies* 46, no.2 (2014): 329–49.

Sachedina, Abdulaziz. *The Islamic Roots of Democratic Pluralism*. Oxford University Press, 2001.

Sachedina, Amal. *Cultivating the Past, Living the Modern: The Politics of Time in the Sultanate of Oman*. Cornell University Press, 2021.

Sachs, Jeffrey D. and Andrew Warner. "Natural Resource Abundance and Economic Growth." *Development Discussion Paper 517A*, Harvard Institute for International Development, 1995.

Al-Sadr, Muhammad Baqir. *Iqtiṣaduna* (Our Economy). Beirut: Dar al-Taʿaruf, 1982.

"Al-Naẓariyya al-Islamiyya li-Tawziʿ al-Maṣādir al-Tabʿiyya" (The Islamic Theory on the Distribution of Natural Resources). In *Ikhtarnalak*, Dar al-Zahraʾ, 1982b.

Saleh, Heba. "The President Plays Down Saudi Suspension of Oil Deliveries." *Financial Times*, 13 October 2016.

"Gulf States Put Money on Sisi's Egypt with Pledges worth $12bn." *Financial Times*, 13 March 2015.

Saleh, Heba and Kerr, Simeon. "Saudi Arabia to Restart Egypt Oil Deliveries," *Financial Times*, 16 March 2017.

Salvatore, Armando. *Public Sphere: Liberal Modernity, Catholicism, Islam*. Palgrave MacMillan, 2007.

Samin, Nadav. "Daʾwa, Dynasty, and Destiny in the Arab Gulf." *Comparative Studies in Society and History* 58, no.4 (2016): 935–54.

Of Sand or Soil: Genealogy and Tribal Belonging in Saudi Arabia. Princeton University Press, 2015.

Al-Saqqaf, Abdulaziz. "Storm Damage." *New Internationalist*, Issue no.236, 5 October 1992. https://newint.org/features/1992/10/05/storm

Saudi Arabia Monetary Authority (SAMA). "Shariah Governance Framework for Local Banks Operating in Saudi Arabia," 16 February 2020.

Saudi Gazette. "Bahrain Issues New Guidelines for Islamic Banks." *Saudi Gazette*. 19 September 2017. http://saudigazette.com.sa/article/517599/BUSINESS/Bahrain

"Charities Benefit from SR 23m Donated by Crown Prince." *Saudi Gazette*, 10 August 2017. https://saudigazette.com.sa/article/514856

Saudi Leaks. "Saudi Academic Hamzah Al-Salem's Fate Still Unknown after Forcible Disappearance Six Months Ago." *Saudi Leaks*, 25 April 2021. https://saudileaks.org/en/al-salem-2

Seccombe, Ian and R. Lawless."Work Camps and Company Towns: Settlement Patterns and the Gulf Oil Industry." *Occasional Papers Series*, 36. University of Durham, Centre for Middle Eastern and Islamic Studies, 1987.

Sells, Michael. "Saudi Nationalism, Wahhabi Daʿwa, and Western Power." In *When Politics Are Sacralized: Comparative Perspectives on Religious Claims and Nationalism*, edited by Nadim H. Rouhana and Nadera Shalhoub-Kevorkian, 275–306. Cambridge University Press, 2021.

Sethi, Aarti. "Why Two Hundred Ordinary Hindus Did Not See a Dead Muslim Child on a Railway Platform in North India." *Kafila Online*, 27 June 2017. https://kafila.online/2017/06/27/why-two-hundred-ordinary-hindus-did-not-see-a-dead-muslim-child-on-a-railway-platform-in-north-india

Seznec, Jean-Francois. "The Sovereign Wealth Funds of the Persian Gulf." In *The Political Economy of the Persian Gulf*, edited by Mehran Kamrava, 69–94. Columbia University Press, 2012.

Seznec, Jean-Francois and Samer Mosis. *The Financial Markets of the Arab Gulf: Power, Politics and Money*. Routledge, 2019.

Shah, Nasra M. "Labour Migration from Asian to GCC Countries: Trends, Patterns and Policies." *Middle East Law and Governance* 5, nos.1–2 (2013): 36–70.

Shah, Nasra M. and Philippe Fargues. "Introduction," Special Issue on Migration in the Gulf States: Issues and Prospects. *Asian and Pacific Migration Journal* 20, nos.3–4 (2011): 267–72.

Al-Sharekh, Alanoud and Courtney Freer. *Tribalism and Political Power in the Gulf: State-Building and National Identity in Kuwait, Qatar and the UAE*. I. B. Tauris, 2023.

Shushan, Debra and Christopher Marcoux. "The Rise (and Decline?) of Arab Aid: Generosity and Allocation in the Oil Era." *World Development* 39, no.11 (2011): 1969–80.

The Siasat Daily. "Saudi Arabia to Allow Foreigners to Purchase Property." *The Siasat Daily*, 30 March 2023. www.siasat.com/saudi-arabia-to-allow-foreigners-to-purchase-property-2557825

Simmel, Georg. "The Stranger." In *Georg Simmel: On Individuality and Social Forms*, edited by Donald Levine, 143–50. Chicago: University of Chicago Press, 1971 (originally published in, Soziologie: Untersuchungen über die Formen der Vergesellschaftung. Leipzig: Duncker & Humblot, 1908).

Singer, Amy, *Charity in Islamic Societies*. Cambridge University Press, 2008.

Sluglett, Peter. "La Monarchie dans le monde arabe: mythes et réalités." In *Monarchies Arabes: Transitions et Dérives Dynastique*, edited by Rémy Leveau and Abdellah Hammoudi, 143–62. La Documentation Françaises 2002.

Smith, Benjamin and David Waldner. *Rethinking the Resource Curse*. Cambridge University Press, 2021.

Smith, Kristin Diwan. "The Kuwait Finance House and the Islamization of Public Life in Kuwait." In *The Politics of Islamic Finance*, edited by Clement Henry and Rodney Wilson, 168–90. Edinburgh University Press, 2004.

Souaiaia, Ahmed E. "Theories and Practices of Islamic Finance and Exchange Laws: Poverty of Interest." *International Journal of Business and Social Science* 5, no.12 (2014): 34–52.

Stafford, Timothy. "An Emerging Philanthropic Superpower? Kuwaiti Humanitarian Efforts in Syria and Beyond." Conservative Middle East Council (UK). April 2017.

Steinberg, Guido. "The Wahhabi Ulama and the Saudi State: 1745 to the Present." In *Saudi Arabia in the Balance: Political Economy, Society, Foreign Affairs*, edited by Paul Aarts and Gerd Nonneman, 11–34. New York University Press, 2006.

al-Subaiey, Maryam. "The Invisible Army." In *Gathering the Tide: An Anthology of Contemporary Arabian Gulf Poetry*, edited by Jeff Lodge, Patty Paine and Samia Touati, 171–72. Ithaca Press, 2012.

Tabaar, Mohammad Ayatollahi. *Religious Statecraft: the Politics of Islam in Iran*. Columbia University Press, 2018.

Tabash, Mosab I. and Raj S. Dhankar. "Islamic Banking and Economic Growth: Empirical Evidence from Qatar." *Journal of Applied Economics and Business* 2, no.1 (2014): 51–67.

Takriti, Abdel Razzaq. "Political Praxis in the Gulf: Ahmad al-Khatib and the Movement of Arab Nationalists, 1948–1969." In *Arabic Thought against the Authoritarian Age: Towards an Intellectual History of the Present*, edited by Jens Hanssen and Max Weiss, 86–112. Cambridge University Press, 2018.

Monsoon Revolution: Republicans, Sultans and Empires in Oman 1965–1976. Oxford University Press, 2013.

Tetreault, Mary Ann. "Bottom-Up Democratization in Kuwait." In *Political Change in the Arab Gulf States: Stuck in Transition*, edited by Mary Ann Tetreault, Gwenn Okruhlik and Andrzej Kapiszewski, 73–98. Lynne Rienner Publishers, 2011.

Stories of Democracy: Politics and Society in Contemporary Kuwait. Columbia University Press, 2000

"Autonomy, Necessity, and the Small State: Ruling Kuwait in the Twentieth Century." *International Organization* 45, no.4 (1991): 565–91.

Times of Oman. "Expats Can Now Own Properties Outside of ITCs," *Times of Oman*, 9 March 2022. https://timesofoman.com/article/114152-expats-can-now-own-properties-outside-itcs

Tinker-Salas, Miguel. *The Enduring Legacy: Oil, Culture and Society in Venezuela*. Duke University Press, 2009.

Tobin, Sarah. *Everyday Piety: Islam and Economy in Jordan*. Cornell University Press, 2016.

Tok, Evren, Rachael Calleja and Hanaa El-Ghaish. "Arab Development Aid and the New Dynamics of Multilateralism: Towards Better Governance?" *European Scientific Journal* 1 (2014): 591–604.

Toth, Anthony B. "Control and Allegiance at the Dawn of the Oil Age: Bedouin, Zakat, and Struggles for Sovereignty in Arabia, 1916–1955." *Middle East Critique* 21, no.1 (2012): 57–79.

Tripp, Charles. *Islam and the Moral Economy: the Challenge of Capitalism.* Cambridge University Press, 2006.

Turak, Natasha. "The UAE Is Now Offering Citizenship to Foreigners and the Economic Gains Could Be 'Transformative.'" *CNBC*, 1 Feb. 2021. www.cnbc.com/2021/02/01/the-uae-is-offering-citizenship-to-foreigners-sees-economic-potential.html

Ulrichsen, Kristian Coates. "Migrant Labor in the Gulf." In *The Gulf States in International Political Economy*, edited by Kristian Coates Ulrichsen, 167–241. Palgrave/MacMillan 2016.

"The Politics of Economic Reform in Arab Gulf States." *Center for the Middle East*, Rice University's Baker Institute for Public Policy, June 2016.

Unnikrishnan, Deepak, "The Hidden Cost of Migrant Labor: What It Means to Be a Temporary Person in the Gulf." *Foreign Affairs*, January/February 2020. www.foreignaffairs.com/articles/india/2020-02-07/hidden-cost-migrant-labor

U.S. Energy Information Administration (US-EIA). Country Analysis Brief: Qatar, 28 March 2023. www.eia.gov/international/content/analysis/countries_long/Qatar/qatar.pdf

al-Uwaisheg, Abd al-Aziz. "Kayf Naḥaṣan Niṭām Rusūm al-ʾArāḍiy al-Bayḍāʾ" (How Can We Improve the Fee System on "White Lands?") *Al-Watan Online*, 4 December 2015. www.alwatan.com.sa/Articles/Detail.aspx?ArticleID=28738#

Valeri, Marc. "Simmering Unrest and Succession Challenges in Oman." Carnegie Endowment for International Peace. January 2015.

"The Ṣuḥār Paradox: Social and Political Mobilisations in the Sultanate of Oman since 2011." *Arabian Humanities* (online), 4 (2015). http://journals.openedition.org/cy/2828; DOI: https://doi.org/10.4000/cy.2828.

"Oligarchy vs. Oligarchy: Business and Politics of Reform in Bahrain and Oman." In *Business Politics in the Middle East*, edited by Steffen Hertog, Giacomo Luciani and Marc Valeri, 17–41. London: Hurst & Co., 2013.

"High Visibility, Low Profile: the Shiʿa in Oman under Sultan Qaboos." *International Journal of Middle East Studies* 42, no.2 (2010): 251–68.

Oman: Politics and Society in the Qaboos State. Oxford University Press, 2009.

Vassiliev, Alexei. *The History of Saudi Arabia.* NYU Press, 1998.

Vitalis, Robert. *America's Kingdom: Mythmaking on the Saudi Oil Frontier.* Stanford University Press, 2006.

vom Hau, Fulya Aypadin. "Regulating Islamic Banks in Authoritarian Settings: Malaysia and the UAE in Comparative Perspective." *Regulation and Governance* 12, no.4 (2018): 466–85.

Vora, Neha. "Expat/Expert Camps: Redefining 'Labour' within Gulf Migration." In *Transit States: Labour, Migration and Citizenship in the Gulf*, edited by Abdulhadi Khalaf, Omar Al-Shehabi and Adam Hanieh, 170–97. Pluto Press, 2015.

"From Golden Frontier to Global City: Shifting Forms of Belonging, 'Freedom,' and Governance among Indian Businessmen in Dubai." *American Anthropologist* 113, no.2 (2011): 306–18.

"Producing Diasporas and Globalization: Indian Middle-Class Migrants in Dubai." *Anthropological Quarterly* 81, no.2 (2008): 377–406.

Wald, Kenneth D., Adam L. Sliverman and Kevin Friday. "Making Sense of Religion in Political Life." *Annual Review of Political Science* 8 (2004): 121–43.

Wallin, Matthew. "US Military Bases and Facilities in the Middle East: Fact Sheet." American Security Project, June 2018. www.americansecurityproject.org/fact-sheet-us-military-bases-and-facilities-in-the-middle-east

Warde, Ibrahim. *Islamic Finance in the Global Economy*, 2nd edition. Edinburgh University Press, 2010.

Weiner, Scott. "The Politics of Kuwait's Bidoon Issue." Sada: Carnegie Endowment for International Peace, October 20, 2017. https://carnegieendowment.org/sada/73492

Wells, Madeleine and Rivka Azoulay. "Contesting Welfare State Politics in Kuwait." *Middle East Report* 272 (2014).

Wilkinson, John C. *The Imamate Tradition of Oman*. Cambridge University Press, 1987.

Willoughby, J. "Ambivalent Anxieties of the South Asian – Gulf Arab Labour Exchange." In *Globalization and the Gulf*, edited by J. W. Fox, N. Mourtada-Sabbah and M. Al-Mutawa, 223–43. Routledge, 2006.

Wilson, Rodney. "Etatisme versus Market Driven Islamic Banking: The Experiences of Iran and the Arabian Peninsula Compared." In *The Political Economy of the Persian Gulf*, edited by M. Kamrava, 125–45. Columbia University Press, 2012.

"The Development of Islamic Finance in the GCC." Kuwait Programme on Development, Governance and Globalisation in the Gulf States, London School of Economics, May 2009.

Winckler, Onn. "Labor Migration to the GCC States: Patterns, Scale, and Policies." Middle East Institute, February 2010.

"Labor and Liberalization: the Decline of the GCC Rentier System." In Political Liberalization in the Persian Gulf, edited by Joshua Teitelbaum, 59-85. Columbia University, 2009.

Woertz, Eckart. *Oil for Food: The Global Food Crisis and the Middle East*. Oxford University Press, 2013.

Wohidul Islam, Muhammad. "Al-Mal: The Concept of Property in Islamic Legal Thought." *Arab Studies Quarterly* 14, no.4 (1999): 361–68.

World Bank Group. *Towards a National Jobs Strategy in Kuwait: Overview*. World Bank, 28 September 2022. http://documents.worldbank.org/curated/en/099155109292260319/P16615507094f70ac09ff10e025ddcfd40b

Wright, Steven. "Political Absolutism in the Gulf Monarchies." In *Routledge Handbook of Persian Gulf Politics*, edited by Mehran Kamrava, 346–56. Routledge 2020.

Al-Yahya, Khalid and Nathalie Fustier. "Saudi Arabia as a Global Humanitarian Donor." In *Gulf Charities and Islamic Philanthropy in the "Age of Terror" and Beyond*, edited by Robert Lacey and Jonathan Benthall, 169–98. Gerlach Press, 2014.

Yergin, Daniel. *The Prize: The Epic Quest for Oil, Money and Power*. Touchstone, 1991.

Young, Karen E. "Sovereign Risk: Gulf Sovereign Wealth Funds as Engines of Growth and Political Resource." *British Journal of Middle Eastern Studies* 47, no.1 (2020): 96–116.

Zeghal, Malika. "Veiling and Unveiling Muslim Women: State Coercion, Islam and the 'Disciplines of the Heart.'" In *The Construction of Belief: Reflections on the Thought of Mohammed Arkoun*, edited by Abdou Filaly-Ansary and Aziz Esmail, 127–49. Saqi Books, 2012.

Zaman, Muhammad Qasim. *Modern Islamic Thought in a Radical Age: Religious Authority and Internal Criticism*. Cambridge University Press, 2012.

"The 'Ulama of Contemporary Islam and their Conceptions of the Common Good." In *Public Islam and the Common Good*, edited by Armando Salvatore and Dale Eickelman, 129–55. Brill, 2004.

Zaman, Nazim and Mehmet Asutay. "Divergence between Aspirations and Realities of Islamic Economics: A Political Economy Approach to Bridging the Divide." *IIUM Journal of Economics and Management* 17, no.1 (2009): 73–96.

Zawya. "Oman Sticks to Target of Implementing Income Tax by 2024." *Zawya*, 20 September 2022. www.zawya.com/en/economy/gcc/oman-sticks-to-target-of-implementing-income-tax-by-2024

"Job Security Fund Benefits over 10,000 Omanis who Lost Jobs," *Zawya*, 19 October 2021. www.zawya.com/en/economy/job-security-fund-benefits-over-10-000-omanis-who-lost-jobs-en81syy0

Zysow, Aaron. "Zakat." Encyclopaedia of Islam, 2nd edition. Brill Online, 2013 http://referenceworks.brillonline.com/entries/encyclopaedia-of-islam-2/zakat-COM_1377

Index

Accounting and Auditing Organization for Islamic Financial Institutions (AAOIFI), 145, 151, 157
Alwaleed bin Talal Foundation/Alwaleed Philanthropies, 122, 124
Al-'Alayli, (Sheikh) 'Abd-allah, 95
Al-Aouda, (Sheikh) Salman, 75, 86–87
Arab nationalism, 22, 85, 109, 120, 127, 143, 146
Arab Oil embargo (1973), 24
and oil price "shock," 24, 31, 91, 118
Arab Spring, 53, 74, 86, 145, 149, 168
ARAMCO, 21, 69, 91, 99, 136
Autocracy, 6, 9–10, 17, 19, 22, 68, 74, 92, 94, 107, 111, 118, 149, 154, 166–67, 169, 171, 173

Bab Rizq Jameel, 136–37
Bahrain, 1, 3–5, 7, 25, 68, 77, 90, 104, 135, 152
and Islamic Banking and Finance, 145, 152, 158
and Shi'a, 4, 68, 164
Bahwan family (Oman), 129, 135
Bhabha, Homi, 89, 110
bidūn, 54, 70–72
in Kuwait, 71–72
in Saudi Arabia, 71
Bin Bayyah, (Sheikh) Abdallah, 36–37
Britain
and Dhofar revolution, 21
as imperial power in Gulf, 9, 18–19, 25, 46, 88–90, 98
and oil exploration, 1–2, 9, 21, 23, 31, 89–90
and Security of Gulf States, 9, see also United States security of Gulf States
and state-formation in Gulf, 20–25
Bukhamseen family (Kuwait), 130, 156

Charitable giving, 4, 27
encouraged by ruling elites, 113, 116, 138, 173
and *da'wa*, 115–18, 128–29, 132, 138
and foreign residents, 57, 68, 105, *see also labor, foreign*
by governments, 112, 114, 120–21, 123, 126, 128, 134
and implications regarding politics, 112–27, 136, 139
to imported labor, 114, 130–32, 139
by members of royal families, 113, 117, 120–27, 138, 170
motivations for, 37, 112, 115, 138
multilateral agencies, 114–19
by non-governmental agencies, 112, 120–21, 123, 127–29
and poverty, 39–41, 135, 137–38
by private actors, 112, 122–23, 129–30, 132, 134–35
sadaqa, 39, 132
and transparency, 112, 134
zakat, 132, 135, 138, See also zakat
Citizenship
in Gulf states, 27, 37, 66, 68–70, 88, 102, 107, 130, *see also Government Distributions to all citizens*
and naturalization, 44–45, 68–72, 92–93, 102, 107
Consumption
as an organizing principle, 17, 24, 28, 48, 50, 72, 81, 166, 171
Coronil, Fernando, 14, 167

Dhimma, dhimmi, 44–46, 109

Ecuador, 14
Eid bin Mohamed al-Thani Foundation, 125, 132
and *dyuf Qatar*, 131–32
and ḥafiẓ 'ala na'ima, 132

Index

Employment
  private sector, 53, 62, 65, 67, 69, 133
  public sector, 48, 50, 52–57, 86, 97, 101
Fanon, Franz, 89
Foreigners, see also labor, foreign
  as "stranger," 92–93
  and perception of threat, 91, 94, 96, 109
  and property ownership, 104–5
  and social cohesion, 92–93

Ghazali, Abdelhamid, 35
Government Distributions, 4, 16, 37
  to all citizens, 4, 10, 12, 16–17, 27, 47, 50, 54–55
  to merchants/private sector, 23, 64–66
  and poverty alleviation, 33, 51–52, 57, 66–67, 77–78, 113, 125, 133
  and response to oil price downturn, 49–50, 53, 55–57
  to royals, 47, 58–62, 78–80
  to students, 51
  to tribes, 54, 62–64, 80–81

al-haraka al-dusturiyya al-islamiyya (HADAS, Islamic Constitutional Movement), Kuwait, 128
Hierarchy, 14, 17, 23, 27, 34, 45, 48–49, 52, 62–64, 69, 73, 92, 96–100, 103, 110–11, 138, 166, 168–69, 172

Ibadi Islam (Ibadism), 31, 121, 148, see also Oman Ibadism
Ibn Baz, (Grand Mufti) 'Abd al-'Aziz, 86
ijaara, 143, 159
Instrumentalism, 10–11
International investments of GCC States, 19, 21, 24–25
International Islamic Charitable Organization (IICO), 116, 118
International Islamic Council for Da'wa and Relief (IICDR), 116, 118
International Islamic Relief Organization (IIROSA), 116–17
Iran, 3, 11, 14, 21, 85, 90, 103, 117, 129, 153
Iraq invasion of Kuwait, 84, 127
  and Gulf War, 25, 85–86, 103, see also United States Intervention
  and Kuwait royal family, 85
  and Muslim Brotherhood, 127
  and Sahwa response, 86
  Saudi Arabia host foreign troops, 25, 86
Islam, normative tradition, 11, 32–44, 140
  and belonging (*intīma'*), 28, 44, 68, 88, 95–96, 108–9
  and charity (*zakat* and *sadaqa*), 27, 39–41, 106, 112–14, See also zakat
  common good (maslaha), 33–37, 47, 76, 123, 136, 141, 162, 166, 173, See also maslaha
  equity (qist), 28, 33–35, 39, 43, 46, 49, 51, 54, 81, 83, 86, 140, 142–43, 157
  and good works (saliḥāt), 33, 38, 165
  and *haqq*, 39, 172
  justice (*'adl*), 11–12, 16, 33–36, 76, 83
  as political resource, 4, 11, 14, 16–17, 22, 32, 41–42, 72, 74–75, 81–85, 114, 116, 167–68, 171, See also Shari'a in Constitutions
  and resources, 33
  and umma, 42–44, 88, 108, 111, 131, See also umma
  and wealth, property, resources, 37–39, 42–43, 79
Islamic Banking and Finance, 4, 16, 27–28
  and collaborations between royals and business, 48, 62, 65, 100, 156–57, 171, see also Royals in Business
  and compensation of Shari'a scholars, 158
  corporate social responsibility, 165
  and criticisms of, 147, 159–63
  and debt, 159
  and development, 147–49
  and enrichment, 145, 155
  and "financial lobby," 166
  and global capitalism, 65, 148, 166
  and government regulation of, 146–54
  growth of, 145–46
  history of, 143–45
  and interests of ruling elites, 66, 148, 154–58, 166, 173
  in Malaysia, 149, 153–54, 162
  and micro-finance, 163–64
  origins, 85, 140–41
  principles, 141–42
  Shari'a boards, 118, 134, 145, 148, 150–53, 157–58, 161, 164, 171
  and *takāful* (Islamic insurance), 131, 152, 165
  tools/instruments/contracts, 142–43, 159–60
  in UAE, 145–46, 149, 153–54, 164
  and zakat collection, 157, see also zakat
Islamic Development Bank (IDB), 78, 118–19, 144, 147, 162–63
Islamic Economics, 31, 140–41

Index

Jamaʿiyyat al-Islaḥ al-Ijtimaʿi, 128–29
Jamaʿiyyat Ihyaʾ al-Turath al-Islami, 128
Jameel, Abdellatif, 136

kafala (for non-citizens), 99–101, 170
  appeasement of, 100
  and *kafīl*, 130
  and nation building, 101
  purpose of, 99
  reforms of, 130
King Abdallah International Foundation for Charity and Humanitarian Deeds, 122
King Faisal Foundation, 122
King Salman Humanitarian Aid and Relief Center (KS Relief), 117
Al-Khorafi family (Kuwait), 65
Kuwait
  Al Sabah and Islamists, 85, 127
  Al Sabah royal family, 19, 60, 62–63, 85, 119, 130, 146, 156
  and bidūn71, See also bidūn
  and charitable foundations, 66, 121, 127–28, 135, See also Kuwait Fund for Arab Economic Development (KFAED)
  and Islamic Banking and Finance, 146, 150, 152, 156, 160, *see also Kuwait Finance House*
  and merchants, 63–65
  and Muslim Brotherhood, 84–86, 127, 129, 146, *see also Muslim Brotherhood*
  National Assembly (Parliament), 5, 10, 23, 36, 57–58, 64–65, 80, 82, 85, 127–28, 165
  and political participation, 5, 10, 23, 80–81, 85, 154
  and ruler's allowance, 58, 60, 80
  and Salafi movement, 84–85, 127–29, See also al-Tajammuʿ al-Salafi al-Islami (Salafi Islamic Gathering), Kuwait
  and Shiʿa, 68, 70, 129, 133
  and zakat collection, 133, 170, *see also zakat*
Kuwait Finance House, 145–46, 160, 165
Kuwait Fund for Arab Economic Development (KFAED), 119

Labor Force
  national and imported, 26, 28, 46, 57, 91–92, 94, 100, 169
  public sector and private sector, 52–54, 62, 65, 69, 86, 97, 101
labor mobilization, 91
labor, foreign, 4, 23, 26, 88
  and access to resources/services, 27, 95, 97, 99, 107, 110, 114
  Arabs (non-GCC), 88, 90, 93–96, 98–99, 104, 108–11
  Asians, 93, 95, 98–99, 103, 108–11, 131
  blue collar, 93, 100–1, 104, 106, 111
  and deportations, 72, 103
  Europeans, 88, 93–94, 97, 99, 104–5, 108–10
  hierarchization of, 93–94, 96–99, 107, 110–11, *see also United States and labor hierarchy/segregation*
  importation/recruitment of, 23, 26, 28, 69, 94, 98, 101–2
  and lodgin, 102–5
  and mustaʾamin, 108–9, 169, 172, *See also Mustaʾamin, Mustaʾamān*
  numbers/proportions in GCC states, 91, 94, 96, 103
  organization of, 98, 107, 110
  and property ownership, 97, 104–5, 110
  relationship to sponsor (*kafīl*), 99–100, 106, *see also kafala*
  role in nation-building, 88, 93–94, 98, 101, 107–10, 139
Luwati, Luwatiyya, 66

maṣlaḥa, 35–37, 41, 43, 81, 162, 173–74
Mawdudi, Abu'l Aʿla, 31, 140
Modernization, 46, 76, 107, 141, 173
  and legitimation, 15, 24, 47–48, 77, 90
mudaraba, 142–43, 159–61
Munif, Abdelrahmam, 24, 89, 109
murabaḥa, 143, 159–60
musharaka, 142–43, 157, 159–61
Muslim Brotherhood, 2, 84, 116, 125
  in Kuwait, 85–86, 127–29
  in Qatar, 77, 125, 137
  in Saudi Arabia, 84
Muslim World League, 115–18, 120
Mustaʾamin, Mustaʾamān, 45–46, 108–9, 172
Mutawaʾa, 41, 84, 86

occupation of Grand Mosque of Mecca (1979), 84
Oil and gas industry
  companies in Gulf, 62, *see also United States oil companies*
  exploration and state formation, 20, 31, 59, 63, 90, *see also Britain oil exploration*
  and labor unrest, 91
  and price downturn (2014–21), 14, 49, 105, 126
  rents, 1–6, 9–10, 15–16, 29, 41, 47, 49, 94, 143, 168

reserves, 3, 5, 7
revenues, 2, 10, 16–17, 47–48, 78, 110, 119
and "secrecy," 10, 58, 79, 112
Oman
  Al BuSaʿid royal family, 9, 20, 59, 61, 63, 79, 156
  and charitable giving, 121, 129, 135, 137, *see also* Oman Charitable Organization [OCO]
  and Ibadism, 5, 20, 31, 121, 148, 172
  and Imamate, 20–21
  and Islamic Banking and Finance, 148–52
  and majlis al-shura, 23, 77
  and poverty eradication, 67, 135
  and Shiʿa, 68, 121, 148
  and "universal" Islam, 137, 148
Oman Charitable Organization (OCO), 121
Organization of the Islamic Cooperation (OIC), 115, 118

Political Participation, 10, 17, 23–24, 68, 74–76, 82, 168, *see also* Kuwait and political participation
Public–private collaborations
  in business, 171
  in Islamic banking and finance, 144, 157

Al-Qaradawi, (Sheikh) Yusuf, 35–37, 41, 43, 69, 116
Qatar
  and charitable foundations, 66, 120–21, 125–26, 135, 137, *see also* Qatar Charity and Qatar Foundation
  and Islamic Banking and Finance, 150–52
  and majlis al-shura, 23
  and Muslim Brotherhood, 77, 125, 137
  and Salafi movement, 125, 137
  Al-Thani royal family, 9, 19, 61–62, 79, 125, 137, 156
Qatar Charity, 125–26
Qatar Foundation, 126–27
Qutb, Saʿid, 38, 140

Al-Rajhi Bank, 146–48, 156, 160
Al-Rajhi family (Saudi Arabia), 129, 146–48, 156, 160
Rentier State(s), 6, 9–10, 15, 47, 100, 167
  and rentierism, 94, 167
  Theory of, 9–10, 171
ribaʾ, 39, 86, 140–41, 143, 146, 159, *see also* Islam, normative tradition
Rodinson, Maxime, 11, 141, 167

Royals
  in business, 48, 58–62, 64
  and land ownership, 59–60

Al-Sadr, Baqir, 42, 140
Sahwa movement (Al-Sahwa al-Islamiyya), 75, 86–87
Al Saʿid, (Sultan) Saʿid bin Taimur, 21
Al Saʿid, (Sultan) Haitham bin Tariq, 62, 137
Al Saʿid, (Sultan) Qaboos bin Saʿid, 12, 16, 21, 61, 63, 121, 156
  response to Arab Spring, 86–87, 148
  and sectarianism, 66, 137
Al Saʿud, (Prince/King) Faisal, 63, 71, 115, 123, 143, *see also* King Faisal Foundation
Al Saʿud, ʿAbd al-ʿAziz bin Abdul Rahman ('Ibn Saʾud), 20, 22, 41
Saudi Arabia
  Al Saʿud royal family, 9, 41, 59, 79, 82, 84, 86–87, 117, 121, 137, 143, 147
  and bidūn, 71, *see also* bidūn
  and charitable giving, 115–16, 118, 121
  and Islamic Banking and Finance, 148, 150, 155, 157, 164
  and *majlis al-shura*, 66, 79–80
  and Muslim Brotherhood, 84
  and NGO law (2015), 122–23
  and oil concession with U.S., 20
  and poverty eradication, 67, 122–23, 133
  and Rohingya, 71
  and Sahwa, 75, 77, 80, 86, *see also* Sahwa movement (Al-Sahwa al-Islamiyya)
  and Shiʿa, 68–69, 77, 117, 120
  and Vision 2030, 67, 123
  and "white lands," 60, 75, 133
  and zakat collection, 133, *see also* zakat
Saudi-Wahhabi statehood
  1744-1818, 20
  1824-1891, 20
  1913-, 20
Shariʿa
  in Constitutions, 3, 31, 36, 86, 110
Al Sheikh family, 61, 83, 168
Al Sheikh, (Grand Mufti) ʿAbd al-ʿAziz, 83, 168
Shura, 18–19, 23, 37, 58, 77
Social contract, 10, 24, 48, 54, 72
sukūk, 142–43

al-Tajammuʿ al-Salafi al-Islami (Salafi Islamic Gathering), Kuwait, 128
Al-Thani, (Sheikh) Hamad bin Khalifa, 61, 126

Al-Thani, (Sheikh) Tamim bin Hamad, 61
Tribal dynastic monarchy, 19, 23
Tribes and tribalism
  and formal identification, 63
  in Gulf today, 63, 68, 72, 81, 114, 134–35, 139
  in Gulf, pre-independent state, 1–2, 18–20, 41, 62–64, 89
Tunisia, 12–14, 75, 82

ulama, 11, 36
  authority in modern state, 11–12, 28, 34, 46, 84
  authority in pre-modern state, 22
  independent, 40, 74
  official, 12, 20, 22, 36–37, 133.
umma
  and dhimmi, 44–45, 109, See also Dhimma, dhimmi
  in modern Gulf today, 5, 46, 76, 106, 116, 172
  in normative tradition, 11, 15–16, 30, 37, 42, 47, 70, 72, 95–96, 109, 169
United Arab Emirates (UAE), 2–5, 25, 56, 70, 99, 103–4, 106, 154, 169

Islamic Banking and Finance, 145–46, 149, 153–54, 164
United States
  intervention in the Gulf, 85, 103
  and labor hierarchy/segregation, 91, 98
  oil companies, 9, 19, 23, 90–91, 95
  security of Gulf States, 6, 9, 25, 84, 86
Al-Utaibi, Juhayman, 84–85

Al-Wafa' Women's Philanthropic Society, 123–24, 130
Wahhabiyya, Wahhabism, 20, 22, 41, 115, 137
  in Saudi Arabia, 20–21, 32, 115, 137, 143
waqf/awqāf, 12, 122, 125–26, 130, 135
World Assembly of Muslim Youth, 115–18

Zakat, 16, 39–42, 112, 132–35, 138, 157, 170
  collection in Sa'udi state pre-oil, 41
  and "evasion," 134
  imposed in Kuwait, 133, 157
  imposed in Saudi Arabia, 133
  and revision of in Kuwait, 170
  and revision of in Saudi Arabia, 133, 170
Al-Zamil family (Saudi Arabia), 65, 155–56

Books in the Series

1 Parvin Paidar, *Women and the Political Process in Twentieth-Century Iran*
2 Israel Gershoni and James Jankowski, *Redefining the Egyptian Nation, 1930–1945*
3 Annelies Moors, *Women, Property and Islam: Palestinian Experiences, 1920–1945*
4 Paul Kingston, *Britain and the Politics of Modernization in the Middle East, 1945–1958*
5 Daniel Brown, *Rethinking Tradition in Modern Islamic Thought*
6 Nathan J. Brown, *The Rule of Law in the Arab World: Courts in Egypt and the Gulf*
7 Richard Tapper, *Frontier Nomads of Iran: The Political and Social History of the Shahsevan*
8 Khaled Fahmy, *All the Pasha's Men: Mehmed Ali, His Army and the Making of Modern Egypt*
9 Sheila Carapico, *Civil Society in Yemen: The Political Economy of Activism in Arabia*
10 Meir Litvak, *Shi'i Scholars of Nineteenth-Century Iraq: The Ulama of Najaf and Karbala*
11 Jacob Metzer, *The Divided Economy of Mandatory Palestine*
12 Eugene L. Rogan, *Frontiers of the State in the Late Ottoman Empire: Transjordan, 1850–1921*
13 Eliz Sanasarian, *Religious Minorities in Iran*
14 Nadje Al-Ali, *Secularism, Gender and the State in the Middle East: The Egyptian Women's Movement*
15 Eugene L. Rogan and Avi Shlaim, eds., *The War for Palestine: Rewriting the History of 1948*
16 Gershon Shafir and Yoar Peled, *Being Israeli: The Dynamics of Multiple Citizenship*
17 A. J. Racy, *Making Music in the Arab World: The Culture and Artistry of Tarab*
18 Benny Morris, *The Birth of the Palestinian Refugee Crisis Revisited*
19 Yasir Suleiman, *A War of Words: Language and Conflict in the Middle East*
20 Peter Moore, *Doing Business in the Middle East: Politics and Economic Crisis in Jordan and Kuwait*
21 Idith Zertal, *Israel's Holocaust and the Politics of Nationhood*
22 David Romano, *The Kurdish Nationalist Movement: Opportunity, Mobilization and Identity*

23 Laurie A. Brand, *Citizens Abroad: Emigration and the State in the Middle East and North Africa*
24 James McDougall, *History and the Culture of Nationalism in Algeria*
25 Madawi al-Rasheed, *Contesting the Saudi State: Islamic Voices from a New Generation*
26 Arang Keshavarzian, *Bazaar and State in Iran: The Politics of the Tehran Marketplace*
27 Laleh Khalili, *Heroes and Martyrs of Palestine: The Politics of National Commemoration*
28 M. Hakan Yavuz, *Secularism and Muslim Democracy in Turkey*
29 Mehran Kamrava, *Iran's Intellectual Revolution*
30 Nelida Fuccaro, *Histories of City and State in the Persian Gulf: Manama since 1800*
31 Michaelle L. Browers, *Political Ideology in the Arab World: Accommodation and Transformation*
32 Miriam R. Lowi, *Oil Wealth and the Poverty of Politics: Algeria Compared*
33 Thomas Hegghammer, *Jihad in Saudi Arabia: Violence and Pan-Islamism since 1979*
34 Sune Haugbolle, *War and Memory in Lebanon*
35 Ali Rahnema, *Superstition as Ideology in Iranian Politics: From Majlesi to Ahmadinejad*
36 Wm. Roger Louis and Avi Shlaim, eds., *The 1967 Arab-Israeli War: Origins and Consequences*
37 Stephen W. Day, *Regionalism and Rebellion in Yemen: A Troubled National Union*
38 Daniel Neep, *Occupying Syria under the French Mandate: Insurgency, Space and State Formation*
39 Iren Ozgur, *Islamic Schools in Modern Turkey: Faith, Politics, and Education*
40 Ali M. Ansari, *The Politics of Nationalism in Modern Iran*
41 Thomas Pierret, *Religion and State in Syria: The Sunni Ulama from Coup to Revolution*
42 Guy Ben-Porat, *Between State and Synagogue: The Secularization of Contemporary Israel*
43 Madawi Al-Rasheed, *A Most Masculine State: Gender, Politics and Religion in Saudi Arabia*
44 Sheila Carapico, *Political Aid and Arab Activism: Democracy Promotion, Justice, and Representation*
45 Pascal Menoret, *Joyriding in Riyadh: Oil, Urbanism, and Road Revolt*
46 Toby Matthiesen, *The Other Saudis: Shiism, Dissent and Sectarianism*
47 Bashir Saade, *Hizbullah and the Politics of Remembrance: Writing the Lebanese Nation*
48 Noam Leshem, *Life After Ruin: The Struggles over Israel's Depopulated Arab Spaces*
49 Zoltan Pall, *Salafism in Lebanon: Local and Transnational Movements*
50 Salwa Ismail, *The Rule of Violence: Subjectivity, Memory and Government in Syria*

51 Zahra Ali, *Women and Gender in Iraq: Between Nation-Building and Fragmentation*
52 Dina Bishara, *Contesting Authoritarianism: Labour Challenges to the State in Egypt*
53 Rory McCarthy, *Inside Tunisia's al-Nahda: Between Politics and Preaching*
54 Ceren Lord, *Religious Politics in Turkey: From the Birth of the Republic to the AKP*
55 Dörthe Engelcke, *Reforming Family Law: Social and Political Change in Jordan and Morocco*
56 Dana Conduit, *The Muslim Brotherhood in Syria*
57 Benjamin Schuetze, *Promoting Democracy, Reinforcing Authoritarianism: US and European Policy in Jordan*
58 Marc Owen Jones, *Political Repression in Bahrain*
59 Dylan Baun, *Winning Lebanon: Populism and the Production of Sectarian Violence, 1920–1958*
60 Joas Wagemakers, *The Muslim Brotherhood in Jordan*
61 Amnon Aran, *Israeli Foreign Policy since the End of the Cold War*
62 Victor J. Willi, *The Fourth Ordeal: A History of the Muslim Brotherhood in Egypt, 1968–2018*
63 Grace Wermenbol, *A Tale of Two Narratives: The Holocaust, the Nakba, and the Israeli-Palestinian Battle of Memories*
64 Erin A. Snider, *Marketing Democracy: The Political Economy of Democracy Aid in the Middle East*
65 Yafa Shanneik, *The Art of Resistance in Islam: The Performance of Politics among Shi'i Women in the Middle East and Beyond*
66 Shirin Saeidi, *Women and the Islamic Republic: How Gendered Citizenship Conditions the Iranian State*
67 Jessica Watkins, *Creating Consent in an Illiberal Order: Policing Disputes in Jordan*
68 Nora Derbal, *Charity in Saudi Arabia: Civil Society under Authoritarianism*
69 Tine Gade, *Sunni City: Tripoli from Islamist Utopia to the Lebanese "Revolution"*
70 Chloe Skinner, *Occupier and Occupied: Israel, Palestine and Masculinities across the Divide*
71 Miriam R. Lowi, *Refining the Common Good: Oil, Islam and Politics in Gulf Monarchies*